Stott

WORLD OF ORNITHOLOGY

GUINEA FOWL OF THE WORLD

OTHER TITLES AVAILABLE

Lewis Wright's Poultry
Dr J Batty

Pheasants of The World
Dr Jean Delacour

Cult of The Budgerigar
W Watmough – Revised by Cyril Rogers

Practical Poultry Keeping
John Portsmouth

Poultry House and Appliances
A D.I.Y. Guide

Bantams
W F Entwisle

Cockfighting and Game Fowl
Herbert Atkinson

Poultry Colour Guide
Dr J Batty and Charles Francis

GUINEA FOWL OF THE WORLD

by

R. H. Hastings Belshaw

PUBLISHED AND DISTRIBUTED BY:
Nimrod Book Services,
P.O. Box No. 1,
Liss, Hampshire, GU33 7PR.

First Published 1985
ISBM 0 – 947647 – 20 – 1

Printed by:
UNWIN BROTHERS LIMITED
The Gresham Press, Old Woking, Surrey
A Member of the Martins Printing Group

Publishers:
Nimrod Book Services
(Fanciers Supplies Ltd)
P.O. Box 1, Liss,
Hants. GU33 7PR
England.

ACKNOWLEDGEMENTS

A list of works and authors to whom I am indebted for information will be found in the bibliography. I would also like to express my sincere thanks for various forms of assistance to the following:

Tom Adam, Dengold Guinea Fowl Ltd., Aberdeenshire.
P. de Backer, Director of the Royal Zoological Society, Antwerp.
Harry Brown, Manchester, Iwoa, U.S.A.
David Cairns, Ark Foods Ltd., Norfolk.
J.C. Cauchard, author of 'La Pintade'.
Tom Corbett, London.
Dr. R. Faust, Director Zoological Gardens, Frankfurt.
I.C.J. Galbraith, British Museum of Natural History.
Robert Galliano, Galor, France.
Dr. J.F. Giovannetti, Institut d'Elevage et de Médecine Vétérinaire des Pays Tropicaux, Paris.
T.G.H. James, Egyptian Antiquities Dept. of British Museum
John Karmali, F.R.P.S., Nairobi.
N.H. Lambert, M.R.C.V.S., Dublin.
Mrs Li Tianmin, Embassy of The Peoples' Republic of China, Dublin.
Dr. D.F. Marais, Klein Africa Game Farm, Transvaal.
Elizabeth Neuman, Dublin.
H.E. Dr. Brian O'Ceallaigh, Irish Embassy, Cairo.
M.J. Petitjean, Laboratoire de Spermiologie du Magneraud, France.
The Editor and staff of *Poultry World,* London.
Drago Radić, Dublin.
Donald Risdon, Tropical Bird Garden, Rhode, Somerset.
Geraldine Sardella, New Jersey, U.S.A.
Raymond Sawyer, World Pheasant Association.
Marcella Senior, Trinity College, Dublin.
The Director and staff of the Station des Recherches Avicoles (I.N.R.A.), Tours, France.
Loyle Stromberg, Pine River, Minnesota, U.S.A.
Claus Trogisch, Walsrode, Fed. Republic of Germany.
Gerrit Van Gelderen, Dublin.
The Director of the Vogelpark, Walsrode, Fed. Republic of Germany.
Jim and Jane Williams, Washington, D.C., U.S.A.
Dr. H.E. Wolters, Zoologisches Forschungsinstitut, Alexander Koenig Museum, Bonn, Fed. Republic of Germany.

Especial thanks are due to Dr. Kevin Dodd, Veterinary College of Ireland and to Peter Olney, Curator of Birds, Regents Park Zoological Society, London, both of whom provided constructive criticism and helpful suggestions.

Dr. Marianne Neuman, M.D., Dublin, who instintingly devoted so much time perusing and checking the text and for her invaluable assistance with translations and communications.

To my children, Marcus who executed the drawings and sketches, Alan for his assistance with flock maintenance and Karen, Lara, Sarah and Michael for various helpful services.

I dedicate this book to my wife Deirdre, whose unenviable task it was to type the manuscript and without whose unfailing encouragement and support it would never have been written.

December, 1984. R. H. Hastings Belshaw

CONTENTS

DISTRIBUTION

MAPS

SHOWING LOCATION

OF

WILD SPECIES

(Described in Chapter 2)

Parts of Africa where species are located are also covered in Chapter 2.

KEY

AGELASTES and ACRYLLIUM — Map 1

N	*A. niger*
A	*A. meleagrides*
V	*Acryllium vulturinum*

AFRICA

KEY

GUTTERA Map 2

P	*G. p. plumifera*
Ps	*G. p. schubotzi*
K	*G. pucherani pucherani*
1	*G. e. verreauxi*
2	*G. e. sclateri*
3	*G. e. schoutedeni*
4	*G. e. chapini*
5	*G. e. kathleenae*
6	*G. e. seth smithi*
7	*G. e. edouardi*
8	*G. e. suahelica*
9	*G. e. barbata*

AFRICA

NUMIDA MELEAGRIS   Map 3

G1	*N.m. galeata*	H1	*N.m. mitrata*
G2	*N.m. sabyi*	H2a	*N.m. uhehensis*
G3	*N.m. marchei*	H2b	*N.m. rikwae*
G4	*N.m. blancoui*	H3	*N.m. marungensis*
T1	*N.m. meleagris*	H4	*N.m. maxima*
T2	*N.m. somaliensis*	H5	*N.m. papillosa*
T3	*N.m. major*	H6	*N.m. damarensis*
T4	*N.m. strasseni*	H7	*N.m. limpopoensis*
T5	*N.m. toruensis*	H8	*N.m. transvaalensis*
T6	*N.m. intermedia*	H9	*N.m. coronata*
T7	*N.m. macroceras*	G =	grey breasted
TH	*N.m. reichenowi*	T =	tufted
GH	*N.m. callewaerti*	H =	helmeted

*G4, *T3, *T6, *T7, *H2A, *H2B, *H4, *H6, *H7, *H8,

FOOTNOTE * Whether the precise status of above should be considered a race or a distinct subspecies merits further investigation.

AFRICA

G2
G1
G1
G1
T1
T1
T1
G1
G1
G1
G4
T4
T1
T2
T2
T4
G3
T3
T2
T4
T7
T5
H1
G3
GH
H3
TH
GH
GH
H1
H2b
H2a
H1
H3
H1
H3
H3
H4
H1
H1
H1
H1
H5
H5
H8
H7
H6
H9
H9

INTRODUCTION

The principal intention of this book is to describe and illustrate the natural species and modern strains and to reinstate in popularity the keeping of guinea fowl. Information about the guinea fowl is usually provided in meagre amounts and widely dispersed throughout the range of books on ornithology and poultry keeping. It seems time that this unfairly neglected family was accorded more space to itself. At the risk of irritating aviculturalists on the one hand and poultry keepers on the other, it is felt that a book which combines as many aspects and accumulates as much information as possible will still be of interest to both. If anyone is stimulated to experiment more widely with guinea fowl than before, then this effort will have been worthwhile.

A survey presented on a wide front and addressing such divergent interests, touches by necessity only briefly on many topics. Its manifold aim is to make the adventurous aviculturalist more aware of the selection of natural species and subspecies available; to outline the development of recent techniques which can provide an opportunity for the show breeder to create wider ranges of ornamental varieties and, similarly, to enable the poultry farmer to increase the scope and rate of production. Finally, increasing numbers of people are interested in raising poultry while employing natural foods in order to restore the nutritional value and flavour so often missing in factory style products. For those who are seeking something more unusual than chickens and turkeys but are reluctant to become involved with game birds, no better choice could be made than the common guinea fowl. They are dynamic, amusing to observe, easy to rear and can certainly be profitable. They make a superb table bird, the texture of the flesh resembles a cross between turkey and pheasant, but its flavour possesses a uniquely distinctive nuance. Unlike game they are always in season and so fill awkward gaps in the culinary calendar. In late spring and summer they are prolific egg layers. The eggs have a rich yellow yolk and are of fine creamy flavour, eagerly sought after by gourmets.

The number and variety of specimens kept by zoos and aviaries has been in somewhat of a decline during the past few decades. This may partly have been due to the upsurge of interest in the orders of water birds, raptors and the many delightful and exotic species imported in earlier years from South America and Australasia. At present there are in Europe and the United States of America only limited numbers of the highly colourful and elegant vulturine guinea fowl, which is not more difficult to breed and rear than some of the commoner pheasants. It's magnificent plumage and gracious manner make it as big an attraction to the visitor as any other specimen in the bird garden. Many of the crested species are also highly attractive in appearance and relatively easy to maintain. A number of varieties are currently flourishing in European aviaries.

It is worth remembering that two other species, the Black and the White Breasted guinea fowl are fairly rare – the latter is now being considered as an endangered species. Steps have yet to be made by responsible conservationists to obtain some stock for captive breeding in order to assist in preserving this most interesting bird from extinction.

The author has kept and bred guinea fowl in various parts of Great Britain for over thirty years, some as ornamental varieties alongside peafowl and pheasants and some in commercial flocks on free range. Whether in pen or plantation, their hardiness, extraordinary blend of intense curiousity, extreme wariness and volatile temperament ensure that while they possess diverse attractions for different people, they will never be boring.

COLOUR ILLUSTRATIONS

A variety of Species is now given in colour, thus showing the diverse nature of the Guinea Fowl Family (Numididae)

Plate 1 Mural on Old Shrine of Ibibio Chief's Wife showing Guinea Fowl as Symbol of Fecundity

Plate 2 VULTURINE GUINEA FOWL
Top Left: Side View, Male; Right: Front View Male. **Bottom**: Side View Female

Plate 3 Group of Vulturine Guinea Fowl foraging in the wild state in Kenya

Plate 4 **Top:** White Breasted Guinea Fowl (photo: OKAPIA)
Bottom: Kenya Crested Guinea Fowl

Plate 5 **Top** Left: Head of N.M. Papillosa – Wattle Nosed Guinea Fowl
Right: Crowned Guinea Fowl Heads (courtesy: Dr. Marais)
Bottom Left: Young Kenya Crested Guinea Fowl (approx. 6 months)
Right: Crowned Guinea Fowl Chicks Hatching in Wild (courtesy Dr. Marais)

Plate 6 **Top** Left: Year Old Reichenow's Guinea Fowl
Right: Pair of Mitred Guinea Fowl

Bottom Left: White African Guinea Fowl
Right: Lavender Blue Guinea Fowl

Plate 7 Zambesi Crested Guinea Fowl living in dense forest (courtesy/photo: P. Johnson)

Plate 8 Flock of Mitred Guinea Fowl at Water Hole, Kenya (courtesy/photo: Jacana)

Plate 9 **Top** Left: White Breasted Guinea Fowl (similar to Pied). Right: Lavender Guinea Fowl
Bottom Left: Pile or Pied Guinea Fowl. Right: Pearl/Grey Guinea Fowl (Standard)

Plate 10 **Left:** Pearl Grey with Head Detail (painting by Kurt Zander)
Right: Sennar Tufted Guinea Fowl (Note: Nasal Bristles) (photo: Farouk, Zoological Gardens, Gisa)

Plate 11 Lavender Guinea Fowl (painting by Kurt Zander)

Plate 12 **Top** Left: Domestic Guinea Fowl Eggs showing Variations in Colour
Right: Egg at point of hatch with shell removed
Bottom Left: Domestic Chick Pearl Grey. Right: Domestic Chicks, White and Pied

Plate 13 **Top** Left: Four week old Keets (open range). Right: Eight week old Keets (open range)
Bottom Left: Helmet and Wattle development (four months ornamental variety)
Right: Helmet and Wattle development (six months ornamental variety)

Plate 14 **Top** Left: Intensive egg production. Right: Packing day old Keets
Bottom Left: Large scale incubation. Right: A big intensive unit

(courtesy Galor, France)

Plate 15 **Top** Left: Sex linked day old's on feeder (courtesy Galor)
Right: Intensive system – floor reared Guineas (courtesy Galor)
Bottom Left: Artificial insemination using dosage regulator, mobile bench and clamp (courtesy Galor)
Right: Chicken and Guinea cross, marked hybrid vigour (photo: Dr. Marais)

Plate 16 **Top** Left: Hatching Keets (courtesy: Arkfoods Ltd) Right: Rearing Keets under gas burners (courtesy: Arkfoods Ltd)
Bottom Left: Cranium with Helmet removed showing connecting aperture
Right: Helmet dissected laterally showing honeycomb tissue

1

GUINEA FOWL IN HISTORY

CHAPTER 1

GUINEA FOWL IN HISTORY

History and folklore in Europe and Africa; Outline of dispersal by traders and settlers; Recent developments within the poultry industry

Guinea Fowl belong to the order of birds known as Galliformes which includes turkeys, grouse, pheasant, curasows and the farmyard chicken. The chart in chapter two indicates the precise relationship. Their particular family name is *Numididae,* by which were known the ancestors of the only domesticated fowls to originate from the African continent within historical times. The fossilised remains of guinea fowl approximating to *Numida meleagris* have been found in Czechoslovakia, these have been dated back to the upper Pleistocene Era, about 2,500,000 years ago. In that period however, elephants and lions were roaming as far north as England.

The importation of guinea fowl into the southern Mediterranean area preceded the turkey by several millennia and even the jungle fowl by some hundreds of years. The variety and predominance of the latter is mainly due to the skill of the early Indian and Burmese peoples who seem to have bred it since neolithic times with the result that it arrived in the west as a well domesticated fowl.

The original character and habits of the guinea fowl, on the other hand, only began to undergo transformation during the past 50 years in spite of about 4,000 years of sporadic cultivation. The first historical reference to them is found in murals of the Eygptian fifth dynasty, in the Pyramid of Wenis at Saqqara c. 2400 BC. Aviaries were quite fashionable in this period amongst the wealthy landowners who maintained them as an attractive feature of their walled gardens. These birds were either still indigenous to Egypt or imported down the Nile from Nubia and further south ie, the land of Punt, — Sudan, Ethiopia and Somalia, along with lepoards and other exotic fauna, gold, ebony, frankincense, ivory and slaves. By the time of Queen Hatshepsut c. 1475 BC the Eygptians had extended the scope and range of their trading with other seafaring peoples. The jungle fowl had reached Eygpt and China. Poultry thenceforward were cultivated on a much larger scale and with a considerable degree of expertise. Records of this period refer to the use of "walk in" type incubators, constructed with mud bricks and heated by burning camel dung. The largest could hold up to 90,000 eggs, mainly jungle fowl and guinea fowl and many of them claimed up to 70% hatches. Lacking thermometers, the maintenance of constant incubation temperatures was a family secret as jealously guarded as those of the pottery kilns. Guinea fowl depicted in Hieroglyphic form, known as the 'N.H' bird, were examples of *N.m. meleagris,* the nasal tufts often resemble the helmets. They may also be seen in the reconstructed chapel of Sesostris I at Karnak c. 1900 BC and in the later 18th dynasty

Figure 1 – 1 Example with incised spots, Chapel of Sesostris I at Karnak C 1900 BC

Figure 1 – 2 18th Dynasty Hieroglyph in Tomb No 99 Thebes (shows helmet and nasal tuft)

tombs at Thebes c. 1570 to 1300 BC. the accuracy of the representation is amusingly varied. It is known that these fowl were still in Egypt during the Ptolomaic period when we can picture them being enjoyed by Anthony and Cleopatra.

We are not certain whether the Greeks obtained any guinea fowl from Eygpt, but they were well established as domestic fowl on Greek farms by 400 BC. The Phoenicians had circumnavigated Africa 200 years earlier. Both they and the Greeks were then trading around the known world. Scyrax, a fifth century BC Greek explorer related that:

If one sails through the pillars of Hercules, keeping Africa on ones left hand, there opens not far from the Cape of Hermes a wide Gulf called Kotes. In the middle of this Gulf lies the town of Pontion and a large reedy lake called Kephasias. There live the birds called meleagrides and nowhere else, except where they have been taken from that place.

Heyn in 1888 quotes Mnaseas who claimed that guinea fowl originated in the West Atlantic land of Sicyon, also thought to be the main source of electron or amber. Sophocles describes them as, "Weeping tears of electron".

A Greek legend recounted in Ovid's *Metamorphoses* relates that upon the death of the hero Meleager, his sisters wept until they died of grief. This stirred the compassion of the Goddess Artemis who rescued them from Hades by turning them into guinea fowl. The white spots on their plumage represent the tears shed by the sisters. Some people have attributed the origin of their Greek name to this legend, but Mr Hyams in *Animals in the Service of Man,* may be on equally firm ground in his contention that 'meleagrides' is a corruption of 'melanargis', meaning black and white.

Mr Hyams has suggested that Phoenician seamen also brought the birds from West Africa and had domesticated them in Carthage and other Phoenician cities where they were discovered by the Romans. Whether or not they were imported to Rome by Mark Anthony or Octavian, guinea fowl became celebrated by the Romans only during the early empire period which began after the fall of Eygpt in 30 BC. They had sacked Carthage and Greece 150 years earlier. The various names which they conferred on them, i.e. Pharaoh's chickens, Carthaginian hens and Numidian hens leave the source from whence they were obtained still undecided. Pliny the elder in his natural history published AD 77, stated that they were the last bird to be added to the Roman menu and that they were in great request from Numidia, both eggs and flesh were considered table delicacies. Ben Jonson in 1637 translates from Horace's *Country Life,* "the ginny hen could not go down my belly then more sweet than olives". The emperor Caligula offered them as sacrifices to himself when he assumed the titles of deity, and they were still an expensive luxury when Terentius Varro a contemporary of Lucullus stocked them in his magnificient aviary at Casinum. They are represented in a fresco in the house of the Vettii at Pompeii and in a mosaic at the baths of Diocletian in Rome. They are also depicted feeding on herbage and fruits on a 4th century AD mosaic in the Museum of Rome, and in black figures around a 5th century BC Greek skyphos or drinking cup in the New York Museum of Art.

It seems therefore fairly certain that during the first century AD guinea fowl from both East and West Africa were being stocked in Italy and Greece. We do not known how widely the Romans distributed them in Europe but we may reasonably conjecture that some land owners kept them on their estates across the empire. Guinea fowl bones have been found at the Roman Limes camp now called Saalburg in the Taunus mountains of West Germany and a leg bone with a metal ring on it was discovered in the ruins of the Roman town of Silchester in England. With the advent of the dark ages nothing more is

Figure 1 – 3 Greek skyphos, VI BC (The Metropolitan Museum of Arts, Rogers Fund, 1941 —41:162:125)

heard of them in Northern Europe but it is significant that they are still known by the old classical names of 'faraone' (Pharaoh's birds) in Italy and 'meleagrides' or 'Agriornitha Noumidias' (Numidian Gamebird) in Greece.

During the late 14th and 15th century Portuguese traders rediscovered them along what became known as the Guinea Coast of East Africa. They reintroduced them to a Europe eager for the novelties which were pouring in from the east along the caravan roads of "the great Turk" or Moslem empire and the new world or "West Indies". People were often unsure from which direction the latest curiosity had arrived. The French described them as 'Poules de Turquie' and also 'Poules d'Inde'; had they come from Africa or across the Atlantic? By 1555 the argument was settled and they were accepted as 'Poules de la Guinée,' turkeys became 'Dindon'. Finally they adopted the name 'Pintade' from the Spanish and Portuguese 'Gallena Pintada' (painted hen).

Similar confusion occurred in England due to the coincidence of guinea fowl and turkey fowl both being introduced between 1530 and 1550. The latter had reached Spain and Portugal from Mexico in 1524 and if their indigenous and more appropriate name of 'Totolin' had been retained, the subsequent mistake might have been avoided. The English, smitten with the original French misnomers, were left sorting out 'Ginny birds' and 'Turkey birds' for the remainder of the century. In Germany they were described more aptly as 'Perlhuhn' (pearly hen).

Shakespeare when writing *Henry IV* in the 1590's, committed both historical and factual errors which were pointed out by JE Harting in *The Ornithology of Shakespeare.* In Part one, Act two, Scene one, turkey hens are referred to in the carriers' saddle bags, but only guinea hens could have fitted in these; neither of course were in England until the reign of Henry VIII. The Bard was sufficiently enlightened by the time he wrote *'Othello'* in 1604 — Act one, Scene three, "Ere I would say, I would drowne myself for the love of a Gynney Hen, I would change my humanity with a Baboone" — part of Iago's speech to Rodrigo who contemplates drowning himself for love of Desdemona. By this time ginny hen was being used as a slang term for courtesan or prostitute.

One of the most famous and respected early works on birds, *'Ornithologia'*, 1685 by Francis Willughby and John Ray, recently reprinted by the Scolar Press, contains a section on the 'Guinney Hen', it points out that they were also known as 'Mauretanian hens' and adds that some birds have been seen in England which were brought out of 'Sierra Lyone' and these birds have a crest of dark feathers on their heads instead of a horn, this was the first known English reference to the species *Guttera.* Ray's last work, *Synopsis Methodica Avium* provided the basis from which Linnaeus in 1735 compiled his classification of birds and introduced the two terms generic and specific for each species. The Latin designations under which both birds were classified demonstrate the persistent confusion about their relationship and origins. Guinea fowl became *Numida meleagris* and the turkey was labelled with the astonishing compound — *Meleagris gallopavo.* The jungle fowl became *Gallus* and the peafowl became *Pavo.* The enthusiasm with which both birds were adopted was a measure of their culinary superiority to the native birds. Within 150 years the guinea and turkey had utterly displaced the peafowl and swan as the major table bird for festive occasions.

It it difficult to trace the detailed history of breeding guinea fowl in Africa. The only written records were made by European naturalists and explorers in the 18th and 19th centuries. Techniques of animal husbandry had spread south and west from Eygpt after 2,000

Figure 1 – 4 4th Century AD Roman Mosaic (Museo Nazionaie Romano)

BC. The two predominant areas where domesticated guinea fowl are recorded were in southern Sudan around the White and Blue Niles and in the hills where game is scarce and the tribesmen became skilful stock breeders. The other area was West Africa. Here, along the great rivers, agriculturally based kingdoms and empires reach back over 1,000 years and many have oral traditions of keeping and breeding guinea fowl. Notable amongst these are the Manding peoples of the Mali Empire, approximately 1,200 AD to 1,800 AD centered in the Kangaba area of the upper Niger, the Hausa of northern Nigeria, the Dagomba in northern Ghana, the Dan of northern Liberia and the Ivory Coast, the Dogon in Mali, various groups in Benin, Togo and the Biafran area of southern Nigeria. The mural shown in Plate 1 was executed on the shrine wall of an important Ibibio woman, the guinea fowl image symbolises her fertility and status.

Until recently many of the other peoples of Africa had not troubled to domesticate any of the guinea fowl or Kanga as they are best known in the eastern region. Subspecies of the popular genus *Numida* were so common everywhere that they were usually hunted as game, they could also be captured alive and fed in cages for use as required. Nests and eggs were eagerly sought in the laying season.

In South Africa, the only domesticated guinea fowl for a long time were birds of *galeata* stock from Europe, imported by white settlers. This was also the case with turkeys in the USA. These domestic guineas were flourishing in Cape Colony during the late 19th century, pure white and lavender strains are also recorded at that time. Some settlers had also tried unsuccessfully to domesticate *Coronata,* the larger indigenous subspecies. These invariably reverted to their wild state at the first opportunity and the few who remained in confinement became more unpleasantly aggressive as they got older. Before 1950 there are occasional records of cross breeding between *Coronata* cocks and the imported domestic Guinea hens. The crosses were larger than the imported guineas and had the blacker plumage of the *Coronata* but the lighter coloured legs common in European stock.

Guinea fowl feathers were highly valued in all parts of Africa (as they are by milliners around the world), and were worked into cloaks and headdresses for the chiefs and shamans. Because of it's renowned fecundity in egg production, related in Africa to seed sowing, the bird acquired in many regions a fertility symbolism equivalent to that of the owl for wisdom in parts of Europe. Guinea fowl images and motifs were frequently incorporated into conventionalised designs for clothing and other articles used at weddings and in female initiation ceremonies.

Native peoples along the Zambesi are reported to have had a superstitious fear of the crested guinea fowl and treated its flesh as taboo, because it was generally only observed flitting around the deepest and darkest parts of the forest and was therefore considered to be subject to spirit transmigration. In these areas, the belief was that the birds bodies could be entered by spirits of the recently deceased who were then guided to the world after death. This is part of the universal folk belief where the flight from the body after death of the spirit or soul is represented by a bird such as the dove, petrel, crow or nightjar.

At the end of the rain season in East Africa, the first sighting of the guinea flocks emerging into the fields from wooded shelter was the accepted signal to begin planting and sowing. The interest was probably mutual. This invariably took place during the first half of February which was regarded as the beginning of the year. Tribes in Uganda, when plant-

A
Pointed Primary showing Elongated spots at edge

B
Strong Rounded Secondaries give Powerful Lift-off
Note: Barred Edges

C
Spotted and Finely Speckled vane of body plumage has thick downy base

Figure 1 – 5 Three Guinea Fowl feathers

ing in the fields would imitate the guinea fowls 'song' with their own version — O–Kol, O–Kol, mi–i tokoch— (plant, plant, there is luck in it).

On the huge savannas of the east and south, flocks of thousands of birds, especially around the water holes, used to be an accepted feature of the landscape. Because of its ability to evade predators, in Africa as in other parts of the world where it is now acclimatised, the guinea fowl's only serious enemy is man. During the past 50 years, human depletion of the wild flocks has become increasingly severe over most parts of the continent and there is now an accelerating decline of almost all subspecies. At the speed by which human population rates on the sub–continent are exploding, many subspecies may, unless protected, be in danger of extinction before the end of this century. In Kenya the annual rate of increase is 4% i.e. the population will double in 17 years. In South Africa it is increasing by 60,000 per month. Gabon, one of the few 'quiescent' countries has set up an institute to study ways of curing its population 'problem' which is only increasing by 1.1% per annum. Recently some of the African nations have found it expedient to set up hatcheries and poultry farms for guineas as well as other fowl.

The guinea fowl as a fertility symbol rapidly found its niche in folklore further north. In the warmer areas of western Europe where the guineas began laying sufficiently early, their eggs were highly prized for the Easter fertility celebrations. They are named as amongst the eggs eaten, in English, French and German records, along with those of turkey, duck, goose, seagull, peafowl, hen and plover. Their value in 19th century France, was reckoned at five times the price of hen eggs. The blunt ended shape was popular for executing designs and paintings. The exceptionally tough shell was ideal for and almost certainly the last to break open during the egg rolling, tapping and other contests, games and dances conducted in the shadow of the maypole. They were numbered amongst the coloured eggs hidden in central European gardens, supposedly by the Easter hare as paschal gifts for the children. The egg as a potent symbol of the cosmic life force was revered in Africa as in other parts of the world. As well as occupying a central place amongst the gifts at Spring fertility festivals and wedding celebrations, it was a powerful vehicle for magic. Amongst the Hausa peoples, a guinea fowl egg was broken against the front door of the house of a newly married couple to invoke good luck. One buried under the doorstep would prevent the entry of malicious spirits. A lonely wife could summon her husband by placing an egg on the roof and willing it to draw him homewards. It's use as a benificent force was exemplified in the new year's Nyanku–Sai purification festival in Ghana where the royal ancestors were invoked, in front of an egg presented by the king, to bless the crops and the state. The egg was then thrown in the river and if found to be unbroken, the omens were good for the coming year. Eggs and other special foods were also ceremonially eaten to perpetuate the magical strength of the kingdom. The same power can equally be harnessed for harmful purposes. Eggs and fowl are used in ritual curses and sacrifices on every continent.

WORLD DISTRIBUTION

Guinea fowl stocks in Europe were often supplemented by fresh imports during the 18th and 19th centuries when the landed gentry sought them as additional game for their estates. They were frequently seen in Bristol arriving on the slave ships. The same transport carried them westward to the Americas' and by the early 1700's so many had been settled in the Carribean and parts of central America that they were fast becoming part of the wild fauna, especially in the larger islands of Cuba, Jamaica, Hispaniola and Puerto Rico.

Colonists from Europe took guinea fowl and other poultry along with them not only to the Americas' but to the 'Far East'. In an early account of the East India Company, Fryer, in 1698 records, "Fowls for game they have several, the best of which is the guinea hen".

The birds gained instant acceptance in China, with it's ancient traditions of aviculture and early supremacy in domestic duck breeding techniques. From the early 18th century, they were cultivated widely in small units over the entire country and named Pearl Fowl.

in Chinese phonetic alphabet: zhēnzhūjī.
Their successes in cultivation are evidenced by the fact that in India guineas are still known as Chinese Fowl (Hindi: Chīn kī murgi).

A shipment was brought from India to New Zealand in 1864. The guineas were released in several locations but they did not become widely established. A few flocks may still exist in remote areas but they have not been seen in significant numbers since 1930. Several attempts at establishing feral flocks in Australia from 1870 onwards were also unsuccessful. They have been reported breeding on some of the Capricorn Island group and a few were liberated on Heron Island during 1960 — 70. (Lavery 1974) (Kikkawa and Boles 1976).

They were introduced on the Hawaiian Islands in 1874 and some birds still exist on Hawaii but their status is unknown. (Hawaiian Audubon Soc. 1975).

They are regularly noted, sometimes as 'Galeenys', in conjunction with other poultry, in the earliest colonial records of the North American States. This name (from Galina) was common local currency in many parts of the English speaking world and has not completely died out. In 1796 Stedman stated in a report on Surinam that, "They had also there, the tame Galeenys". In 1869 RM Blackmore in *Lorna Doone* writes, "Men is desaving and so is Galanies". From no less a stylist than Jane Austen, letters 1884 ed. comes the phrase "Bantam cocks and Galinies".

Under conditions established for pheasants, guineas multiplied rapidly into large feral flocks, a few examples can still be seen in Ireland. They proved equally elusive for the furred and feathered predators of Europe and parts of America but they can be captured quite easily while roosting at night however, with the aid of bright lights and nets. The estate owners who found them frustrating as a sporting bird, (they preferred to run from the guns rather than take to the wing), were only too pleased to donate their birds around the local farmers and obtain more space for pheasants. By the 19th century most farms maintained a flock which served the dual purpose of providing meat for festivals and also to sound the alarm at the approach of any intruder. Their loud cries at any unusual sound could be heard over a wide distance at night and often succeeded in deterring both two and four legged marauders. On free range they have also been known to attack and kill rats and snakes.

Their popularity as table birds reached a peak in Britain during the Victorian period and this state of affairs lasted until the economic instability which occurred after the first world war. Prices which had scarcely changed for a century rose dramatically. Cost consciousness overtook producer and consumer alike. Guinea, turkey and goose were luxury birds and even in this class, the smaller guinea was discounted as an economic competitor. Fewer people remained on the land to cope with even routine chores and the surviving agriculturalists concentrated on breeding faster maturing chickens and turkeys, with increased egg production. Census figures show the rapid decline in numbers of guinea fowl in some western nations up to as recently as 1960. In the USA about one million birds were reared in 1939, by 1954 numbers had fallen to two hundred and fifty thousand and remained static for the rest of the decade. The post war period in Britain witnessed guinea fowl on hotel menus much less frequently than oysters. In the central European nations all poultry stocks were decimated by the second world war. Prior to this event; France, Italy, Austria, Hungary, Poland and Roumania all recorded a widespread consumption of guineas and had regularly exported surplus birds to Germany and Great Britain. Italy was fortunate to have a group of biologists and poultry fanciers who were interested in cross breeding subspecies of *Numidae* which could be obtained without difficulty during the 1920's and early 30's when African access was easily available. Among them was Prof Ghigi, one of the leading authorities of the period on guinea fowl. They obtained many fertile hybrids from *galeata, meleagris* and *mitrata* at the Italian Government's poultry research unit in Rovigo. Further experimental work took place during the pre war years and some of the larger and more successful strains which resulted, were supplied to other parts of Europe. These new strains constituted the basic stock from which the large breeding establishments have produced their own selective variations during the past 25 years. The application of modern genetics and scientific management enabled breeders to achieve equivalent successes to those obtained with turkeys. The principal objects were the same, to increase egg production by extending the normal laying period so that day old chicks could be made available on a year round basis. Traditionally, table guineas had only been available to the market at certain seasons and the supply had never been sufficient to allow marketers to popularise the birds. In a growing number of countries nowadays guinea fowl may be purchased from the shops as a feathered carcass like game or prepared in oven ready packs, fresh or frozen, during any month of the year. The particular aim of some breeders was to develop very fast maturing strains and in this respect one Norfolk company had notable success during the last decade, following 15 years selective breeding. Their initial 5 or 6 stock lines were Italian, as these mixed strains apart from being up to 50% heavier possessed characteristics required for intensive breeding which is now accomplished exclusively by artificial insemination. Local strains which possessed higher fertility factors were also incrossed. The original northern European birds which are descendants of the West African *galeata,* were not found easily adaptable for these purposes. The Norfolk company's breeding stock, under a strictly controlled environment, are now capable of laying periods extending from 9 to 10 months out of 12. Growth rates of the keets or young birds are similar to those achieved under intensive conditions for turkeys and chickens. Their breeding hens average 160-170 settable eggs per season and have a 92% successful hatching level.

Live weights of 2¼ to 3 lbs (approx 1 kg to 1.4 kg) which are the optimum variations sought by the British restaurant trade are obtained in 8/9 weeks. The company also exported day old chicks and birds to countries as varied as Japan, Canada, Nigeria, Kenya and Zambia.

In western Europe and France in particular, many farmers prefer to purchase day old chicks or keets and rear them to their own feeding formulae. Breeders are therefore geared extensively to day old keet sales, with a greater orientation to egg production and hatchability. During the early sixties successful artificial insemination techniques for guinea fowl were developed and employed at the Station Experimentale d'Aviculture du Magneraud in western France. The methodology is now well proven and is expanding rapidly through breeding establishments around the world.

As a result of successfully applied intensive control methods and the artificial insemination development which also speeded up breeding selection techniques, the production of guinea fowl in France tripled between 1962 and 1972. It rose from approximately 4% to over 12% of the total poultry market and compared favourably with duck production. During 1970 average monthly production of day old keets was 1.6 million rising to 3 million in July alone.

Previously more than half of all keets were reared in the south where the warmer weather favoured range and outdoor pens. Now the intensive systems of the north western region account for about 60% of stock. A large hatchery may house from 20,000 to 50,000 breeding birds in cages. The progeny varies from 120 to 175 live keets per hen over a ten month laying season, the cost of those reared during winter being 25% higher. The remainder of the national stock is grown outdoors and individual small farmers produce over 25% of the total output. The rate of development was also accelerated by the avidity with which new consumers took to guineas as a change from mass produced chickens, even at a higher price and slightly smaller size. Another reason for the huge success of the French guineafowl industry is the degree of national co–operation which exists between the hatcheries, growers, veterinarians, centres of expertise like the Institut Technique pour l'Aviculteur (ITAVI); Syndicat des Selectioneurs Avicoles Francais (SYSAF) and the Ministry of Agriculture's Institut Nationale de la Recherche Agronomique (INRA) working through its various poultry research stations.

A severe setback was encountered in the years following 1973 when infectious enteritis arrived, affecting the intensive growers in particular, destroying many flocks and this raised the cost of day old keets. Production peaked again by 1976 – 77 but the rapid rise of about 13% flooded the market and a further epidemic of severe enteritis the following winter combined to put many growers out of business. Slower but steady progress has since been made with the annual output at around 50,000 tonnes and the results of selective breeding have now shown an increase over the first 10 years of 30 to 40 g per bird. The favourite market weight is approximately 1.5 kg. Consumption in Germany and Italy is lower and in Britain it is still under 1,000,000 per annum.

There is a considerable degree of interest in the Soviet Union where work and studies are particularly concerned with guinea fowl egg production as these are very popular and breeding is directed towards increasing the quantity laid per annum. This is not surprising when the commercial benefits are considered. In spite of the smaller size its nutritional value is almost equal to that of the hen egg, it is easily transportable due to the almost unbreakable shell and its 'keeping' qualities are more than five times greater.

The increasing popularity of guineas for the table is reflected in the USA and many other countries, however, production has not yet developed on such large or intensive scales. In 1975 one of the most prominent American hatcheries had only 1,500 laying fowl and was exporting keets to Canada and some of the South American nations. In the same year total production across the country was estimated at under 3,000,000 per annum. In general, breeders supplied their own local markets. The majority of birds were grown on small farms in the southern and central states, New York, California and in a few hatcheries in the mid west. There is apparently a large market for keets of 1 lb to 1½ lb (500 gm to 750 gm), which would allow a faster turnover than in Europe. Some farms in the US and Australia have been raising substantial flocks of White or 'White African' birds for an eager market. They anticipate this variety will become as great a favourite as the white turkey, because with the 'oven ready' carcass there are no dark pin feathers and and the flesh is slightly paler.

Production in Great Britain was adversely affected by the importation during 1980 of large quantities of frozen oven–ready guinea fowl from the large intensive farms of France, Belgium and Holland. These could be retailed at two thirds of the primary cost of producing the birds in Britain because of the economies of scale and more advantageous farm pricing systems in some of the EEC countries. Stricter controls which were introduced at the end of 1982 went some way towards establishing a basis of fairer competition but the magnitude of intensive broiler production in north western Europe still sways the balance in the favour of these units.

One major breeder in Aberdeenshire now concentrates on hatching keets of hardy free range strains to supply at day old to farmers and small holders who want to rear the birds to their own feeding programmes. These are absorbed by local markets whose customers are prepared to pay a little extra to obtain home fed birds.

The Norfolk intensive hatchery is still supplying several thousand eight week old 1 kg carcasses per week to the English market. The breast and limb configuration is claimed to be superior to those from other European hatcheries.

Traditional extensive methods of raising guinea fowl are still practiced widely. Growers argue that because the birds are on free range, total food consumption by the time they have attained 2½ lbs live weight (1.1 kg) at 16 to 18 weeks old is only a little more costly than for the broiler raised bird. They are usually fed on a home mixed fish meal and cereal ration with broiler crumbs added. This is supplied ad lib in outdoor hoppers and the rest of the diet is foraged by the birds themselves. It is also, not unreasonably, claimed that the more mature bird, raised on foodstuffs partly of its own choosing, possesses a more distinctive and gamey flavour. An obvious drawback is the paucity of production due to the traditional breeding methods practiced, with egg output at 90 to 110 eggs per hen. There are patently many combinations of intensive and extensive methods which could be employed to advantage, especially by growers with large expanses of rough terrain and suitable climates.

It would be unfortunate, now that the means are available, if short term commercial considerations were to prompt growers and marketers to present broiler guineas in the same manner as chickens and turkeys, thus sacrificing the breed to the mass demand for inexpensive white meat. Guineas should be fed so as to maintain their recognised flavour and quality and this is an important marketing point. Nor should they be offered merely as a substitute for game. If it is not debased, the guinea will always command a price commensurate with its high status. The expanding application of breeding by artificial insemination (A.1.) will rapidly alter the pattern of short supply as it did in western Europe. In turn this should satisfy and stimulate demand throughout the rest of the world.

Figure 1 – 6 Black Guinea Fowl **(Courtesy: Antwerp Zoo)**

2

THE SPECIES

Distribution Maps are shown in the Prelimary Section (p vii and xiii)

Figure 2 – 1 An old print showing conventional grouping of poultry, including the Guinea Fowl

CHAPTER 2

THE SPECIES*

Description of natural species and subspecies with notes on avicultural procedures

Classification of birds into different categories, species and subspecies has been an ongoing developing procedure by ornithologists since the 18th century. As new similarities and distinctions are noted and registered, it frequently becomes necessary to reallocate some species, genera and even families and also introduce new ranking concepts to contain them properly, such as super families, subfamilies, etc. In order to show the precise relationship between guinea fowl and other gallinacious species a chart is included to indicate the most recent designations. This may also dispel a certain confusion for some aviculturalists when consulting the older reference books where guinea fowl are often classified under the family *Phasianidae*.

The actual nomenclature, dealing with what name should be used for a particular bird or subspecies is also confusing in respect of guinea fowl. During the late 19th and early 20th centuries, many ornithologists were compiling lists of African birds, sometimes without reference to, or knowledge of, each others work. The result is that in various reference books several subspecies and even distinct species, particularly in the genera *Numida* and *Guttera,* overlap or have been given two or three different names with regard to race and form; e.g. *Guttera edouardi verreauxi* is referred to as *G e pallasi* and also *G cristata.* In the case of some subspecies there is still disagreement or doubt, even in the vernacular. Many of the distinguishing characteristics between some of the *Numida* subspecies lying in the belt across central and southern Africa are relatively slight e.g. colouration of bare skin and wattles. Here one is occasionally tempted to substitute the terms intermediate variation or deme. If, as is now agreed, the subspecies are all capable of interbreeding and since many of them overlap geographically it is easy to understand how isolated pockets of hybrids and variants could develop.

The trinominal classification of *Numididae* is mainly but not exclusively based on the check lists of JL Peters *Birds of the World,* 12 vols and Howard & Moore 1980, which follows the order known as the Basel sequence. This was proposed by Ernst Mayr at the 11th International Ornithological Congress in 1954. Additional details such as previous names are provided with each specific description, where this would seem to aid clarification. Thirty eight natural species and subspecies are currently recognised. These are divided between four genera and seven species.

* For illustrations of the species see the Colour Section facing p xvi

The huge diversity of the African climate creates an equally diverse breeding season amongst the guinea fowl population. Generally speaking, all the species nest during or close to the wet, lush periods of the year when the temperature is warm and food is most plentiful. In some parts of the continent where there can be extended droughts lasting for several years, the helmeted inhabitants have been known not to breed at all over an entire season. Breeding in these areas is therefore cued by the advent of the rains and acclerated plant growth as well as by length of daylight.

Some local areas vary from the normal standard where they are affected by altitude, mountain ranges and coastal winds, but the following may be applied as a rough guide. In West Africa the wet season is usually July to October, in some parts it begins two months earlier. In Central Africa the rains occur north of the equator, from April to June and in September to October. South of the equator they occur between November and April and again in July and August. Some areas may have more extended long rains and no short ones. In the east, Kenya, which is best known for the excellent climate of its high plateaux, also has extreme contrasts. The long wet season extends from March to May with a shorter one between October and December. The north eastern area is semi arid and the Masai lands in the south are almost equally hot and dry.

Northwards, the Sudan has a wet summer and dry winter with almost no rain in the extreme north at any time. Further down the east side, Moçambique has its hot wet season from October to March; the same months are hot and dry in Zimbabwe and Zambia. Angola and Namibia are dry and cool from June to September but hot and wet from October to May. In the Republic of South Africa, rainfall in the central areas is unpredictable with droughts and torrential rains often alternating. Night frosts occur along the western coastline from April to October. The eastern side is warmer and the northern strip is sub–tropical.

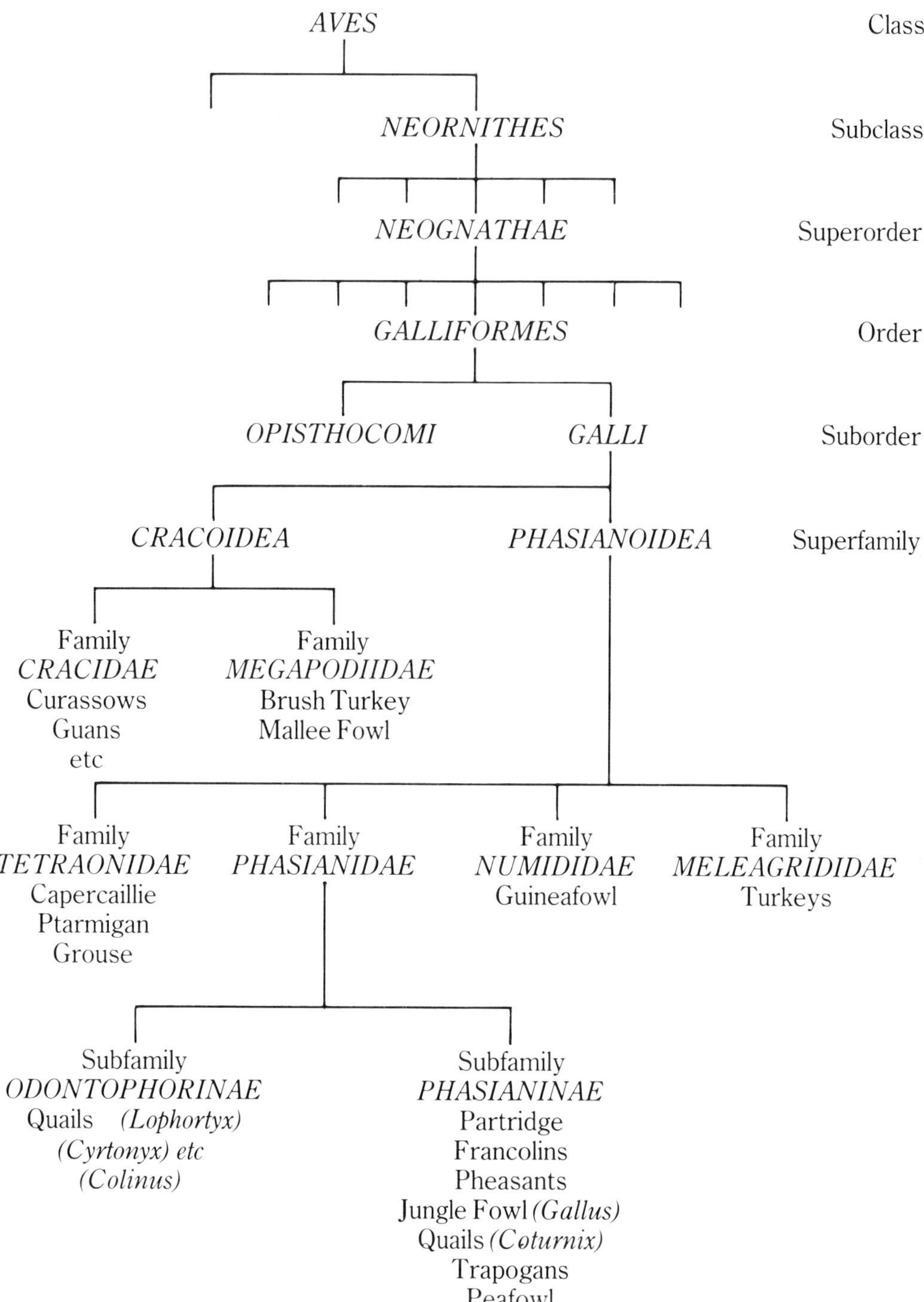

Figure 2 – 2 Classification

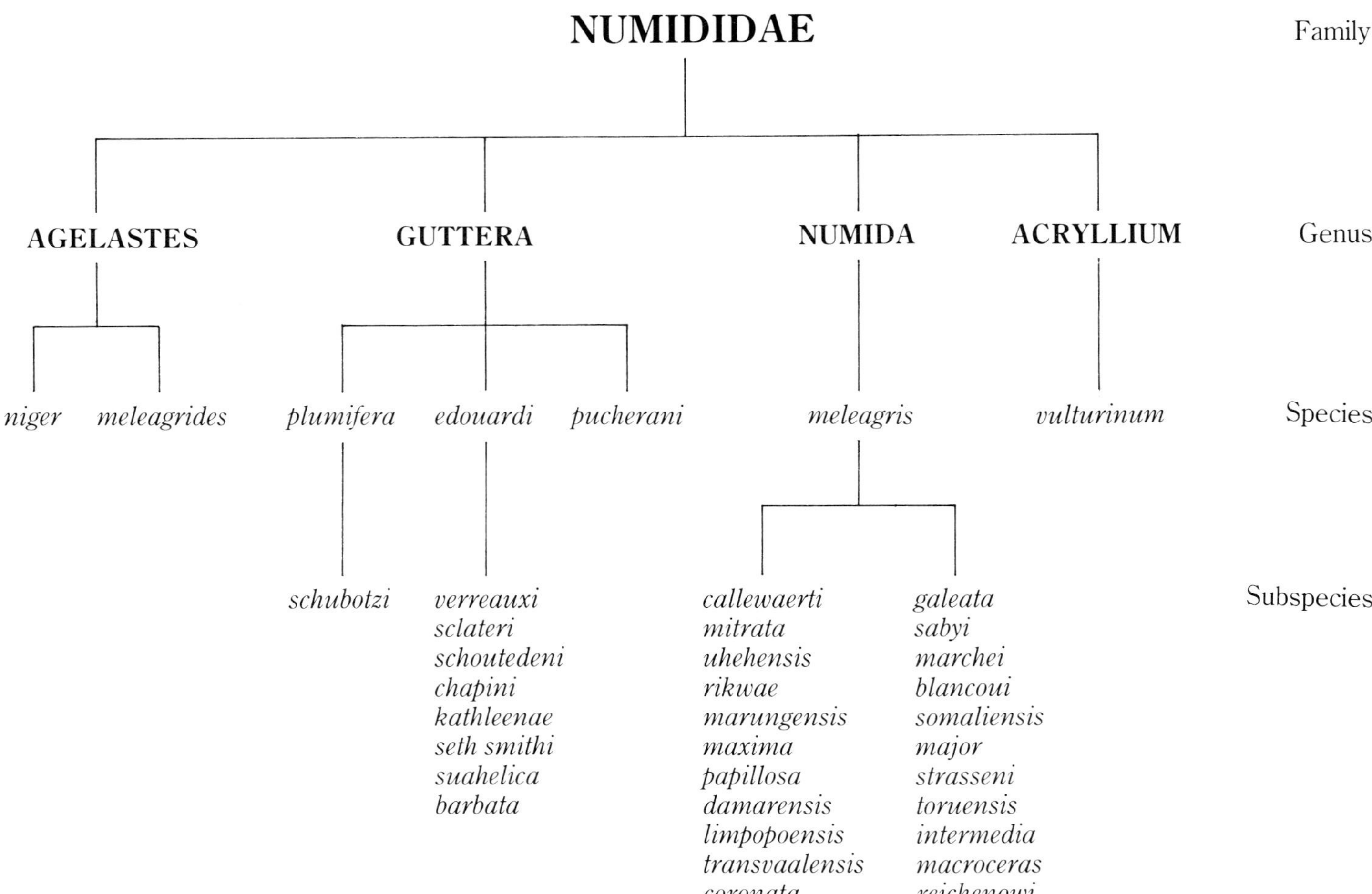

Figure 2 – 3 *Numididae* Family

GENUS ACRYLLIUM (Gray) 1840

Acryllium vulturinum (Hardwicke 1834)

Vulturine guinea fowl: Fr. Pintade vulturine, Gr. Geier-perlhuhn

Distribution

Eastern Ethiopia, Somali Republic, Kenya, eastern Uganda, north eastern Tanzania

Habitat

Common in the desert areas, arid grasslands, patches of scrub and thorns, Acacia woods and tree covered high plains. They can be seen roving in small flocks of anything from 25 to 70 birds. Often their heads are just visible moving through the long grasses. A few have been spotted in the dense forest on/Mount Massabit in Kenya.

Characteristics

Length 61 to 70 cms. Wing length 290 to 320 cms. Sometimes called the Royal guinea fowl, it has the most striking colours and the most elegant shape of any of the members of the family. It is larger and taller with a long thin neck, small bare head and strong bluish white curved beak. The bare skin of head and neck is greyish blue, the iris is crimson. A broad band of short velvet like chestnut feathers extends around the back of the cranium from ear to ear, producing an effect like a monk's tonsure. The feathers of lower neck and upper mantle extend into very long pointed hackles, black with stripes of white and cobalt blue. The upper parts of the body and abdomen are black, dotted with white spots. The breast has long bright cobalt blue patches on either side. Wings and tail are black with white stripes. The central tail rectrices are long and pointed with the laterals much shorter. The edges of the outer secondaries are pale mauve and the white spots on the flanks are ringed with lilac (mid mauve). The legs and feet are grey brown. The male has a blunt spur on one or both legs and is often slightly larger, otherwise the sexes look alike.

The chicks are barred and mottled brown, buff, tawny yellow and black with black stripes or patches on nape. The head carries black spots rather than stripes.

In the natural state, the nest is a hollow lined with some grass and sited under scrub or beside a tussock of tall grass. Eggs 8 to 15 usually more than 12, pale cream or buff, glossy and pitted with buff/white specks. Approximately 51 x 38 mm long, incubated by the hen they hatch in 24 days.

These birds rarely fly except to roost. They can run at great speed and survive long periods away from water. They absorb drops of dew from the greenstuffs on which they commence feeding well before dawn and utilise their metabolic water more efficiently, like most desert animals. The fact that they are even more addicted to insects than the other guinea fowl genera accounts for an additional moisture supply. Otherwise their food range is similar to the helmeted species.

The calls are softer and more agreeable than other guinea fowl but they can be noisy when going to roost, both cock and hen produce a long repetitive sound, transcription — *Kée–kée–kée–kée,* the hen has a softer note also, *Ou–ée ou–ée.*

Husbandry

As aviary birds, they are represented in many of the large collections in Europe and America. This handsome and gentle bird is always a big crowd atttraction. They acclimatise well and are not as difficult to maintain in Northern Europe as the Fireback Pheasants. Damp, severe frost and snow are injurious to them and during these conditions they should be indoors. It is unnecessary to heat their night shelter providing it is well insulated, unless in extreme wintery conditions with frost exceeding minus 5°C. It is advisable to cover their floor with a thick layer of straw or similar material to protect their feet during low temperatures. They are tame and non–aggressive in disposition so mix well with other birds. Being used to desert conditions, they will thrive best if their outside run has the advantage of as much full sunlight as possible. It must also be well drained.

Incubation and rearing works best with bantams or turkey hens. Eggs can also be hatched in incubators. Diet should comprise pheasant crumbs, greens, grains, soft fruits and finely minced meat, they will always welcome live insects.

This species is more prone to respiratory complaints than *Numida.*

GENUS AGELASTES

Agelastes niger (B P Hall 1961)

Phasidus niger (Cassin 1857)

Black guinea fowl: Fr. Pintade Noir, Gr. Schwarzesperlhuhn

Distribution

From Cape Lopez Gabon, south and west Cameroon to northern Congo, Ituri Forest in Zaire and Loango Coast.

Habitat

Confined to the equatorial rain forests of west and central Africa as far east as Aruwimi. Parties of 10 to 25 have been encountered wandering on the forest floor. It is not hunted for food by the local people as the flesh is said to be dry and to have a peculiarly disagreeable flavour. This is fortunate for its own preservation.

Characteristics

Length 42 to 46 cms, wing 203 to 218 mm. The smallest of all the guinea fowls; its head is bare except for a short band of downy velvet like black feathers which extend in a straight line from the culmen over the crown towards the occiput. The beak is greenish brown and the bare skin of head and neck pink or occasionally orange yellow. The head has no crest or protuberance. There are a few downy black feathers growing sparsely on the neck. The plumage is a sooty black, faintly pervaded with brown. The wings and tail have no other shading. The tail rectrices are long but not pointed. The eye is grey brown, legs and toes brown. The male has one to three blunt spurs on the rear of the tarsi, the female is usually not spurred but occasionally has one. Otherwise the sexes look alike. The spurs are laterally compressed and grooved. The immature birds have a patch of white on the abdomen, tawny markings on the crown and red brown vermiculations on breast and innermost secondaries.

The call is a peeping trill or soft low whistle repeated many times.

Food comprises insects, frogs, forest fungi and green leaves. The eggs are said to be a pale brown with yellow or violet clouding on a thick pitted shell approx 42 mm x 34 mm long. Prof A Ghigi held the opinion that the Black guinea fowl and the Congo peafowl were more closely related to the francolins.

Both species of *Agelastes* have transversal scales on the rere of the tarsi, resembling those of the pheasant family.

In spite of its rather chicken like appearance and longer tail, Dr J P Chapin has affirmed that this bird really belongs to the *Numididae.* If one examines its second metacarpal, one can see no backward process tending to bridge the gap between that and the third metacarpal, this is always present in the true *Phasianidae.*

B P Hall in *The Bulletin of British Ornithology* 1961, "On the relationship of the two genera *Agelastes meleagrides* and *Phasidus niger*", has analysed the very slight differences in their plumage, texture and tails, she pointed out the close resemblances between the immature birds and the chicks of each genus. In this she has been supported by R E Moreau and Dr Chapin who have agreed that the two birds are really geographic representatives of a single line of guinea fowl and should be subsumed under a single generic name. The proposal was therefore made that *Phasidus* should be considered a synonym of *Agelastes* and henceforth be known as *Agelastes niger.*

Husbandry

Some specimens have been maintained in aviaries for periods lasting several years. The most recent instance was in Antwerp Zoo, in 1959 and during the early 60's, but these birds have not yet been bred successfully in captivity. They require a full tropical environment with a lot of space which restricts the possibilities of breeding to a limited number of highly specialised aviaries.

GENUS AGELASTES

Agelastes meleagrides (Buonaparte 1849)

White Breasted guinea fowl: Fr. Pintade a poitrine blanche,
Gr. Weissbrüstiges Perlhuhn, Am. Turkey guinea fowl, Dth Kalkoenparelhoen.

Distribution

Western Ghana, Ivory Coast and Liberia.

Habitat

These birds are now extremely rare and have only been recorded in the lowland tropical forests of the above countries. They remain in the dense cover and are not often encountered. Small parties of up to six as well as pairs have been seen. The forest dwellers in Liberia used to trap them and occasionally find their nests.

Characteristics

Length 46 to 50 cm, wing 207 to 227 mm, tail M. 130 to 150 mm, F. 120 to 150 mm, tarsus 70 to 75 mm. The head and neck are bare except for a few white feathers sparsely distributed on neck and throat. The head has no protuberances or wattles and the bare skin is bright rose–red fading to milky white on the nape. The upper mantle and breast are white. The rest of the plumage is dark brown to black, the primaries being margined with grey and the secondaries with sepia, finely vermiculated with white dots on the outer webs. Eyes are brown, legs and feet are olive and the beak greenish brown. The male has small spurs, otherwise the sexes look alike. Both have transversal scales on rere of tarsi.

The eggs are a pale red brown pitted with white specks approx 45 mm x 35 mm.

Food comprises seeds, berries, worms, insects, and leaves.

The familiar call is a low deep *kok–kok–kok–kok.*

The chick has the head and neck covered in black down feathers. On the lower neck and chest the down is dark rufus to black, there is a white patch on the abdomen.

Husbandry

The Frankfurt Zoological Gardens acquired three young birds in 1963, one of these died prior to reaching full maturity. The other two were females and flourished until 1973. They both laid a considerable number of infertile eggs over a period of several years. Despite strenuous efforts, the zoo was unable to secure a male bird to mate with them. No others have been obtained since. The Zoo is confident that they would have been able to breed successfully in the spacious tropical environment which was provided. The Berlin Zoo has also had specimens but did not succeed in breeding with them.

Aviary food

Finely minced meat and greens, pheasant crumbs, fruit, live insects and grit. The floor of the forest species should be partly sand and gravel and mainly woodland peat and leaf mould, where the birds can scratch for insects and worms. A captive breeding programme would obviously be of great value in order to preserve and eventually redistribute this species which is diminishing faster than the rain forests themselves. Protective regulations are understandably difficult to enforce over the area of its natural habitat.

GENUS GUTTERA (Wagler 1832)

Crested guinea fowl: Fr. Pintade a Huppe Noir, Gr. Haubenperhuhn, Afrik. Kuifkoptarentaal, Dth. Kuifparelhoen, Swah. Kororo, Kiku. Ngerekere,

Tonga. i kangele, Chindao. i khangatori

Distribution

Members of this genus are widely distributed in the thickly forested area of South, Central, East and West Africa.

Habitat

Unlike *Numida* they prefer the humid tropical forest, opting for deciduous rather than evergreen areas. They can also be observed at the edges of the forest and in the adjacent clearings but they rarely stray far from the thick bush and undergrowth. When surprised they fly into the branches and vanish amidst the leafy camouflage. They are never encountered on the open plains. The species *Guttera plumifera* in particular, inhabits dense areas of virgin forest and tracts of 'Magongo', (*Sarcophrynium arnoldianum*), which dominates previously cleared areas.

Characteristics

The head and upper neck are bare apart from a thick mop of black feathers which ornament the head. The feathers rise from an adipose cushion of fibrous tissue, extending from between the nostrils backwards over the crown of the head. The shape, height and thickness of the crest varies considerably and the colouration of bare skin on certain areas of the head and neck is different in each subspecies. The neck skin is arranged in tight folds which are most noticeable around the nape. Most species lack the familiar gape wattles of the *Numida* genus, but in some of the *Guttera edouardi* subspecies (see illustration of *G E Schoutedeni*), the skin extends in a broad pendulous fold from the base of the cheeks. Sometimes there are distinct tufts of bristle at the base of the mandibles. The *Guttera edouardi* group have a wide collar of dark unspotted feathers from the base of the bare neck, spreading downwards in front well onto the upper breast and in some cases forming a mantle over the back.

In the adult birds, a section of the trachea extends into a curve or loop which is supported by a pocket shaped cavity between the wishbones of furcula as it passes to the lungs. In specimens of chicks which were examined, this feature was found to be undeveloped. This additional loop may contribute to their unique trumpeting call. A similar sound is produced by the crane family which has a 1.5 metre trachea coiled in loops. The Crested guinea fowl are noted for their unusually upright stance which is not normally adopted by the helmeted group. In size they are similar to the smaller members of the latter and have the same rounded body contours and thick plumage.

Apart from *Guttera plumifera* they have three distinct cries. A harsh grating alarm note and a short double note when on the move. Most distinctive of all is the musical trumpeting call with various rhythms, produced while standing upright and with the neck extended, usually after feeding and in the evenings before roosting. This has been described as *tatti–tatti–tatti–tattarara–tarara–tattarara,* repeated at different speeds. Their food includes insects, spiders, snails, small vertebrates, grass, leaves, seeds, berries and kernels.

They are monogamous like all the genera.

A smaller number of eggs are laid in a hollow on the ground in as much cover as possible, in thick scrub or forest areas. The colour varies from light brown to off white, pitted and speckled, narrow and pointed at one end, large and rounded at the other, average size 50 mm x 41 mm. The incubation period is shorter than that of Numida, 23 to 25 days. Most of the chicks have a large blue spot on the crown of the head. By 5 to 6 months old they are often as large as their parents and have developed adult plumage.

Husbandry

Guttera plumifera, Guttera pucherani and at least six subspecies of *Guttera edouardi* have been imported into Europe and have bred successfully. Prof Ghigi crossed *Guttera edouardi edouardi* with *Guttera edouardi barbata* in the 1920's. *Guttera pucherani* was bred in England as early as 1912 by Gurney and quite regularly in Europe ever since. Crested guinea fowl imported from Sierra Leone, probably *Guttera edouardi verreauxi,* had been seen in England before 1685.

In the aviary it is understandably more difficult to induce imported specimens to breed and they have been found to require fairly large spacious enclosures with an environment simulating the forest conditions closest to those from which they derive. All the *Guttera* species suffer from the cold and require permanent heating in northern latitudes.

GUTTERA PLUMIFERA PLUMIFERA (Cassin 1857)

Plumed guinea fowl: Fr. Pintade plumifère, Gr. Schlichtfederiges Haubenperlhuhn

Distribution

Cameroon, Gabon, Loango coast and Congo.

Habitat

Primary forest. It prefers to remain in the dense areas of forest, not appearing at the outer perimeters or in scrub or clearings like members of the other two species. A flock of from 10 to 40 when not breeding, will roost in one large tree if possible. They are more difficult to observe than the other crested species, usually seen feeding on the forest floor, they disappear silently into the trees when disturbed, without sounding an alarm.

Characteristics

The black crest plumes are tall, slender and profuse, rising straight upwards, they begin between the nostrils and continue in a narrow band over the crown of the head in a full arc, with the tallest plumes in the centre. This bird has rather well developed wattles, depending from the corner of the gape and ranging in colour from dirty yellow to slate grey; about 13 mm on the cock and 4 mm on the hen. The bare skin around the head and neck is dark slate blue grey. There are two blue tufts of hair like bristles on either side of the base of the upper mandible. The body, shape and plumage are similar to the *Guttera edouardi* species, a dense black, covered with large white spots. Some of the wing feathers have a white margin. On the inner webs the spots are irregular; on the outer webs the spots run in lines and have a bluish tinge. It does not have the usual black collarette and each neck feather is terminated with a very large pearl shaped white spot bordered with blue. Eyes brown, beak blue grey, legs and toes light bluish grey. Length 20 to 22 ins. (50 to 55 cm). Wing span of 235 to 242 mm in the male and 215 to 230 mm in the female. Tail 110 mm, beak 24 to 26 mm.

The call has been described as a series of harsh discordant sounds, *Ka–ka–kak–kar–ka–kak,* not as loud or piercing as the other crested species and silent when alarmed. The flock when feeding makes a distinctive quacking sound.

The chick has black down on the crown, neck and rump with pale chestnut on cheeks and over ear coverts, the sides of neck, chest and wing are deep russet, underparts pale buff, two pale chestnut stripes on either side of forehead which almost meet on the crown and diverge towards the occiput. The young bird has short black feathers on neck and head with tiny wattles at the corners of the gape.

A nest found in August had nine white eggs of the usual shape, laid on dry leaves 48 to 49 mm x 37 to 38 mm.

Native hunters can call them up with a nasal *Kow* sound, repeated until they hear the birds responding with a low *kak–kak–kak* and eventually they appear from the undergrowth. Their flesh has been described as dry and peculiarly strong flavoured. This is possibly because they eat quantities of forest fungi as does *Agelastes niger.*

GUTTERA PLUMIFERA SCHUBOTZI (Reichenow 1912)

Distribution

Found in Zaire. From the Ubangi river eastwards to the Semliki river and Lakes Albert and Edward.

Husbandry

Similar in all respects to *Guttera plumifera plumifera* except that it has large rough patches of orange coloured skin on cheeks and nape of neck. It has been bred successfully in the Royal Zoological Gardens of Antwerp, where chicks were born as recently as 1968.

GUTTERA PUCHERANI PUCHERANI (Hartlaub 1860)

Kenya Crested guinea fowl: Fr. Pintade huppé de Pucheran, Gr. Pucherans Haubenperlhuhn

Distribution

Somali Republic, Kenya, Tanzania, Zanzibar and Pemba Islands. From the Juba river in the north, south to the Pangani river, coastal region and inland to Kilimanjaro. Common in the Sokoke–Arabuku forest and inland from the coast. Birds from the Jombeni mountains are somewhat larger. Outside the breeding season, flocks of up to 50 birds have been observed in semi–open vegetation.

Description

Some ornithologists have maintained that this is another subspecies of *Guttera edouardi* but we have no evidence of natural interbreeding and as the colouring and the neck skin formation is distinct from the others, most modern works afford it separate status. The body plumage is uniformly grey/black and covered with medium sized bright blue spots, these are large and very distinct on the primary coverts. There are long distinct blue and white stripes along the primaries and secondaries, these are spaced on a black ground. It is without the black collar common to the *Guttera edouardi* group. The uniformly sized blue spots continue on the neck plumage up to the junction with the bare skin. The skin has a thick double fold around the neck, tightly creased on the lower nape and slightly raised under the ears. The bare skin of head and neck are a bright cobalt blue except for patches of scarlet around the eyes, behind the crest, on chin, throat and front of neck. The black crest is of medium length, thick, fine and slightly crinkled. It extends from the base of the upper mandible across the crown and onto the occiput. The outer edges of the flight feathers have a cream to pale coffee coloured edging. The spotting on the under plumage is finer and the overall impression of the plumage gives a bright blue effect. The eyes are a light red brown, legs and feet pale blue grey.

From a study on *G p pucherani* conducted by Dr T M Crowe (see Bibliography) there appears to be a relationship between the degree of crest curliness and the average climatic temperature. The crest height and extent was also found to be diminished in localities of greater visiblilty. He has suggested that a high crest may be useful as a signaling device where the vegetation is dense.

Husbandry

It has been imported into Europe many times this century and bred successfully. A flourishing colony is currently established in the Walsrode Bird Park, Federal Republic of Germany, where it has been bred for a number of years. In 1980 there were also specimens in Augsburg, Berlin and the USA.

GUTTERA EDOUARDI VERREAUXI (Elliott 1970)

Guttera edouardi pallasi (Stone 1912)
also *Guttera cristata* (Pallas 1764)
Pallas's Black Crested guinea fowl

Distribution and Habitat

West Africa from Guinea Bissau and Sierra Leone as far as Togo and Nigeria. Can be observed in and on the perimeter of dense forest, thick bush and on forested hills up to 2,500 feet (approx 760 m).

Characteristics

The crest is of thick crinkled black feathers longer and not as curly as in *Guttera edouardi edouardi*. Bare skin of face and neck very dark blue. Crimson chin and throat. Plumage base deep black with a chestnut wash, all the feathers are densely covered with tiny spots white in centre surrounded with Cambridge blue. The primaries are dull brown with white edging; the secondaries are black, the three innermost having broad white margins. The outer webs have several bright blue lines. Inner wing lining grey brown, spotted towards the tips of coverts. Beak greenish grey, eyes brown, legs and feet bluish black. Wattles rudimentary.

Length 46 to 53 cm, wings 252 to 272 mm, beak 27 to 29 mm, tail 120 to 135 mm, tarsus 71 to 82 mm. Has been imported and bred in Europe, it is quite belligerent in the aviary.

The chicks, like others of the group are barred on the head and back on a chestnut, black and buff ground, buff shading is paler underneath.

This subspecies was for a considerable time confused with *Guttera edouardi edouardi* from central and southern Africa which was also believed to have the crimson throat. This led Prof Ghigi to believe he had discovered a new subspecies with a dark throat in the Zambesi valley, (see *Ibis* [1944] pages 166 to 171, article by C H B Grant and C W Mackworth Praed).

GUTTERA EDOUARDI SCLATERI (Reichenow 1898)

Distribution

Western Cameroon (Sakbayeme), Edea and adjacent localities on the Sanaga river, also southern Nigeria east of the Niger river.

Characteristics

Similar to *Guttera edouardi verreauxi* except for the crest. This is very short in front, approximately 7mm, the feathers are long and slender and lengthen to approximately 46mm behind the crown of the head. The nostril is exposed as the lower edge is unfeathered. The neck, head and crop are blue, chin is red, beak is pale grey blue, legs and feet are grey, eyes dark brown. Length of wing 243 to 275 mm, tail approx 130 mm, tarsus 75 to 80 mm, and length from 45 to 53 cm.

GUTTERA EDOUARDI SCHOUTEDENI (Chapin 1923)

also *Guttera edouardi schouteneni*
Schoutedens Blue Spotted guinea fowl: Fr. Pintade huppé de Schouteden

Distribution

Southern Zaire and Republic of Congo. South of the equatorial forest, through the Kasai valley and area of Lake Tumba.

Characteristics

The black crest feathers resemble those of *Guttera edouardi verreauxi* but are slightly longer, 40 mm over crown and 27 mm on forehead. The bare skin of head and neck is dark blue, chin and throat red, no red around the eye. The beak is lighter grey and the black collar is more extensive. Tight double fold of neck skin on nape like all *Guttera edouardi* and distinctive pendant fold at throat. The rest of the plumage is similar to *Guttera edouardi seth smithi* except that the overall spotting is smaller and less blue.

Husbandry

It has been bred successfully in the Royal Antwerp Zoo during the late 1950s.

GUTTERA EDOUARDI CHAPINI (Frade 1926)

Distribution

Central and southern Angola especially around Benguella.

Characteristics

Similar to *Guttera edouardi schoutedini* except that the bare skin on the centre of the chin and throat is crimson, face and neck steel blue. Much less spotting on the feathers. The crest feathers are less crinkled but similar in length, wing 260 to 263 mm.

GUTTERA EDOUARDI KATHLEENAE (White 1943)

Distribution

Western Zambia, Southern Zaire and Eastern Angola.

Characteristics

Very similar to *Guttera edouardi chapini*. The bare skin on the chin, lower cheeks and centre of throat is a bright scarlet. Feeding call a deep *tok–tok–tok*. Wing span 260 to 280 mm.

GUTTERA EDOUARDI SETH–SMITHI (Neumann 1908)

or *Guttera cristata seth–smithi*

Distribution

Zaire, Tanzania, Uganda and southern Sudan. North and east of the equatorial forest from the Ubangi river to the rift valley, south to the Semliki river extending into Tanzania as far as the Pangani river. Around Lakes Albert and Edward in Uganda and across the border into Sudan. It occurs in considerable numbers and is the subspecies of *Guttera edouardi* most likely to be seen in east Africa.

Characteristics

It has stronger dark blue spotting on the plumage than other members of the *Guttera edouardi* subspecies. The black crinkly crest, resembling that of *Guttera edouardi verreauxi* is well developed on the forehead where the feathers are approximately 23 mm when straightened and 36 mm on the crown. The bare skin of the throat and front of the neck is ruby to brick red and that on the rest of the head and neck is steel blue. The gape wattles are small and pendant 3 to 4 mm. The eyes are dark brown and it has the usual tight hanging fold of skin around the nape.

Husbandry

Recorded breeding in Uganda from November to January, in Zaire, March. These birds have frequently been bred in Europe and are currently in Holland and the Walsrode Bird Garden in West Germany.

GUTTERA EDOUARDI EDOUARDI (Hartlaub 1867)

also *Guttera lividicollis* (Ghigi 1905), *Guttera symonsi* (Roberts 1917), *Guttera bocagei* (Frade 1926)
Zambesi Crested guinea fowl

Distribution

Zambia, southern Malawi and the Zambesi valley in Moçambique across to the Victoria Falls and southwards from Zimbabwe through the eastern Transval to Natal and the coast north of Durban. Found in groups of 7 or 8 up to small flocks of 20 to 25 birds.

Characteristics

The black crest feathers are short, dense and very tightly curled. The bare skin around the head and neck is very dark blue black. There is a distinguishing triangular patch of ochreous white around and under the ears, sometimes reaching back onto the nape. The plumage is deep black with a hint of dark chestnut but not nearly as definite as on *Guttera edouardi verreauxi*. This is uniformly covered with tiny bluish white spots which are surrounded by indistinct black circles. Around the lower neck there is a wide unspotted black collar which extends down unto the upper breast. The primaries and secondaries are strongly edged with white and the secondaries have longitudinal blue streaks. The eyes are deep red, beak is horn coloured with blue tinge at base. Legs and feet bluish grey. Length varies from 46 to 56 cm (18 to 22 in.), wing span 251 to 280 mm, tail 110 to 120 mm. Nests have been found around Beira in December, Zambesi valley in January.

GUTTERA EDOUARDI SUAHELICA (Neumann 1908)

also *Numida grantii* (Elliot 1871)

Distribution

Tanzania from Ugogo to Lindi, south and west Malawi.

Characteristics

Similar in size and plumage to *Guttera edouardi barbata* but the spotting has only the faintest hint of blue. The bare skin on throat, chin, upper part of neck, sides of head and under the eyes are red, but not quite as strongly defined as in *Guttera pucherani pucherani,* all the rest is blue black.

GUTTERA EDOUARDI BARBATA (Ghigi 1905)

also *Guttera cristata makondorum* (Grote 1912)

Distribution

Extreme south and east of Tanzania, Makonda area and adjacent parts of Mocambique to southern Malawi.

Characteristics

The crest is shorter and more tightly curled like that of *Guttera edouardi edouardi.* the skin of the head and neck is dark blue and black without any red. Its black collar descends to the middle of the breast. There are tiny distinct pale blue spots on the back. Wing approx 275 to 290 mm. It has been bred in Europe on numerous occasions.

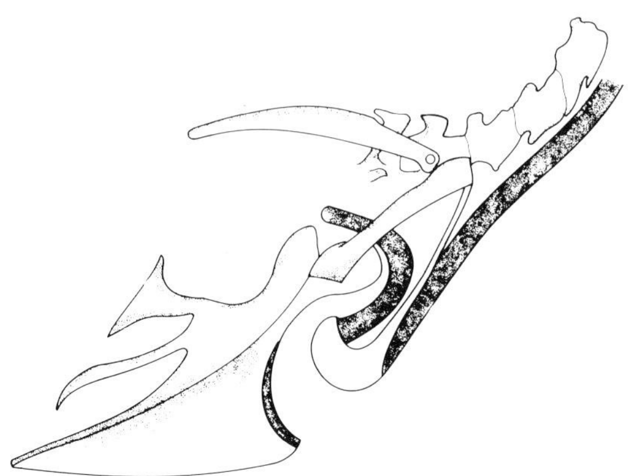

Figure 2 – 4 Sternum and Shoulder-girdle of Guttera showing looped Trachea

SPECIES DIFFERENTIATION

1. Individual members of a species or large subspecies e.g. *N.m. galeata* or *N.m. mitrata* are shown in breeding populations in which a thorough mixing of genes takes place. The genes of a population constitute a gene pool. There is frequent interbreeding which results in gene flow between the interbreeding populations.
2. As a result of separate mutations, different types appear in the populations A and B; individuals who possess the new characteristics are called variants.
3. New characteristics which are advantageous are favoured by selection, the variants increase giving rise to two subspecies; or where we began with the large subspecies, two races, these have recognisable differences but can still interbreed, i.e., there is still gene flow.
4. New variants may eventually appear within each subspecies or each race and some of these may eventually become dominant. In this way different variations accumulate within the subspecies or races A and B.
5. If the differences between the subspecies eventually become so extensive that the natural gene flow is no longer possible, two new species will have been formed.

1 *Numida uhehensis*

2 *Numida maxima*

3 *Numida intermedia*

4 *Numida papillosa*

Figure 2 – 5 Head, Helmets and Wattles compared

Species Differentiation

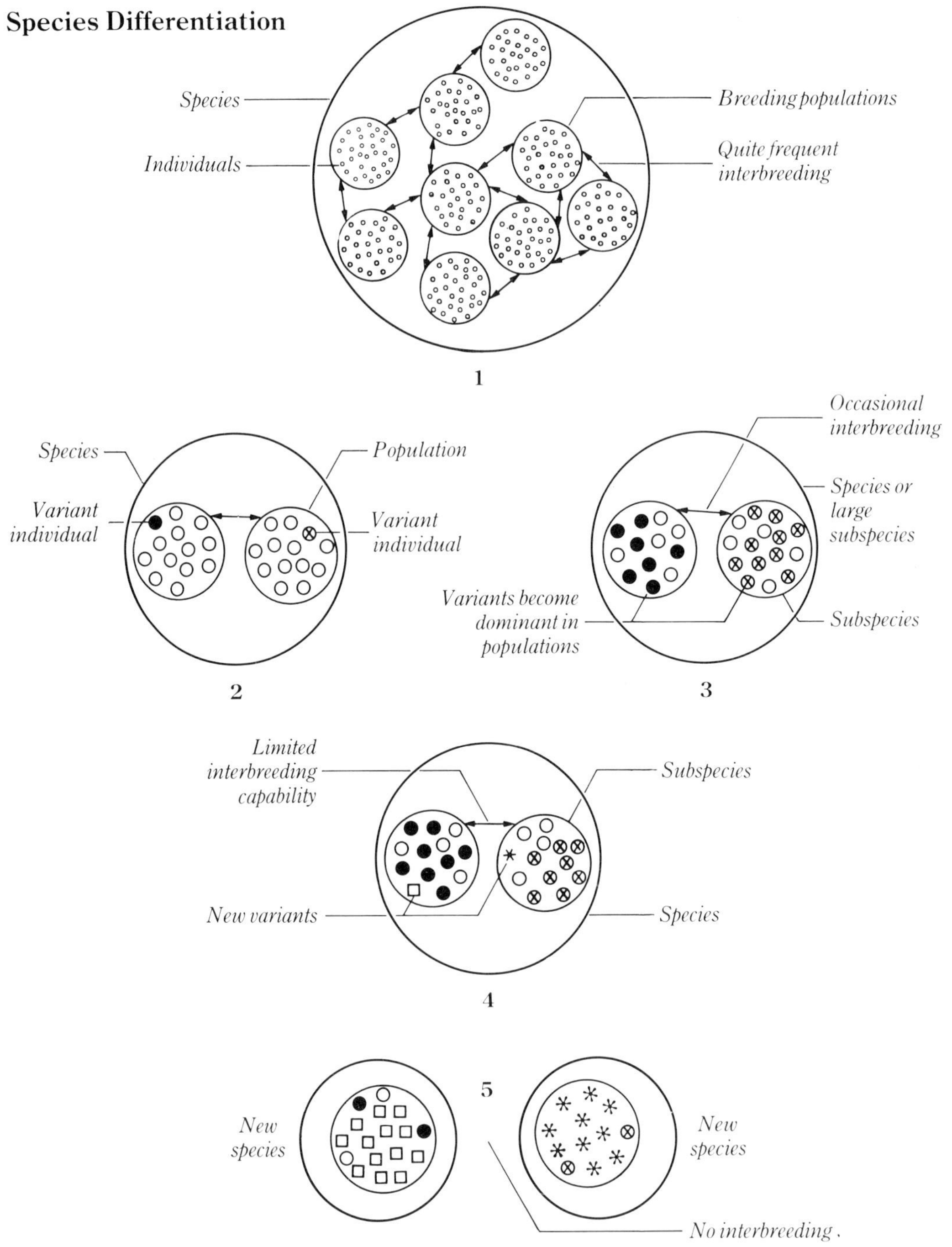

Figure 2 – 6 Species Differentiation Diagram

GENUS NUMIDA

Helmeted guinea fowl: Fr. Pintade casquée/commune, Gr. Helmperlhuhn, Russ. Cessarka, Dth. Witborstparelhoen, Afrik. Gewone Tarentaal, Swah. Kanga/Inkanga/Nganga Sotho and Sechuana, Khaka, Zulu and Xhosa. i-Mpangele, Hausa. Zabon Daji/Zabo, Mandingo. Kammo, Joloff. Nat, Tuareg. Tilel, Egypt, Ouēsa

Distribution

This the best known and most common species. Its numerous subspecies are distributed over almost the whole of Africa south of the Sahara desert. Even to the north, one subspecies inhabits parts of the Atlas mountain range in Morocco and to the east another extends into Arabia.

Habitat

Each subspecies tends to occupy specific geographical locations and in the regions where they overlap, especially north of the equatorial forest, distinct races or tribes tend to occupy local habitats in either successive belts or pockets. They can accommodate to diverse conditions and are found over a wide range of terrain. On the savannahs and farmlands they favour areas where there are small scattered clumps of scrub particularly *Acacia,* which has a symbiotic relationship with ants, a favourite food; here their colouring provides good camouflage in strong light and shade. They will choose locations where there are at least some large trees in which to roost. The Locust bean is another popular tree.

They are rarely found further than 10 km away from water, lakes and large rivers or smaller ones in which the flow does not cease during the dry seasons. They are also common in lightly covered forest districts and high grassy plateaux up to 1,800 m, rocky hillsides, mountain gorges and ravines. During the day they usually walk from place to place covering as much as 20 to 30 miles while foraging. In parts of east Africa towards evening it is customary to see long columns of these birds advancing towards a river or water hole where they drink in orderly fashion, never overcrowding or hustling. Those at the back will wait patiently while the front rows quench their thirst and quickly withdraw.

The flocks are at their largest size during the dry season. Before 1950, numbers up to 2000 or 3000 would not be uncommon around an east African water hole. During the rainy season they divide into smaller breeding groups. They prefer to roost in the highest trees available and although they dislike excessively damp locations, especially for nesting, they can sometimes be found amongst swampy areas of mangroves near the coast.

Characteristics

Numida are easily distinguished by the bony protuberance on the crown of the head from which their name is taken. The helmet reaches full size when the bird is around two years old and as it ages becomes progressively more wrinkled and faded looking. It varies in size and shape according to subspecies and even within each subspecies there is considerable variation. Occasionally specimens have been found without any helmet development, these have only a horny casing or cap over the crown. They have cartilaginous wattles extending on either side of the mandibles or gape, these also vary in size, position and colour. The nostrils have a fleshy membrane around and between them which is usually linked to the wattles. The bare skin on cheeks, throat and nape is somewhat wrinkled or rucked like fine leather. The sparse filoplumes which proceed up the nape with varying profusion in all except the tufted group, resemble hairs more than feathers. The broad tail has 16 rectrices which are short and rounded at the ends and are not much longer than the coverts.

Dr T M Crowe has pointed out that many of these geographic morphological variations seem to be closely correlated with environmental variation. Birds inhabiting hot moist areas tend to have longer denser filoplumes on the neck. These are believed to be sensory structures which enable the bird to monitor environmental effects like wind etc., they may also act as a heat shield.

The plumage is generally black or dark grey and brown with pearly white dots and short transverse bars and stripes of white on the primaries and secondaries and sometimes breast and neck plumage. Details of colouring, size and weight vary considerably between subspecies, interestingly some of the smallest birds are found in Morocco and parts of west Africa and the largest in south central and south Africa. All of the subspecies are extremely wary and alert.

When hungry these birds will tackle almost anything if non toxic and of appropriate size, their food includes even young birds and snakes (see also chapter 4, section on Aviary). While feeding, they will often proceed on a wide front, raising and driving insects and small animals ahead of them, then finally they circle in on them from the sides in a U shaped formation. This is another reason for the congregation of large social flocks during the dry season in addition to the obvious benefits gained for raising the young birds and the reduction of predation levels. The chances of survival as a member of a flock are increased by a factor of 2 or 3 for the adult birds.

Clutches of eggs are from 8 to more than 20 depending on subspecies and climate. They are laid in a well camouflaged nesting hollow often beside a tussock in the open plains as well as in wooded areas. Often two or three hens will share a nest so that one or two are always 'on guard'. The nests are so difficult to see that they are generally only found by accident. They are lined with grasses and leaves and the eggs are often covered with the same material when the parent is absent. In sandy areas the eggs may be covered with sand to help retain moisture or in hot dry rocky places the nest is frequently sited near water where the hen can wet her breast feathers during intervals between brooding.

The egg shells are off–white to light brown, very thick and deeply pitted, they may be strongly or lightly speckled with dark or red brown spots or blotches. They are wide and rounded at one end tapering to a narrow rounded point at the other usually 45 mm to 55 mm in length and 120 mm to 130 mm in circumference. Incubation is approx 27 to 28 days. The hen only isolates herself from the flock just before and during the actual incubation period; the cock usually remains in the vicinity of the nest to assist in guard duty. The hen and chicks rejoin the flock within 2 to 3 days after hatching, by which time the chicks are well able to keep up with the other adults. The colouring of their down varies only slightly between the subspecies. It exhibits the familiar tawny yellow to buff with the distinctive black or brown markings common to most guinea fowl. Usually light brown or black stripes over the crown and nape and along the back. The legs and feet are normally deep orange to coral.

The brown stripes on the crown are the last of the distinctive chick markings to disappear as the new feathers emerge over a 4 to 12 week period. During this time the primaries are dark grey with white patches on the outer webs. The secondaries and coverts are mottled grey brown and white. From mantle to tail, the feathers are red brown and fawn. The emerging wattles and the beak are tinged pink. By the time the chicks are 3 to 4 months old, the smaller flocks rejoin to form the same large flocks which had fragmented, prior to the breeding season. Unless severely disturbed, each major flock keeps to well defined territorial areas although there is some traffic of individual birds between flocks. They have favourite roosting sites in wooded valleys which are patronised continuously over decades, as indicated by the large mounds of droppings beneath specific trees. They roost at twilight and often return to foraging an hour or two before dawn, to take advantage of marauding night insects and the condensation on the herbage. This allows them the luxury of a long noon siesta in well choosen shade while the sun is at its hottest.

Initially, naturalists assumed that there were at least three distinct species of helmeted guinea fowl and it is true that each of these groupings possess certain distinctive characteristics. *N.m. galeata* in west Africa has the dark grey unspotted plumage over collar and breast and the broad red wattles. *Numida m. meleagris* and its allies in the north and east, (known as the Tufted or Bristle Nosed guinea fowl), have the nasal bristles, some have a thick wooly collarette of feathers around the neck and very pale blue wattles. Across the south east, centre and south of the continent stretch the taller, broader helmeted groups with blue green neck skin and narrow wattles. On the distribution map for *Numida,* I have applied these distinctions and designated the three sets as G, T and H respectively, in order to provide greater ease of identification; it also assists in highlighting the directions of genetic drift between the main geographical areas. The adjacent smaller groups of subspecies often differ only in averages but overlap in ranges of measurement and colour gradation.

At the beginning of the 20th century, exhaustive research was carried out by naturalists more thoroughly in some regions than others. In the areas around Lake Victoria for instance, when separate local groups were examined, each set of distinguishing phenotypical characteristics was regarded as constituting a distinct subspecies. Some of these would nowadays be regarded as a local variation or a genetic deme, which is a more or less isolated unit of population within a species or large subspecies. An example might be *N.m. uhehensis* which is isolated and contained on the plateau of that name, well inside the *mitrata* area. It is also currently accepted that the height and curvature of the helmet is a matter of individual variation and therefore it is distinguishable only in a generalised way e.g. by the very broad cranial base or overall size as a typical feature of a subspecies. This was recognised by Oscar Neumann as early as 1898 in his article *Die Helmperlhühner,* but it remained a subject of dispute for many decades. It is therefore quite possible to find individuals, demes or clinal variations within any of the major subspecies, which are after all distributed over vast tracts of territory, exhibiting one or more features, helmet, wattle shape and colour, body size etc., which do not conform to the typical description.

All members of the genus *Numida* are fairly hardy and most of them have been imported and bred in many parts of the world. They require protection from frost and cool damp weather during the winter as they are not as hardy as the domesticated varieties. Specimens most likely to be seen in zoos or bird gardens are *N.m. mitrata, N.m. reichenowi, N.m. galeata, N.m. coronata* and *N.m. meleagris.*

NUMIDA MELEAGRIS GALEATA (Pallas 1767)

Numida zechi (Reichenow — variation)

Grey Breasted guinea fowl

Distribution

West Africa from Cameroon to Senegal and up through Nigeria as far as Air in Niger. North of the rain forest up to the desert.

This species was introduced into Cape Verde Islands, St Thomas and Annobon circa 1683 and was abundant by 1709. It was also introduced around the same period to St. Helena, Cuba, Jamaica, Puerto Rico, Dominican Republic, Haiti and central America, where they quickly became naturalised. In 1960 they were still common on Annobon, the Agalega Islands and on some of the Cape Verde Islands. They no longer occur on Ascension, St. Helena, Madeira or Porto Santo. In the West Indies they are now extinct on Puerto Rico and Jamaica but still feral on Cuba, Isle of Pines and the Dominican Republic. Domesticated strains are of course widespread.

Habitat

Wide ranging and adaptable, they inhabit open plains and farmland, forest clearings, plateaux, mountain gorges and rocky hillsides. Favourite spots are near a river bank where thick bush and high trees are plentiful, also tracts of ironstone country and dry bush, or mangroves swamps near the coast.

Characteristics

The bare skin of chin, throat, lower neck and along nape is brownish black, dark grey in front of helmet. Pale bluish white on sides of head and cheeks and around eyes, ears and sides of upper neck. Medium sized umber coloured helmet, usually with a backward curve. Rows of stiff dark filoplumes proceed up the nape. The large broad wattles on either side of the head are usually scarlet with a bluish white base but sometimes they are half bluish white and half scarlet or even just scarlet tipped. The fleshy membrane around the nostrils and down to the corner of the gape on either side is scarlet to deep red. Beak yellowish to pale brown, eyes clear brown. The plumage is black, occasionally washed or streaked with dark chestnut brown and covered with large pearl white spots ringed with deep black outer circles. It has a wide slate grey collar washed with purple or pale lilac extending from the lower throat down over the upper breast and back around the mantle. The primaries are more barred than speckled, strong parallel lines of spots and short transverse white bars. The spotting from the lower breast and along the flanks to the undertail feathers is particularly large. The feathers on the lower back and tail coverts have very fine dense net like spotting, producing a grey cobweb effect. Legs and feet are grey brown. The hen is similar to the cock but usually slightly smaller. Length 48 to 59 cm, beak from base of nostril 22 to 26 mm, wing 250 to 275 mm, tail 120 to 150 mm, tarsi 68 to 75 mm. Mating usually occurs in April or May depending on the region and chicks are weaned by August or September. Eggs have been found in Secoto as late as October; 8 to 15 eggs are common sized 50 mm x 39 mm with the normal guinea fowl shape, light brown to off white, deeply pitted blotched or speckled with reddish brown.

This species is the principal ancestor of the domestic and feral guinea fowls spread around the world, prior to the modern hybrids which are now being disseminated rapidly. As might be expected of a subspecies which covers such a vast part of west Africa there is a high degree of variation in size and other characteristics. Many of the agricultural societies along the Gambia, Volta and Niger rivers have long traditions of breeding these birds. One such colony is described in the 19th century by Graf Zecchi who in fact claimed the birds which he found there as a separate subspecies. This was established among the community in the area of Krachi in Togo. Here the birds were much smaller, being around 48 cm long with high helmets and very large kidney shaped red wattles. The skin on the nape was coloured blue. As many of the domesticated birds undoubtly escaped over the centuries to breed back with the wild subspecies, it is almost impossible to determine which characteristics may have been influenced by domestication and which would have been natural variations. Both the albino and the black mutations were noted in the 19th century in different areas. The Cape Verde birds were also small. They were the only imported species to have survived as they flourished in the inaccessible mountain ranges where it was too difficult to hunt them.

NUMIDA MELEAGRIS SABYI (Hartert 1919)

Distribution

Western Morocco, in the Atlas mountain region mostly between the Bou Regreb and Sebou River, near Fez and south of Marrakesh.

Habitat

It can be found in small groups along the wooded ravines and in the foothills.

Characteristics

Closely related to *N.m. galeata,* the shape and colouring are similar but this bird is usually smaller in size; length 470 to 500 mm. The helmet and wattles are also smaller and completely red, the legs are almost black. The main distinguishing feature is the unspotted collar which is distinctly wine tinted. The head is pale grey. It breeds earlier, laying 8 to 12 eggs from the end of March onwards.

It's numbers have suffered severe reduction since about 1960 and only scattered pairs have been recorded recently. It is sometimes confused with groups of feral guinea fowl which can be seen in the foothills and locally in coastal areas as far as Derna, near Tobruk in eastern Libya.

NUMIDA MELEAGRIS MARCHEI (Oustalet 1882)

Gabon Helmeted guinea fowl

Distribution

The Savannahs of Gabon to the lower and middle Congo river, bounded northwards by the Ubangi river up to the central African Republic and across to the southern tip of Cameroon.

Characteristics

This is usually a slightly larger bird than *galeata*. The feathers of the mantle and upper breast are washed with a darker blue shade. The lateral wattles are red and have the broad form of galeata but are smaller. The feathering of the collar often has small white bars. Its characteristics merge with those of *N.m. galeata* along the lower Niger. It's length is 500 to 580 mm.

NUMIDA MELEAGRIS BLANCOUI (Grote 1936)

Distribution

Western Cameroon, Ouham basin to Gore in the north and to Bouca and Batangafo in the east. Type specimen from east Logone river.

Characteristics

Feathering resembles *galeata*. The wattles are blue white with red tips and there are small bristles at the base of the culmen. It is considered to be an intermediate form between *marchei* and *strasseni* (see *Oiseau* page 65 by G M Lucien Blancou, 1939).

NUMIDA MELEAGRIS MELEAGRIS (Linne 1758)

Numida ptylorhyncha (Leeson 1831)
Tufted guinea fowl/Bristle Nosed guinea fowl, Tufted Sennar guinea fowl, Fr. Pintade à pinceau.

Distribution

From the Lake Chad region eastwards across Chad and Sudan, the Kordofan province and the White Nile as far south as Bahr el Ghazal. It continues eastwards through northern

Ethiopia and Djibouti across to Yemen and Asir in Saudi Arabia. It may be found in steep mountain areas or in the marshlands of the White Nile and its tributaries.

Characteristics

This is the ancestor of the stock cultivated in Eygpt and probably in parts of the Roman empire. It has been bred sporadically by the hill farmers of the southern Sudan. Quite a large bird, 540 to 600 mm in length. Its black plumage is thickly spotted with white dots; the outer web of the secondaries is finely vermiculated and not barred. It has a thick tuft of hairlike bristles growing from the membrane on the cere between the nostrils. Its lateral wattles are large, and usually pale blue–white, in some regions the lower part is red. The slightly curved helmet is dirty yellow at the base changing to maroon at the tip with red brown culmen; skin of face and neck pale blue white, the beak is horn coloured, eyes dark brown, legs and feet are sepia. The nape feathers are dense and dark brown or black. The juvenile bird often has a feathered breast tuft which disappears before reaching adulthood. Many of the birds seen in Arabia have blue green neck skin and less bristles which suggests a transition to *N.m. mitrata.* Colonies of *N.m. meleagris* and *N.m. somaliensis* have flourished sporadically since the 1920's in the Egyptian Zoological Gardens at Giza.

NUMIDA MELEAGRIS SOMALIENSIS (Neumann 1899)

Distribution

From Ethiopia, the Harar, Galla and Arussi districts eastwards to the coast of the Somali Republic, southwards to Juba land and the Lorian swamp in Kenya.

Characteristics

Very similar to *N.m. meleagris* but slightly smaller and with a lower helmet. It has bright red tips on the pale blue white wattles. It is more commonly observed than *N.m. meleagris.*

NUMIDA MELEAGRIS MAJOR (Hartlaub 1884)

N. ptylorhyncha neumanni (Erlanger 1904)
N.p. baringoensis (Grant 1914)
N.p. var. inermis (Dubois 1915)

Uganda Bristle Nosed guinea fowl

Distribution

Central African Republic, southern Chad and Sudan, Zaire, eastern Ubangi–Shari district, upper White Nile and southern Ethiopia west of the Arussi–Galla plateau, south to the savannahs of the Uelle, Semliki rivers, nothern Uganda, north western Kenya to the Rift Valley.

Characteristics

Its general colour is darker than *N.m. meleagris,* often with a blue black sheen. The spotting on the breast and under plumage is large sharp and clear. The nasal tufts are shorter but well defined and the wattles are pale blue white. Helmet dark brown, the skin on the rear of neck and throat dusky flesh shade with blue patches around the ears. Base of beak red brown, tip buff, eyes brown, legs and feet dark brown. Sometimes there is a pale brown bristled papilla over the nostrils. The sides of the upper neck are thickly covered with small black feathers. Length 550 to 610 mm. Towards the southern Uelle, the helmet is low but to the west, it is taller like that of *strasseni.*

A small flock has been observed in company with four lions, mutually ignoring each other, the guinea fowl seeming to be in no fear.

NUMIDA MEGEAGRIS STRASSENI (Reichenow 1911)

Ubangi Bristle Nosed guinea fowl

Distribution

Eastern Cameroon to the middle and upper Shari and lower Ubangi rivers northwards from the Central African Republic into Chad.

Characteristics

There is a blending of features with *meleagris, major* and *galeata.* It differs from *N.m. meleagris* in that the neck and breast feathers have a distinct blue or purple wash usually unspotted and unbarred. The outer secondaries, including the edges, have pepper and salt speckling. The straw coloured nasal bristles are short and hair like and the lateral wattles are blue white. Length 520 to 570 mm.

NUMIDA MELEAGRIS TORUENSIS (Neumann 1904)

Distribution

The upper Semleki valley, southern base of Mt. Ruwenzori on the Zaire and Uganda border eastwards to the Toro district. The Shari area of north eastern Zaire into the Central African Republic.

Characteristics

Generally resembles *N.m. meleagris.* The wattles are still short and wide and wholely blue white. The nasal tufts are shorter than *major* and reduced in number. There is a violet or blue wash over the chest plumage, the colour and markings on the secondaries are similar to *N.m. papillosa.* There is a dark blue patch on the bare skin of the head from the lower lores to the nape.

NUMIDA MELEAGRIS INTERMEDIA (Neumann 1898)

Distribution

South western Uganda in the Ankole district, Zaire, west shore of Lake Victoria south to Kagera, north western Tanzania.

Characteristics

Another of the *meleagris* group. The wattles are broader than long and oval shaped but the terminal ends are bright red. The nasal bristles are almost gone and the edges of the secondaries are barred and speckled. Length 570 to 610 mm.

NUMIDA MELEAGRIS MACROCERAS

Pencilled guinea fowl

N.p. omoensis (Neumann 1904)
N.p. rendilis (Lonnberg 1911)

Distribution

Southern Ethiopia and Kenya. From the Turkwel river and southern end of Lake Turkana southwards to the top of the Rift Valley and the Meru district.

Characteristics

Length 540 to 580 mm. The helmet is longer than the others of the *meleagris* group. The wattles are blue white and the nasal tufts are well developed. The breast is more finely barred and washed with blue grey. Fine spotting on the plumage runs in distinct lines, hence its pencilled appellation.

NUMIDA MELEAGRIS REICHENOWI (Ogilvie-Grant 1894)

Reichenow's guinea fowl
N. ansorgei (Hartert 1899)

Distribution

Southern Uganda, Kenya and Tanzania. From east of Lake Victoria and southwards through the Kilimanjaro district down to the Singida and westwards to the eastern edge of the Wembere steppes by Tabora. There are large numbers in the Taita district of Kenya.

Characteristics

Closer in configuration and plumage colour to *N.m. mitrata* but slightly larger. The helmet is taller than any of the *meleagris* group but not so broadly based over the cranium as those of the birds further south. The lateral wattles are usually blue white but sometimes partly red. Like *N.m. major* it sometimes has a small hornlike papilla on the cere between the nostrils. It has a thick band of soft woolly feathers, frizzled and curled around the neck, strongest on the nape. Length 530 to 620 mm. The helmet has been recorded up to 56 mm in height, it has regularly been imported and bred in Europe, a colony can currently be seen in the Walsrode Bird Park.

NUMIDA MELEAGRIS CALLEWERTI (Chapin 1932)

Distribution

From the Kasai district of Zaire westwards to northern Angola.

Characteristics

This is probably an intermediate form between *N.m. marchei* and *N.m. marungensis*. It has narrow lateral blue wattles with red tips, the neck feathers, breast and mantle are blue but not so deeply shaded as *strasseni,* the tone varies from brownish blue to lavender and they are finely barred with white. The edge of the outer secondaries has broad white bars. There are no nasal bristles and the helmet is often low, sometimes resembling a horny cap. Length 570 to 610 mm.

NUMIDA MELEAGRIS MITRATA (Pallas 1767)

Mitred guinea fowl
N. mitrata coronata (Gurney)

Distribution

Coastlands of east Africa from southern Kenya and Tanzania to the Zambesi river in Moçambique and across to the borders of Zimbabwe and south east Zambia. Instances occur as far south as Natal and the borders of eastern Cape Province. They were introduced to Arabia (Asir and N Yemen), the Malagasy Republic where they are now listed as native, Grande Comore, Anjouan, Mayotte, Zanzibar, Pemba, Mafia and as far as Rodrigues. In Mauritius they were released in 1769 and became plentiful in the 19th century but are now quite rare.

Characteristics

As this is another widely distributed subspecies there are considerable variations. In the south it has occasionally been confused with members of the Crowned guinea fowl group. The helmet is more broadly based over the cranium than Reichenow's guinea fowl or any of the tufted group, it is always quite large but rarely exceed 33 mm. It is sometimes vertical and sometimes curved backwards. The bare skin on the sides of the neck and head is a bright blue green, dark on nape and throat. The feathers on the nape are thicker and not so hair like as *galeata* or *coronata* but not thick and woolly like the birds further north. The membrane around the nostrils and front of eye is red. The wattles are narrow and lateral, usually bright red but occasionally with a touch of blue white at the base and under the eyes. There is a hanging fold of dark coloured skin along the centre of the throat. The forehead and rear of the helmet are sometimes red. The white spots on the plumage are quite large and distinct, the outer margin of the secondaries is boldly barred with white. On the neck and breast feathers the spotting is very fine often producing a grey appearance. Eyes dark brown, legs and feet grey black. length 550 to 600 mm.

Before 1950 these birds were a common sight over all the areas which they inhabit; the numbers are now noticeably fewer and one has to make special excursions to be able to observe large flocks. These have been decimated by sportsmen as it is probably the most popular game bird in east Africa. It is now most numerous in the Masai lands of Kenya and Tanzania. It has been kept in a semi domesticated form in Zanzibar for several hundred years. It is often imported and has been bred in zoos and bird gardens around the world.

NUMIDA MELEAGRIS UHEHENSIS (Reichenow 1898)

Distribution

Confined to the Uhehe plateau in the southern highlands of Tanzania, it is bordered on the north and east by the Usungwa mountains.

Characteristics

The helmet is low and broad at the base and distinctly red coloured. The wattles are narrower than those of *mitrata* and three quarters red, otherwise similar to *mitrata*.

NUMIDA MELEAGRIS RIKWAE (Reichenow 1900)

N. frommi (Kothe 1911)

Distribution

South western Tanzania, between Lakes Rukwa and Tanganyika.

Characteristics

Yet another variant of *mitrata*. The helmet is claimed to be more pointed at the apex with a red tint, and a red spot under the lower mandible. The upper part of the neck feathers is banded with white and the lower half is spotted. The wattles are blue white with red on tips and forward edges.

NUMIDA MELEAGRIS MARUNGENSIS (Schalon 1884)

N. coronata marungensis
N.m. bodalyae (Bolton 1934)

Distribution

From the Katanga district of Zaire eastward to Lake Tanganyika and lower Ruzizi valley, south to the Kafue river in Zambia. In Kasongo, up the Luazaba to Marungu.

Characteristics

It has similarities to both *N.m. mitrata* and *N.m. coronata* with a more pronounced neck feathering nearly as thick as that of *N.m. reichenowi*. The wattles are narrow and pendant like the *coronata* group, cobalt blue tipped with red. The sides of the head are pale greenish blue and the nape is black merging to dark blue at the sides. The upper breast plumage has larger spotting than *mitrata* but the helmet is similar in size, both it and the forehead are orange coloured.

NUMIDA MELEAGRIS MAXIMA (Neumann 1898)

Distribution

Highlands of southern Angola.

Characteristics

It is still listed as a separate subspecies. It is similar in all respects to *marungensis* except that it lacks the orange coloured helmet and forehead. The variation is usually large — 610 to 630 mm.

NUMIDA MELEAGRIS PAPILLOSA (Reichenow 1894)

Wattle Nosed guinea fowl

Distribution

Southern Angola, northern Namibia and Botswana. From the Etosha Pan across to Lake Ngami and the Okavango marshes in the western Kalahari desert. Common on the northern plateau of Namibia known as Ehirovaherero.

Characteristics

The helmet is broad, long, almost cylindrical and arching backwards over the nape. The wattles are long and narrow like *coronata* and the tips are red, as is the membrane on the cere and around the top of the head. There are large well developed wart like papillae on the cere. The beak is light brown; the sides of the head are light blue green, and further down the sides of the nape and front of the neck are a bright blue green to lilac. The upper part of the wattles are the same shade. The spotting on the plumage is larger than *coronata* but similarly arranged and the filoplumes on the nape are more pronounced.

NUMIDA MELEAGRIS DAMARENSIS (Roberts 1917)

N. Mulondensis (Monard 1934)

Distribution

To be found in Namibia, east of the Windhoek area and southwards to the Orange river.

Characteristics

Similar to *papillosa,* it has the well developed red papillae over the cere. The helmet is also very long but laterally flatter like that of *coronata.*

NUMIDA MELEAGRIS CORONATA (Gurney 1868)

Crowned guinea fowl

Distribution

Zimbabwe, southwards from Harare, Botswana, Transvaal and Natal, Orange Free State and eastern half of Cape Province. It merges with *mitrata* on the Zambesi river.

Characteristics

Quite a large bird like the others of the southern tribes, the helmet is broad at the base, covering the whole crown of the head. It is sometimes vertical and sometimes slightly curved, but laterally flatter and less rounded than that of *papillosa.* There are usually no papillae on the cere but the raised membrane around the nostrils is roughter and sometimes distinctly wart like. The filoplumes on the nape are very sparse and fine. The gape wattles are vertically long and narrow with the tips and often the lower half, bright red. The top of the head around the base of the helmet, nasal membrane and base of the mandibles are also red. The rest of the bare skin on the sides of head and neck and upper portion of the wattles is a paler greenish blue than mitrata. The lower throat feathers are finely marked with rows or stripes of white spotting. The plumage generally has a black ground covered with white spots, these are largest on secondaries and abdomen. Legs and feet are blue black, eyes brown, length 560 to 620 mm, weight 1.4 kg to 1.8 kg, helmet 50 to 80 mm, along upper margin and 25 mm along base. Wing approx 275 mm, tail 140 to 160 mm, tarsi approx 70 mm. Unlike the situation in East Africa, *N.m. coronata* and its closely connected tribes in southern Africa have not diminished as much as the other game birds and animals. It can still be seen in small flocks close to the main roads in Natal and eastern Cape Province. It does not seem to have been native to the western Cape and has been introduced there on numerous occasions. It was imported to Stellenborsch and around Table Mountain as a sporting bird by Cecil Rhodes and several times since then. Flocks have also been brought in by farmers to help them fight crop pests, like caterpillars, beetles, borers, etc. Around some of the farmsteads they multiplied and often became quite tame to the extent of roosting on the out–barns. The farmers encouraged them as they proved useful sentinels when leopards or other large wild animals approached the farmstead. As a result of interbreeding with the domesticated guinea fowl and the reversion of many of the offspring to the wild, many of these flocks now have mixed genepools and some birds are often observed which have pale coloured legs, white breasts and flights or lavender plumage. The feral hybrids are not as large as their domesticated parents and lack the resistance to predation of their *coronata* ancestors. This factor is causing some concern, as it could jeopardise the favourable ecological balance which the wild flocks seem to have established.

NUMIDA MELEAGRIS LIMPOPOENSIS (Roberts 1924)

N. mitrata limpopoensis (Roberts)

Distribution

North eastern Transvaal, in the lowlands east of the Nyl river; across Moçambique to the coast.

Characteristics

An intermediate variation between *coronata* and *mitrata*. There are no papillae on the cere between the nostrils and the lower throat feathers are barred. Length, 570 to 610 mm.

NUMIDA MELEAGRIS TRANSVAALENSIS (Roberts 1924)

Distribution

North western Transvaal, western Zimbabwe to Chobe river and eastern Botswana.

Characteristics

An intermediate variation between *papillosa* and *coronata.* There are small raised papillae on the cere, the helmet is high and broad and the feathers of the lower throat are barred.

Figure 2 – 7 Common Guinea Fowl (From *Lewis Wright's Poultry* J. Batty)

3

THE COMMON GUINEA FOWL

Figure 3 – 1 Common Guinea Fowl
Top: In the snow
Bottom: A Silkie and A Guinea Fowl in Harmony

CHAPTER 3

THE COMMON GUINEA FOWL

Description of common Guinea Fowl and ornamental varieties; notes on anatomy, physiology and life cycle.

THE PEARL GREY GUINEA FOWL

The commonly known domestic bird will be designated as the Pearl Grey as this name possesses the widest currency. At first glance rather like a small bronze hen turkey, the Pearl Grey shares with the latter the bald head and dark plumage with white bars and dots. The differences become obvious on closer inspection. The general shape is thick set and the body appears more rounded with a broad short tail almost disappearing under the tail coverts.

GENERAL APPEARANCE

The head is broad and short, approx 3½ ins (8.9 cm) long, tapering towards the beak and carried forward from the body to which it looks small in proportion. The beak is wide and powerful, with the upper mandible curving downwards over the lower one, it becomes more blunt in older birds. This enables it to split and shred a tough husk, or spear a field mouse with equal facility. The skin around head and neck is bare and wrinkled. Towards the upper neck it is rucked like fine leather. There are rows of long stiff hairlike feathers or filoplumes proceeding down the nape. The nostrils are prominent on the sides of the culmen, separated and surrounded by a thin ridge of membrane known as the caruncle. The eyes are large and intensely alert with dark brown irises. Pendulous wattles on each side of the head are fairly flat and stiff. The lower edge usually curves from the base of the mandible to form a triangular point at the rear. These are vascular in texture and may be regarded as secondary sexual characteristics, they probably have a place in individual as well as tribal and sexual recognition. When the bird is excited they dilate slightly and sometimes darken in hue. They dissipate heat in addition to the normal panting method. The crown of the head is distinguished by a protuberance of the frontal bone of the cranium which is covered with a horny casing and known as the helmet or casque. This becomes noticeable on the keet at around 3 months old and continues to develop for a couple of years. The shape and size is determined by the genotype and there is considerable variation in height and degree of backward curve. It may slope steeply to rise almost vertically from the crown. There are also variations in the length and width of the base around the crown.

The neck is rounded, bare at the juncture with the head but from the centre to base carrying long downy feathers onto the breast and upper back or mantle. The breast should be full and well rounded. In native strains or older birds the sternum is sharp and prominent at the base. The back has a strong curve from neck to tail which gives the guinea it's familiar rounded profile. The tibia is 12.7 cm (approx 5 in) and the metatarsal bones are long 7.6 cm (approx 3 in) so are quite lengthy and strongly constructed with long powerful toes — centre 7.6 cm (approx 3 in) other frontals 5.7 cm (approx 2.25 in) three to the front and one slightly raised at the rear 2.9 cm (approx 1.125 in). Apart from the helmet, two other distinguishing features are the absence of spurs on the tarsi of either sex and the scales on the posterior of the tarsi, which are pentagonal in shape and form distinct lines or rows. These are smaller than those of the pheasants which have a row of large transversal scales.

The contour plumage on the body is very thick and smooth due to the luxurious growth of plumules or down, under and at the bases of the feathers. The sixteen rectrices comprising the tail are short — 15.2 cm (approx 6 in) and rounded at the tips, the central feathers being of similar length to the laterals. As the tail coverts extend almost as far as the rectrices the impression of a very short tail is given. The primary remiges on the second and third metacarpals are 23 cm (approx 9 in) and are the only long feathers. The wing coverts are also dense, making the wings look broad and thick. These compensate for the short tail when the bird is in flight by providing greater control, as with the partridge and woodcock. Total wing span is 74 cm — 76 cm (25 — 26 ins). Average total length 55 cm —61 cm (approx 22 — 24 ins).

COLOURING

In the Pearl Grey, the surface plumage background varies from dark slate grey to gleaming blue black, sometimes tinged with dark brown and uniformly spotted with bright white or pearly dots which alter considerably in size on different areas of the plumage. These are ringed with an even deeper black. Many birds have an unspotted collar which is generally slate or blue grey sometimes tinged with purple or bright blue. The spots on the tail are fine with symmetrical patterns. The upper webs of the wing primaries are marked with wavy bars of white, the lower web has narrower parallel bars. The secondaries have a regularly spotted upper web while the lower is spotted and edged with narrow white bars. The underparts are from medium to dark slate, with large spots on the flanks and sides of the breast. The skin on the tarsi and toes is usually dark or grey brown, occasionally retaining the orange or coral shade of the keet stage for the first two years. The wattles are normally three quarters bright red fading to bluish white where they join the head. The sides of the head from the cere backwards and chin are white with tints of blue. Nape, sides of throat, lower neck and over the eye are brownish or blue black. The end of the bill is a straw colour, deepening through dull orange to dark red at the base. On most birds a bright red edging membrane runs around the base of the bill, from the wattles up and around the nostrils. The helmet varies from dirty yellow to dark brown or umber. The body skin has a faint blue tint on the breast, stronger on limbs and back.

ORNAMENTAL VARIETIES OF GUINEA FOWL

Considerable variation in colouring of head and plumage has occurred. Many fine hybrid colours have been developed by breeders in recent years.

The White or **White African** is an old favourite, all it's plumage is a brilliant white, devoid of any kind of spotting or marking. The skin is also a paler pink, similar to a white chicken or turkey, the bare skin around the neck has a light purple hue. Tarsi and feet have a strong tinge of yellow. A mutation of long standing, the pure white was considered quite common in Europe and in Africa during the early 19th century.

The darker pigmented melanistic variety is known as the **Royal Purple** *(Fr. violette).* Here the depth of colour is so dark that the plumage appears black with a purple sheen. The breast and underparts were originally spotted but in recent strains the dominant pearl spot genes have been fully masked. Specimens with completely black down and feathers have also been noted but these appear to be rare.

The **Lavender** *(Fr. Lilas),* may originally have been the result of a cross between the Pearl Grey and White African. The entire plumage is very pale silvery grey with a lavender or lilac tint. The variety of spotting is similar to the pearl grey with white dots in the usual manner which have grey instead of black outer rings. The skin is also paler. Lavender birds without spots *(Fr. Azurée)* are less common.

The genes which affect plumage colouring are considered in two main categories, those which positively or negatively affect the appearance of pearl spots or alter the background colour. The standard pearl grey markings are due to a number of dominant genes which hide or mask many recessive genotypes.

Most of the unorthodox phenotypes are elminated by poultry breeders and growers when first noticed as they are reckoned to thrive less well. This is probably because in a standard flock, the strange or unusual bird is considered an outcast and may be attacked or harassed. It will only be allowed last place at feeders and drinkers when the rest of the flock are satiated. When they are kept in segregated flocks or in large numbers, as the white and pied phenotypes now are, they grow just as fast and well.

An alternate and more common result of the Pearl Grey/White African cross is variously called the **Splashed, Pied, Silver Wing** or **White Breasted** guinea, depending on the position and degree of white patches on the otherwise standard coloured plumage. Usually the breasts and flights are pure white and the remainder of the plumage is the same as the Pearl Grey. These may also appear in Splashed Lavender by crossing this strain with the White African. Specimens with white breast only are known in France under the name 'Buonaparte'.

One of the most appealingly coloured varieties is variously known as the **Coral Blue, Peacock** or **Violet,** *(Fr. bluette).* In this bird the dark blue washed feathers are often fused with spots of a clear coral shade which gives an overall violet impression. This variety is extremely popular with breeding enthusiasts. When it carries pearl spots it is known in France as 'Bleu clair'.

French breeders distinguish two background shades of brown, each with and without spots. The palest, almost a yellowish white on which the spots appear faintly is called **Chamois**; those without spots are known as **Fauve** or Fulvette and flocks of these tan coloured birds have also been developed by an American breeder in Iowa. In the second, the background brown is a darker muddy colour and when it carries the usual spots is known in English as **Dundotte** and in French and German as **Isabelle**. This genotype has an interesting difference because it also carries a sex linkage which has recently been exploited by commercial French poultry breeders (see Chapter 5). The variety without spots has been christened Rachelle by a leading ornamental breeder and authority in the South of France. He has also bred a variety with extended pearl spotting, 'Betelgeuse' and crossed it with other phenotypes to produce specimens with plumage resembling some of the pheasants. A barred strain without spots has also been bred on a South African game farm in the Transvaal.

Some less popular phenotypes have pale downy rings around the eyes and are known as Owls, others have had pink albino eyes but standard plumage colouring, this is a distinctly unfavourable gene combination which renders the subject prone to blindness. As a result of crossings made in Italy between *N.m. mitrata, N.m. galeata* and *N.m. meleagris,* birds have been noted with differing distributions of skin and wattle colouration, i.e. light blue wattles, blue or striped necks and bright blue flecked collar plumage, but no fixed strains appear to have been created from these breeds to date. Opportunities exist here for the ornamental breeder. The helmeted strains have also been out–crossed with *Guttera* and *Vulturinum.*

Occasional crosses with chickens, sometimes known in America as guin–hens, have produced progeny which have always been sterile. Large scale experiments made in France in 1963 and 1966 show that crosses of cock x female guinea are more favourable for the fertility of the eggs but male guinea x hen give better livability for hatched chicks; the offspring possess features of both birds but look rather like young white turkeys. The flesh resembles that of the guinea.

As mentioned in Chapter 2, fertile crosses were obtained between several members of the crested genus *Guttera,* but once the experiments were proven successful, the resultant hybrids do not seem to have been further developed. Interest in the development of ornamental strains has also been strong in the USA and it is still the only country where some show standards are widely if not officially recognised. The following is a copy of a local breeding standard for 'Pearl Greys' as forwarded to the author by an American enthusiast.

STANDARD FOR PEARL GUINEAS—DISQUALIFICATIONS

One or more white feathers in any section of the plumage, gills other than straight wide and flat; crooked back or breast, decidedly wry tail; one pound below standard entails disqualification.

Note: Cut severely for mottled, pinched or drooping gills.

Standard Weight:

Cock	4 lbs
Cockrel	3½ lbs
Hen	3½ lbs
Pullet	3 lbs

Head: Short, broad, wedge–shaped, tapering to the beak, carried horizontally and slightly foward, covered with skin resembling kid, a line of hairlike feathers down the back growing upwards, nostrils very prominent.

Beak: Strong, short and curved.

Eyes: Large, round, very alert.

Helmet: Hard, curving toward the body.

Gills: Flat, stiff, wide, smooth, free from folds or wrinkles, lower edge curved from beak to form a point with rear edge to conform very closely to head, rear should overlap neck where head and neck join (never drop in coil or form a semicircle).

Neck: Round, small/medium length, covered with downlike feathers.

Wings: Large, carried horizontally.

Back: Broad, somewhat curving from neck and descending in gradual curve to the tail.

Tail: Short, carried low.

Breast: Full, well rounded.

Body and Fluff: Rather long, well rounded, fluff full.

Shanks and Toes: Shanks, short, round, smooth. Toes, straight and strong.

SHAPE OF FEMALE:

Gills: Rounded at rear. Other parts as male, except for female's conformation.

COLOUR OF FEMALE:

Same as that of Male.

COLOUR OF MALE:

Beak: Reddish, horn darker at base.

Eyes: Dark brown.

Helmet: Light brown, in young birds nearly black.

Gills: Coral red with no white below or red above, a slightly curving distinct dark line at upper edge of gills; mottled gills very objectionable.

Neck: Bluish brown that sparkles in the sun.

Wings; Primaries: Upper web, light bluish grey, marked with wavy bars of white lower web, evenly and distinctly barred with narrow parallel bars of white, coverts barred about half the length of the feathers, rest pearled.

Secondaries: Upper web brilliant, bluish grey, regularly pearled, lower web edged with narrow parallel bars of white across the lower part of wings.

Back and Tail: Back bluish grey, pearls small, under colour slate. Tail same.

Breast: Body and fluff bluish grey, each feather regularly pearled with large white spots arranged in rows forming an inverted V with angle at shaft, under colour, dark slate.

Legs and Toes: Orange mottled with brown.

Plumage: General surface rich, brilliant bluish grey, pearls varying with size of feathers, under colour, dark slate.

NOTES ON ANATOMY, PHYSIOLOGY AND LIFE CYCLE

The skeletal structure of the guinea fowl differs little from the chicken apart from being somewhat smaller and proportionately more finely boned, 12% — 15% lighter in proportion to live weight. The tarsi or shanks are slightly longer as are the toes. They retain the deep keel or carina on the sternum, this provides the attachment area for the levator muscle, supracoracoideus, which is linked to the upper surface of the wing bone. Birds are as highly specialised in structure as mammals. In order to achieve flight, the body is streamlined and the bones are largely hollow to reduce weight. The skeleton is modified to produce greatest strength at the wing attachments. As might be expected, the large Gallinacious birds need powerful wings to raise their heavier bodies. The depressor and levator muscles are rich in myoglobin, the pigment which can store oxygen at low tensions and causes the familiar red muscle colour. The combined clavicles form a continuous bone connected at the apex of the 'V' by ligaments with the rostrum of the sternum. This is known as the furcula, 'merrythought' or 'wishbone', and helps to support the pectoralis, the depressor flight muscle. The guinea fowl does not tend to fly far but its wing strength matches that of it's legs in it's requirement to take off swiftly and wheel and dodge in the air as on the ground, in order to elude its predators. In addition to the bone cavities and the five pairs of air sacs around the lungs, possessed by all birds, the close alignment and thickness of the guinea fowl's wing feathers allow it to develop air pressure between them and the skin. This factor reduces the birds specific gravity as well as providing useful insulation against heat and cold. The thickened axis and narrower leading edge of the asymmetrical primary feathers allow each one to pass the air quickly over it's upper surface, like separate wings. Rapid flight also demands large quantities of oxygen. The avian respiratory system accommodates by operating differently from that of the mammal. The large air sacs act as a bellows round the rather small lungs which do not have pulmonary vesicles but tiny branching tubes connecting with the windpipe. Air is forced in a continuous current through these tubes and thus around all the cavities, oxygen is also extracted continuously, not just when inhaling. In compensation the heart is relatively large and beats more than twice as fast as that of the human, in smaller birds up to eight or nine times as fast. This ensures the rapid blood circulation needed to absorb the oxygen. The heat thus generated is equivalently greater and results in an average body temperature for guinea fowl of 41.5 deg C / 106.7 deg F, plus or minus 3 deg between midnight and mid–day. The skin contains no sweat glands but because it is thin and loosely attached, half of all the water evaporated by the bird passes through it.

The cranium is composed of two thin dense plates separated by a considerable thickness of bone of a spongy texture. The spongy cavities contain air carried from the long auditive tubes. It has sometimes been rather bluntly alleged that, "birds and reptiles have holes in their heads". A notable feature of the avian skull is the presence of a large hemispherical tympanic cavity on each side of the hind part of the cranium, i.e. temporal bone, this forms the ear drum and is connected to a slit–like opening in the pharynx, behind the hard palate on the roof of the mouth, by the auditive tubes. By this system air gains access across to each ear drum and through the diploë or bone spaces in the cranium. The cavities act as an amplifier of sound which is specially important to birds with their relatively small heads, as the sounds entering their right and left ears would be too tiny to be meaningful in terms of phase or intensity. On the temporal scale, a bird can distinguish up to 200 discrete sounds per second; the human ear is restricted to around 20 per second.

Many families of birds carry crests of feathers on their heads, sometimes luxurious mops like the curassow, extended plumes like the peafowl and some members of *Guttera*, or single feathers like the Californian quails. Few birds however have elongated helmets as do the *Numida* species, one other is the cassowary of New Guinea which although much larger and more aggressive is equally renowned for its alertness and excitability.

In speculating what other function the helmet might perform, it seems possible that it might be related in some manner, e.g. as an additional resonator of external sound, to the high degree of nervous energy exhibited by all the subspecies and their ability to perceive danger and to galvanise themselves into sustained and successful terrestial escape patterns. It has been suggested that the helmet also affords protection to the head when the birds are running at speed through scrub and tall grasses. The genus *Acrillium* however runs even faster but is quiet and non–aggressive. Birds seem to abandon flight whenever conditions permit because when it is possible to survive there, life is easier on the ground, flying uses a lot of energy and food.

It is perhaps significant that those races living closest to the hot central forest regions seem to have smaller helmets and conversely that those inhabiting the regions furthest away tend to possess the largest development of the helmet, e.g. the *mitrata* and *coronata* groups. The helmet would also act as a resonator for the birds loud alarm calls and provide some insulation against head and moisture loss. Physiological and behavioural studies are required, to test these hypotheses. The colour plate shows the helmet dis-ected laterally. The cornified casing and thin extension of cranial bone has been removed on one side to reveal the crimson honeycomb tissue which fills the interior and produces additional red corpuscles. The tissue is connected to the interior of the skull by a half inch long aperture in the cranium beneath the rear of the helmet.

The digestive system of most birds has two unique features. First the crop which is really a dilation of the gullet but can in the guinea fowl amount to 5% of the total body weight. Here the food is stored, and may remain for as long fifteen hours depending on the type of food and the condition of the bird. It allows the bird to swallow a large amount of food in a comparatively short time. The crop has considerable powers of distension, when the membrane is filled with water to normal size, capacity is around 80 cc, when forced filled, the capacity rises to 120 cc. If the bird is hungry and the gizzard has become empty, food may not actually be stored in the crop. Guinea fowl have a fairly rapid digestion and food will normally remain in the system for only a few hours. The food in the crop is moistened by salivary juices from glands in the mouth and throat, generally these are slightly alkaline and contain mucin which acts as a lubricant, also an amylase called ptyalin, an enzyme of low concentration, which initiates a limited breakdown of the carbohydrates to sugars. Up to 25% of the starch may be hydrolysed to sugar in two hours and even be absorbed directly from the crop. Some will also be converted into ethyl alcohol, lactic and acetic acid by the bacterial flora of the crop which also has the ability to retain coarser parts of the food for extra moistening, (see also Chapter 7 for impaction and sourness).

From the crop the food passes on down the gullet to the glandular stomach or proventriculus. Here the real digestion begins with glands secreting juices containing hydrochloric acid, high in the case of an omnivorous bird like the guinea fowl, and the enzyme pepsin which breaks down the dietary proteins. The food next passes into the muscular stomach, ventriculus or gizzard, the other unique feature. This is composed of two thick opposing muscles which are lined with a corrugated layer of horny material called keratin, they act as a grinding machine for particle reduction with the aid of insoluble grit such as granite or flint ingested for the purpose, this reduces it in size as it wears smooth and is eventually passed on down the tract. When the food is ground to a smooth paste by the rhythmic contractions it passes through to the duodenum, a U shaped loop enclosing the pancreas. Here the pH value rises; it has been shown that there is a large out–pouring of nitrogenous material by the duodenum and one third of this is mucus which neutralises the acidity. The remaining endogenous protein dilutes the food and allows the bird to absorb a mixture of amino acids from the small intestine, this will maintain it for a short period even if the diet was deficient in one of the essential amino acids.

At the junction of the duodenum and the small intestine, further secretions are added from the liver and pancreatic ducts. Bile, from the gall bladder and the right lobe of the liver, is the well known green viscous liquid containing pigment, salts, an amylase and an accelerating compound. The pancreatic secretions include a lipase or fat splitting enzyme, another amylase and an enzyme called trypsin which splits protein into peptones and peptides, these in turn are reduced to amino acids by intestinal enzymes. The importance of these secretions was highlighted when uncooked soya beans were fed to a flock in order to increase the dietary protein. These beans are excellent when roasted, but the raw bean contains a trypsin inhibitor which checked the pancreatic secretion and caused the death of the entire flock within a few days.

The final breakdown and absorbtion of the ingesta take place as it is moved down the small intestine by the contraction and dilation of circular muscles in the external walls, this action is called peristalsis. About three hours are necessary for efficient absorbtion of the food in the small intestine, but if the bird is scouring, the time will be much shorter and loss of condition and weight is likely to ensue. At the junction of the small and large intestine are two long culs de sac called the caecal tubes. These fill with ingesta and empty regularly but their digestive function is mainly concerned with water absorption. It is believed that some of the polysaccharides may be processed there by fungal and bacterial colonies. The remaining undigested matter accumulates in the large intestine and is finally voided together with the liquid urine, from the anal duct in the cloaca. The urinary residues appear on the faeces as a white capping.

The cloaca is situated at the end of the alimentary canal and also contains the outlet of the reproductive organs and the bursa which is in the upper wall next to the tail. The bursa of Fabricius is concerned with the production of antibodies. Its growth and involution are analogous with that of the thymus gland in the mammal, reaching a peak of development at 4 to 6 months. A keet under 9 months will have a bursal opening which can be penetrated up to half an inch with the tip of a match, only to be attempted when the bird is dead, as a method of ascertaining the age of a wild specimen. In older birds the opening will be much smaller or closed completely with only a slight lump remaining.

Longer term reactions than those produced by the central nervous system are initiated and controlled by the ductless or endocrine glands. These, in response to environmental conditions, release hormones into the bloodstream and tissues. They are known as the pancreas, the adrenals, thyroid, para–thyroid, gonads, pituitary and pineal glands.

In the pancreas a small groups of cells, known as the islets of Langerhans, secrete insulin, the hormone which determines the sugar level in the blood and supervises the development of glycogen which provides energy for the muscles.

The controlling gland is the pituitary, located at the base of the brain it is closely connected with the optic centre and hypothalamus. Its main function is to act on the other glands by means of seven hormonal secretions. One of these, thyrotrophin, acts on the thyroid glands on either side of the trachea, they influence growth, plumage colouring and moulting. A second hormone, adenotrophin, acts on the adrenal glands beside the kidneys, these control a variety of functions, e.g. regulation of blood pressure, sodium and potassium balances, metabolism of protein and carbohydrate, they provide adrenalin to stimulate muscular activity following an emotional stimulus. They also provide additional sex hormones which combine with those from the gonads to control certain types of sex activity. A third hormone, gonadotrophin, acts on the testes which secrete testosterone. By injecting oestrogen, one of the female hormones, into a young male (caponization), the pituitary is inhibited from producing gonadotrophin, thus creating sterility.

The parathyroids regulate the amount of calcium circulating in the bloodstream and stored in the medullary bone structures. The pituitary is also closely linked with, and partially triggered, by the pineal gland embedded in the brain. This is stimulated by light patterns received by photo receptors in the gland itself as well as via the optic nerve pathway. It also contains one of the body's biological clocks which remembers and responds to the changing length of the daily light period and probably the seasonal cycle as well. During the periods of darkness large amounts of the hormone melatonin are produced which directly affects body temperature and locomotive rhythm change; functioning indirectly via the other glands, it affects growth and sexual maturity.

Some of the female sex hormones are called oestrogens. Several types of these when implanted in the male, may cause temporary sterility. Many of these substances have been synthesised and also produce the female secondary sex characteristics when implanted in the male or increase them in the case of the female. They are used to stimulate blood plasma content, fats, earlier weight increase and improvement of flesh texture. These products are available as pellets, powders or paste and the effects may last from 3 to 8 weeks depending on the preparation. While the appearance of the carcase is generally improved, usually due to better distribution of the subcutaneous fat, the fact that possible side effects may result from residual amounts in the body tissue has, it is felt, been insufficiently investigated

REPRODUCTION

In the male the spermatozoa originate in the testes which are located on the dorsal wall of the abdomen near the top of the kidneys. These produce some of the male hormones known as androgens and during the breeding season they are considerably enlarged. The sperm passes out through the epididymus and down the ducti deferentes where the seminal fluid is secreted and stored. The ducts end in papillae or bulbous ducts hidden below the surface of the erectile organ which becomes swollen and projects into the cloaca during copulation or massage applied during semen collection. The age at which satisfactory volumes of semen production begin, depends on the species or strain and also on the season and lighting environment. Guinea fowl generally mature sufficiently between 6½ to 8 months, again depending on the strain and quality of management. Normally about 50% of males can be expected to provide an adequate volume of high quality semen for hatchery purposes. The guinea cock differs from other domestic poultry in that its volume of semen is considerably lower, i.e. 0.02 to 0.15 ml whereas turkey production is 0.08 to 0.33 ml and medium weight chickens 0.08 to 0.5 ml. It does however contain less extra seminal fluid and cellular debris. It's pH is about 7.4.

As embryos, all birds have similar characteristics but by the twelfth day in incubation, female ovarian development has begun. Only one ovary, usually the left, matures, the other remains in its rudimentary form. The mature female should be at point of lay by 26 to 28 weeks old. She possesses huge numbers of microscopic ova, most of which never develop, they grow in clusters around the ovary and are held in place by a thin membrane which is diffused with blood vessels called the theca folliculi.

In the laying bird a series of the ova are increasingly enlarged by yolk development to ripeness. When ovulation occurs the theca folliculi splits along the stigma and releases the fully ripe ovum comprising yolk and blastoderm to begin it's 24 hour journey. It is at this point that occasionally a blood vessel will rupture and cause a blood spot which can be noticed when the egg is broken out. The ovum enters the oviduct through a funnel shaped mouth called the infundibulum which corresponds to the mammalian fallopian tube. During copulation the female everts the end of the oviduct or vagina which opens into one side of the cloaca so that it faces outwards and is brought into conjunction with the male appendage. The semen is deposited in the oviduct and the spermatozoa swim into tubular shaped primary storage glands in the lining near the junction with the uterus or shell gland. Here they can survive for a considerable period, which varies with the species and may extend for several weeks. The level of fertility rises however to a maximum on the second

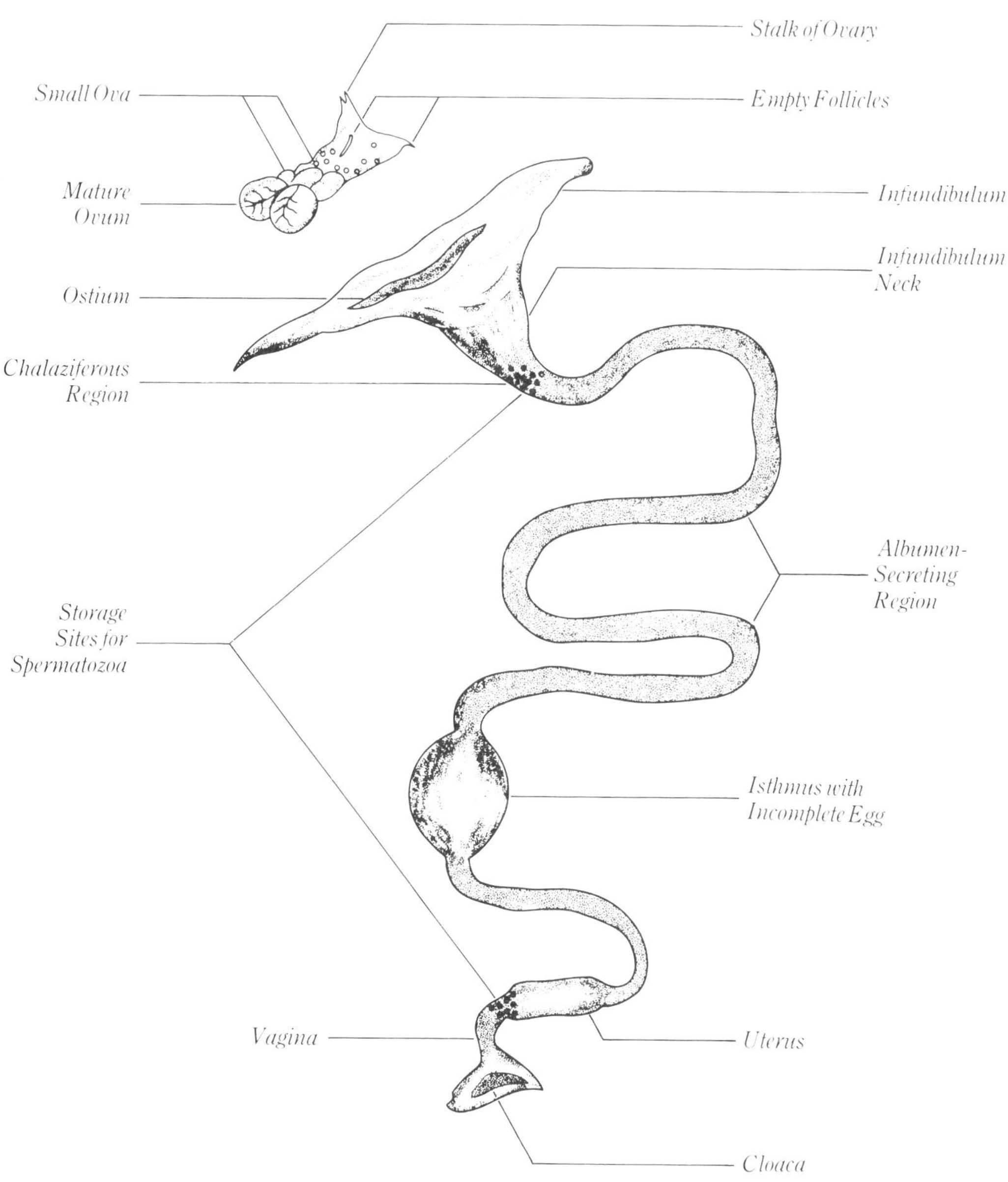

Figure 3 – 2 Female Reproductive System

day after insemination, remains constantly high for a period and then falls away. This high level is known as the 'fertile period' which for guinea fowl is seven days compared with 12 days in chickens and 22 days in turkeys. While the sperm will remain viable for two to three weeks, if the hen is put with a new cock or reinseminated with different semen, the new spermatozoa may fertilise the ova from the second day, the older ones usually being unable to compete with the fresher ones. If the hen were again isolated for seven days she would subsequently produce eggs some of which would be fertilised by the older mate as well as the later one.

By an insufficiently understood process, some of the spermatozoa travel daily the entire length of the oviduct to a smaller storage region in the infundibulum where the ovum is fertilised. The cell created by the fusion between the egg cell and the successful spermatozoon is called the zygote. The ovum then proceeds into the magnum. Here the yolk and germinal disc, known as blastodisc if unfertilised and blastoderm if fertile, collect the dense inner albumen produced by glandular cells lining the magnum walls. The vitelline membrane surrounding the yolk continues at each end in the twisted strands called chalazae. These are often referred to as the 'tread', but they are an integral part of the egg and have nothing to do with semen. They support the yolk and allow it to rotate while acting as buffers, but they are not attached to the shell membrane as is frequently supposed. The blastoderm always moves to the upper side even when the egg is moved around. The ovum passes by peristalsis to the isthmus where the membrane and more albumen is added, then on to the uterus or shell gland where it remains for more than three quarters of its journey. Here it receives about 40% additional albumen and the calcite coating which contains a matrix of proteins for toughness, plus calcium carbonate carried from the birds bone structure by the blood vessels. It finally passes out through the end of the oviduct, which is notable for the great development of it's inner circular layer of muscle. Here the outer shell cuticle and some of the pigments which make up the spots and speckles are formed. The large finished egg can only be laid because the two halves of the pelvic wall are not joined.

EGG AND EMBRYO

The shell of the Guinea Fowl egg is almost three times as tough and strong as that of the chicken. It is more dense and less porous, yet it is only approximately one third thicker than the latter. This protects it against predators and assists the control of moisture retention. From the outside, the crystals are forced together and function like a stone arch, yet it is easily broken from the inside by the chick. It is studded with over 10,000 microscopic pores which permit the intake of oxygen, also bacteria and fungal spores if present; these are exchanged for molecules of carbon dioxide and water vapour by the growing embryo.

The shell is composed of four layers. The transparent outer cuticle, which gives the characteristic bloom to a fresh egg and which disintegrates after storage, prevents rapid moisture loss. Beneath are solid layers of shell, the outer and thicker portion is the palisade in which the pores appear on magnification, as countersunk holes. Both the palisade and mammillary layer are constructed of countless columns of crystaline calcium carbonate which are densely packed on the outside but appear as knoblike mammillae on the inner shell with minute air cushions massed between them. The outer shell membrane is closely attached to the mammillae and the thin inner membrane adheres to it but separates at the broad end of the egg to form the air pocket or sac which acts as a reservoir for respiratory gases. These membranes are also tougher, thicker and less permeable than those of chicken eggs. The air pocket develops as the new laid egg cools and shrinks, increasing in size each day after laying. Four actual layers of albumen enclose the yolk in alternating consistencies. The yolk itself is a structured 50% aqueous solution with concentric rings of white and dark pigmented globules containing compounds and inorganic elements; the colour is influenced by carotenoid pigments like xanthophyll found in constituents of the birds diet such as greens and maize. Most guinea fowl yolks are a deep orange shade. Occasionally a double yolk occurs when two ova have been released in close succession during ovulation and so end up in the same shell. In an infertile egg the blastodisc can be seen as an opaque white spot surrounded by a transparent but mottled area which is really a number of tiny cavities. In the blastoderm the germinal spot is translucent but has a shaft of white yolk connected to it which produces a halo like effect and is named the zona pellucida. There is no mottled effect in the central area.

While a number of spermatozoa manage to infiltrate the yolk membrane, only one actually fuses with the female zygote which has completed the chromosome reduction or meiosis. The fertilised ovum is morphologically, the largest known single cell and the nucleus, allied with protoplasm becomes the blastoderm. The rest of the yolk is food material and not concerned with the subsequent mitosis or cell division. There is a crucial three hour period just after fertilisation when the ovum rotates and causes the materials to organise themselves into a spacial symmetry so that each part or cell division is correctly alligned to form its genotype.

The head of the embryo will always develop at the lowest point. After the egg is laid the temperature drops and development is arrested, as long as it remains below approximately 27° C, until incubation begins. By this time the minute embryo already comprises of from 50,000 to 80,000 cells. During the first 24 hours of incubation, an opaque narrow streak appears in the zona pellucida. While this is developing the blastoderm grows rapidly, surrounding almost the entire yolk by the fifth day. The allantois is then visible, this is a saclike structure which connects with the shell membrane by means of capillaries and passes nutrients to the embryo from shell, albumen and yolk. In the nest, the last and freshest eggs will develop more rapidly than the older ones. The critical periods of mortality are on the fourth and twenty fifth days with up to 10% fatality on each occasion. By four or five days the upper half of the body is complete with head divisions visible, embryo 7—8 mm. The head and tail regions have complete flexion and heart beat is easily observed. At the ninth day the embryo at 28 mm is clearly bird like and recognisable feathers have appeared by the fifteenth day. On day twentyone the embryo should be fully proportioned and by the twentyfifth day it should be lying with the head in the broad end of the shell, the beak with its egg tooth on the tip against the air sac and legs drawn up under the body.

When the enlarged air sac is perforated, the lungs begin to function and the chick will start chipping a circular section of the shell. During the final couple of days when it is actually breathing, it also starts to utter faint 'peeps'. This advertises its condition to a brooding female and may also correlate with adjacent 'peeping' eggs in such a way as to synchronise their hatching times. It may emerge at any time between the twentysixth and twentyseventh day. On hatching, the baby keet should weigh 25 to 30 gs. compared to around 40 gs for the baby chicken.

Some statistics of the egg are tabulated below:

CONTENTS AS PERCENTAGE OF EGG WEIGHT

	Guinea Fowl	Chicken
Yolk	27.9% — 35.1%	31.9% — 34.3%
Albumen	52.1% — 55%	55.8% — 57.1%
Membrane	1%	1%
Shell	12.6% — 15.3%	9.5% — 12.3%

The above figures are averaged from various studies made by M/S Auxilia, Hache and Weizmann (See Bibliography)

APPROXIMATE COMPOSITION OF CONTENTS

	Guinea	Chicken
Proteins	11.2%	11.9%
Lipids	9.5%	9.3%
Minerals	15.4%	12.2%
Liquids	62.1%	65.5%

Energy — 75—95 cal

Vitamins — A, B com., D, E, K–trace

Minerals — Calcium, Magnesium, Phosphorus, Potassium, Sodium, Sulphur, Iron, Chlorine, Iodine, Zinc, Copper, Fluorine, Manganese.

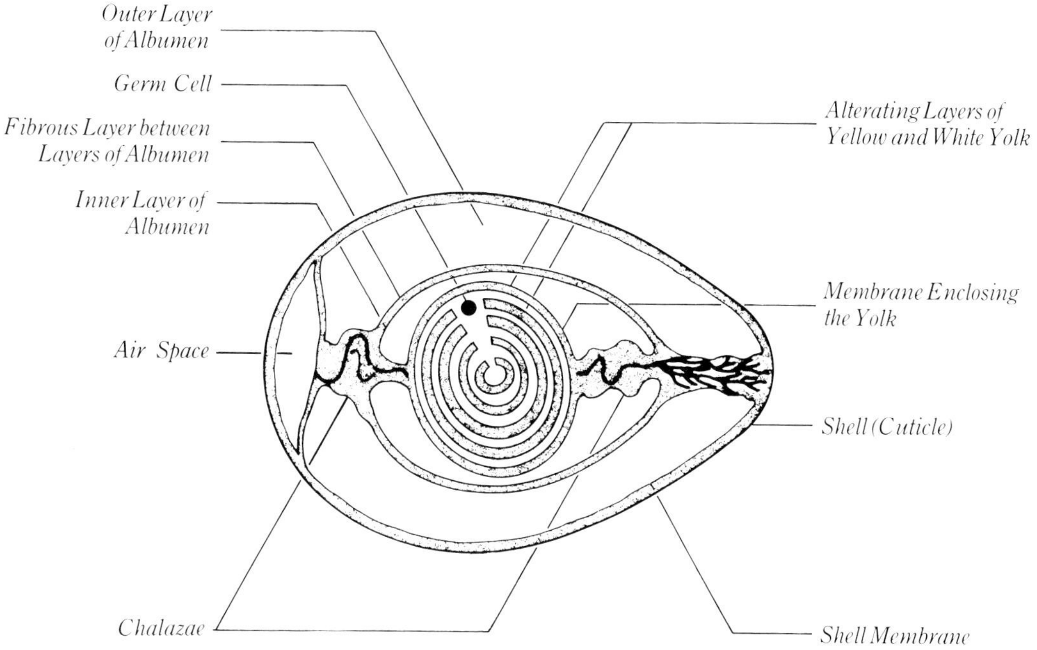

Figure 3 – 3 The Egg

APPROXIMATE EGG SIZE

	Length	Circumference	Weight
Large	57 mm	153 mm	2.10 oz (58 gm)
Medium	48 mm	127 mm	1.75 oz (49.61 gm)
Small	40 mm	110 mm	1.34 oz (38 gm)

4

GUINEA FOWL CULTURE

The Broody Hen (Silkie Cross)

Figure 4 – 1 Guinea Fowl reared in open range park (**Courtesty: Dengold Guineafowl Ltd and Photo: Scotpix**)

CHAPTER 4

GUINEA FOWL CULTURE

WHY KEEP GUINEA FOWL?

Guinea fowl are kept for a variety of purposes which involve quite different goals and management systems. It is proposed to outline the principal methods and systems in this chapter so that intending 'growers' may select from those best geared to individual requirements. So many books on every aspect of normal poultry keeping and aviculture are available that it would be superfluous to reiterate detail, except where guinea fowl require a particular emphasis or deviation from normal procedure.

AVIARY NOTES

When deciding how many and which varieties of bird one intends to stock, remember that adequate space should be set aside to permit isolation of sick or difficult birds and spare pens are needed to accommodate birds while their permanent quarters are being refurbished. Although it may be the intention to sell off the expected progeny, there will inevitably be specimens which one wants to retain and so yet further accommodation or space for expansion should be anticipated.

IMPORTATION OF BIRDS

Most countries have similarly stringent but necessary quarantine regulations for imported birds. These must be strictly observed. Normally the birds must originate from areas which are officially certified free of fowl pest or other such diseases as are currently specified, during the preceding three months. They must then be placed in three weeks quarantine on registered premises and pass a fitness test by veterinary officials of that country to certify them completely healthy and free from all diseases. The birds must be packed in new boxes with sawdust or woodwool litter and travel by disinfected vehicle to the port or airport of embarcation, avoiding any contact with all other birds and poultry. At the point of arrival the importer must take them directly to approved quarantine premises, disinfect his vehicle and burn all container boxes and bedding. The birds must be kept there in complete isolation for at least 28 days or as long as the local officials shall specify. Only authorised persons, suitably disinfected, before and after entry to the premises may attend them during this time.

In the unhappy event of a disease appearing in the birds during their quarantine period, Ministry officials retain the right to order all other birds in the aviary or on the farm to be destroyed, if the quarantine buildings are in the same grounds. Although these rules may seem exacting, they are really not unreasonable and exist to protect all birds and their keepers. If officials are satisfied that one is responsible and concerned, they will be happy to advise and assist. The international community which involves itself with birds is well known for its friendliness.

PENS

Since the aviary and pens will be a permanent fixture, designing for an efficient and ergonomic unit from the start is simpler and less expensive in the long run. The wire fencing should be no more than 1 cm mesh to render breeding pens proof against rodents and small wild birds. Both may introduce diseases and parasites as well as consuming considerable amounts of food. Similar sized mesh in wire or tough plastic should be well secured over the top. Jackdaws will pick at it and cats and rodents, who regard wire mesh as a natural ladder, will try to force entry at the joints. It is often suggested that at the fence base, the perimeter wire mesh should be taken 50 cm below ground level and extended outwards the same distance. In the authors experience, this has not always deterred the brown rat to whom baby keets can offer no defence. These determined rodents have tunnelled almost a meter below ground and three meters horizontally to emerge under a shelter in a grass run. One solution is to lay a heavy duty plastic coated wire mesh 25 cm to 30 cm deep under all pens required to be vermin proof, and secure this to the perimeter fence, which is extended down to meet it, or alternatively put down a concrete screed with drainage channels, leaving the top surface rough with cobblestones and allowing small holes for planting trees and shrubs. One can then spread gravel and sand on top, with peat or shredded bark for the scratching areas. The height of a pen should enable the owner to walk around inside and work in comfort. This also permits small trees and shrubs to attain attractive proportions. The ground dimensions for a breeding pair of guinea fowl or a cock with several hens should be a minimum of 7 m x 3 m.

An open fronted shelter sited at one end of the pen, which should be deep enough to prevent rain and snow from blowing in over the birds and a dry scratching area, are all that is needed for the ornamental strains of guinea fowl in temperate zones. The roosting perches should be about 5 cm thick of natural branches, or timber without sharp angles and set high, so that it is easy to clean out droppings and disinfect underneath. An additional high perch in the open is appreciated, as all species of guinea fowl are always eager to see what is going on around them.

All the imported subspecies, particularly the Crested and *Vulturine* genera, will require heating during the cold and wet months in temperate zones, or in areas with very cold nights. The options are to move them into a large indoor aviary, or to construct indoor sections instead of shelters in their separate pens, which should be at least twice the area mentioned for the ornamental strains. Many bird owners have soil heating cables installed in the runs, 15 cm below the ground; this maintains the sand temperature at around 20 deg C during cold weather. The indoor quarters should be sited so that they and the pens, catch as much sunlight as possible. The front of the indoor section can be inset with double glazing or multiple layers of heavy duty polythene sheeting. If the insulation in the house is really efficient (see section on accommodation for intensive rearing), little heating is necessary. The most important objective is to eliminate all draughts; more birds are lost from this cause than from the sum of likely diseases.

Guinea fowl do not use water for bathing, so a small dusting hollow filled with dry sand should be located to catch maximum sun and warmth. This is essential to keep their plumage in good condition and free of vermin. A little derris and quassia chip dusting powder should be added to the sand occasionally. If the landscaping is as natural as possible, the hen will be encouraged to brood her own eggs in a sheltered hollow which she will select and scrape out for herself. A large variety of trees and shrubs are suitable, taller and faster growing ones can be kept trimmed in proportion. Avoid poisonous species like box and laburnum. Hardy conifers of the pine and spruce variety mix well with fruiting specimens. Berries from the following are also edible — hawthorn *(Crataegus),* guelder rose *(Viburnum opulus),* bird cherry *(Prunus padus),* sea buckthorn *(Hippophae ramnoides),* rowan *(Sorbus aucuparia),* holly *(Ilex aquilfolium),* juniper *(Juniperus communis),* and the *disthicus* and *frigida* varieties of cotoneaster, bramble *(Rubus fructicosa),* ivy *(Hedera helix),* wild rose *(Rosa canina)* and polygonum can be planted outside the fences and trained over but leave plenty of space for sunlight to penetrate. Many satisfactory automatic watering systems are available. The food should be provided in hoppers or troughs designed to prevent spillage. Proprietary game bird crumbs are satisfactory as a basic feeding material. The scratching area in each run provides necessary activity. A good medium is fresh peat in which seeds, grains and insects can be scattered.

The following foods are amongst those naturally available to and popular with most African subspecies. They may provide a guide from which the aviculturalist can formulate dietary compliments with equivalent ingredients. Crop analysis shows that although certain foods when ripe, might be eaten to the exclusion of others for several days by the majority of a flock, individual birds might on the same day consume only a little, or even a quite different type of food. This shows the desirability of providing a choice of foods wherever possible to match individual metabolic needs. When animal protein was being eaten, it would usually constitute one third to one half of crop contents. Levels of the essential mineral nutrients found in the crop were higher than those which are specified in most poultry ration formulae.

Wide varieties of ants, small beetles and larvae formed the major proportion of insects consumed, also eaten were grasshoppers, locusts, spiders, termites, tics, millipedes, centipedes, bugs, weevils, cockroaches, chafers, flies, moths, small wasps, snails, wireworms, cutworms, sawflies and borers. Live insects should be fed as an occasional treat, because if the birds become accustomed to receiving them regularly, their interest in more prosaic foods will fall off. If baby keets seem a bit lethargic a bucketful of ants and pupae will stimulate enthusiastic activity. Green crops which include sainfoin and lucerne are attractive to insects and the latter can be collected very easily with a biologist's suction hoover while walking between the plants.

Favourite green leaves in Africa are those of the wild amaranthus which resembles spinach in appearance and nutritional content of leaf and seeds, clovers, thistle leaves and heads, herb grasses with high nitrogen content, and particularly in wet weather, hot spicy leaves of herbs and bushes.

When it is available, they consume large amounts of *Eleusine coracana* (finger millet) which is high in mineral content. *Pennisetum typhoidum* (bullrush millet) and *Sorghum vulgara* (guinea or kaffir corn), all similar in value to brown rice. Maize is popular when the birds can reach it, as are the other farm cereals. Guineas have a particular fondness for

Figure 4 – 2 Sex Distinction (see text)

Figure 4 – 3 A Commercial – type Guinea Fowl **(Courtesy: Ark Foods Ltd)**

palm kernels, palmyra *(Borassus flabellifer)* has a useful sugar content with vitamins A, B1, B2 and Nicotinic acid. The oil palm *(Elaeis guineensis)* is rich in energy and carotene.

Some other palm kernels have as high a protein content as soya bean, a few are as yet barely classified, seventeen new species of tree have only recently been named in the Korup forest of Cameroon. Seeds of all kinds are taken avidly; sesame *(Sesamum indicum,* sim sim in East Africa or beniseed in West Africa), *Cocconia sessifolia* and Acacia, pigeon and cow peas *(Cajanus cajan* and *Vigna unguiculata)* are notable amongst them, all are protein rich. Cyperus bulbs and fruits of *Tribulus terrestris* (Puncture Vine), *Scutia myrtina* and similar small berries are eaten in season. Guineas have an addiction for apples and orchards in temperate areas are often raided for the windfalls. The locust bean or carob *(Ceratonia siliqua)* is a favourite roosting tree, the seed pods, 100 mm — 300 mm in length, contain a sweet edible pulp which is rich in vitamins, pectin and fructose. When guineas are in the vicinity of the mangrove swamps, they feed voraciously upon the small marine vertebrates, invertebrates and weed. They react with similar avidity when any of these are offered to them.

BEHAVIOUR AND HABITS

Because of their tough and resilient constitution and efficient feather insulation the domestic varieties of guinea fowl fare better than most birds in wide ranging climatic conditions and acclimatise quickly wherever they have been introduced. They are of course at home in the hot equatorial sun but tolerate conditions in Canada, Siberia and Scandanavia of up to 10 deg C of frost and snow in insulated housing without artificial warmth, provided adequate food and suitable frost protection for their feet are made available.

They are naturally gregarious and enjoy flock association, within which, permanent pair bonds are usually established. In a natural environment the guinea fowl mates monogamously within the flock. The coupling is very rapid and usually just preceeds laying. The hen will often make little darting rushes on her toes in front of the cock to attract and entice him. If disturbed on her way to the nest, she frequently drops her egg on the open ground.

In open pens the cock will undertake custody of and mate with 3 or 4 and up to 6 hens but it is noticeable that one or two of these will be the harem favourites and are always the first to be summoned to taste a particularly juicy morsel that the cock may find. In these circumstances it is quite common for two or more hens to share the same nest, incubating side by side with one protecting both clutches of eggs while the other is obtaining food and water.

An onlooker will find it very difficult to distinguish cocks from hens as the colouring and appearance are so similar. There are some general indications. The cock is usually slightly larger and heavier than the hen. There are slight variations in the plumules on the nape and sometimes the wattles are thicker at the outer edges, also wider and deeper on the cock who has a slightly more powerful head development. The latter characteristic is more prominent in certain strains and has even been selectively retained by some breeders in the USA and in Russia.

The hen has a distinctive double noted call sounding like 'come back, come back' or '*kan–gak, kan–gak*', repeated many times. During the mating season in particular, the cocks make darting rushes on tiptoe, with wings partially open, at any other bird outside their own mating group. Quite often one comes across a large agressive hen or a timid cock which provide the exceptions to the general indications. In such a case only a close examination of the cloaca will reveal either the vaginal entrance or the male erectile organ. However, these may not be discernible before 15 to 20 weeks old. The external genital features are more easily distinguished in the early maturing strains developed in Europe (see Sexing).

The behavioural pattern of making darts or rushes with wings raised or semi–outspread at other guinea fowl is common to all the helmeted subspecies. It is often indulged in by both sexes indiscriminately, apart from between pair bonds, at any time of the year. Sometimes it is quite playful and no actual contact is made, at other times the chase may last for hundreds of meters and the victim if caught is severely punished, feathers are pulled out and lacerations inflicted on head and neck. Aggression is strongest at mating time when a pitched battle often takes place before the loser turns and runs, the behaviour in general is often used to establish a pecking order and the keets will be involved in the game by the time they are half grown.

CALLS

The most distinctive call is the high raucous alarm shriek (screech) common to both sexes but produced with greater frequency by the cocks. This is a series of shrill strident notes building up in volume and intensity. It may be uttered for a few seconds or minutes in continuing bursts and is likely to last for as long as whatever is disturbing them remains within sight or hearing. The offending cause may be a potential predator, a stranger, or any colour, shape or sound which seems unusual. The cock also has a shrill single note *chi–chi–chi* repeated and rendered with a variety of emphasis. The hen has a lower extended single note *ka–ka–ka,* frequently uttered after laying, this generally reverts back to the familiar *kan–gak–kan–gak* sequence. When feeding, both sexes have a large repertoir of excited sharp clucks and low squeals, the punctuation becoming sharper with the interest, as when an ants nest is discovered. One is reminded of a running commentary on the nature of the food, as a lengthened squealing will fetch other guineas from many yards away to share the delicacy.

Guineas will co–exist with other fowls provided they are allowed to remain at the top of the pecking order or else there is sufficient room for each class of birds to keep out of each others way. If there should be too many cocks around at mating season, the extra and weaker ones will be harried unmercifully and even killed if they cannot escape. On free range the guinea fowl has often demostrated its courage by attacking and frequently killing predatory rodents like black and brown rats, rattle and copperhead snakes. The intruder will be surrounded and repeatedly pecked by the powerful beaks until life is extinguished.

They have also been known while protecting the keets, to attack and drive away dogs, cats, raptors and crows, the latter are much more aggressive in the USA, Africa and Australia than in Europe. A few birds are often kept with other flocks like turkeys for this express purpose.

JC Skead in his *"Study of the Crowned Guinea Fowl"* describes an eyewitness account of an attack by a Lanner falcon on a quarter grown keet which was defended by four adults. The incident took place in an exposed field where the rest of the flock were feeding about 50 meters away. The falcon made repeated attacks on the keet, wheeling and diving at great speed but each time it was frustrated by the four adults who packed closely around the keet while lunging upwards at the falcon. Eventually it alighted on the field about 15 meters away, two of the guineas instantly rushed to attack it and drove it back into the air. Meanwhile the frightened keet had unsuccessfully tried to fly over to the main flock and was now alone and easy prey. The falcon made a lightening swoop but by this time the rest of the flock, alerted by the four adults, were racing over to surround the keet and reached it in time to fend off the falcon's final snatch. Another incident involving raptors is reported in *World of Wildlife*. Some naturalists in Kenya noted a flock of Helmeted guinea fowl walking over the dry savanah towards the Seronera river which was close by, when a pair of Bonelli's eagles swooped on them. The guineas erupted into a shrieking pandemonium, churning up huge clouds of dust with their wings as half flying and half running they dodged for cover. A lioness hidden in nearby brush joined the chase and swiped at a passing bird with her paw. The chaos lasted only a few seconds and when the dust cleared it was remarked with astonishment that not a single bird had even been injured by any of their predators.

A guinea flock is also popular in the market garden or orchard because of their predelic-tion for beetles and insect pests which infest the produce. They do not scratch up the ground in the manner of chickens and prefer wild herbs and grasses to most of the usual garden crops. They are often brought in by farmers to help them fight crop pests like caterpillars and beetles and complete their task highly successfully.

Despite their loud alarm calls and 'busy body' attitude, they appear to be secretive birds in respect of copulation and egg laying, preferring to perform both these functions as rapidly and quietly as possible. The nesting hollow scraped in the earth may be in a hedgerow or under low scrub and in the guineas absence the eggs will often be covered with dead grasses and leaves. Hens in enclosures can be habituated to laying in nesting boxes either on the ground or even raised, up to a level of 3 or 4 ft. As mentioned, several hens will often lay in a single nesting box. One guinea owner who had been away for a few days discovered over 50 eggs in an old tea chest where no one else had thought to look. In pens or enclosures, the hens who begin to lay in March to May, depending on the cli-mate, will produce about 5 eggs per week providing they are well nourished, continuing until September or October. They usually brood outdoors from May to July in temperate zones. On open range they are steadfast brooders and parents. A hen will continue to cover the eggs even when attacked by a powerful animal like a fox, they have often been found beside the nest with their heads bitten off. In smaller closed areas they are much less reliable brooders and frequently cease to sit after 2 to 3 weeks. Like Pheasants they can be adversely affected or deterred altogether from brooding by bad spring weather conditions. These can also affect the fertility of the eggs, as the cocks ability to produce lively spermatozoa is reduced under ambient temperatures below 20°C. However in con-tinental type climates as in Canada or Siberia, where the ambient temperature may be much lower but the sun is shining strongly, the birds will benefit from the high calorific value and provided they are warm at night will breed satisfactorily.

The fact that the guinea hen lays more copiously under natural conditions in the north-ern hemisphere than in Africa is probably at least partly due to the extended daylight of the northern climate. Even the sexual maturation of the hen requires a full twelve months in equatorial regions where the length of day is always a constant twelve hours. On the range, guineas will create their own dusting hollows, digging deep into fine earth and working it well up amongst their feathers. In strong sunshine they can be found indulging themselves in these by the hour, lying with one or both wings outstretched and tail spread. The abrasive and absorbent action of the soil helps to cleanse the skin and feathers and in conjunction with strong ultraviolet rays dislodges parasites from the feather barbs and makes them more accessible to removal when the bird is shaking out, preening and oiling. Apart from the early keet moults, the adults will usually have the main post breeding moult around the end of October and the beginning of November and a partial moult in late winter. Moulting is controlled by hormone secretions and the time of moulting may be altered by changing artificial lighting patterns and or diet. It should be remembered that metabolic heat loss amongst moulting stock can be rapid during cold conditions, as the birds can only reduce their blood flow near the skin on their feet and wattles.

Like all Gallinaceous birds, the baby keets are precocial. They are born at an advanced stage of development with open eyes and a protective coating of down. As day olds they are smaller but more alert to their surroundings and much faster over the ground than chickens. They resemble pheasant chicks in appearance except for a vivid orange or coral colouration of beak, legs and feet and the distinctive light and dark brown stripes over head and back. The pied varieties show whiter patches in the down and the White African and the tan keets have down with either white or light tan shading. They will start feeding about 24 hours after hatching but can survive up to 48 hours. The guinea hen exercises a higher degree of control over her keets than a foster mother by virtue of their instant response to her wide range of vocal signals. The keets themselves emit a constant stream of excited peeps by which means the hen is always aware of their condition and whereabouts and can react accordingly.

The English term 'keet' often spelt 'keat' derives from old Nordic 'cytlying' or 'keetlyng' which up to Tudor times was applied to the young of many animals and later came to be specifically used for young domestic guineas from day olds to maturity, it is usually still reserved for the domesticated, as opposed to the wild species.

GUINEAS ON THE FARM

Many farms maintain a small flock of 10 to 50 guinea fowl which roam at large around the outer bounds and stockyard, finding their own provender from the loose seeds and grains and the quantities of insects which accumulate under the stacks of hay, straw and manure. They fly out to the fields in the morning, roost sometimes in the trees or return to the safety of the farm buildings in the evenings. They survive with remarkably few casualties, to provide the occasional farm dinner, a few eggs in season and to act as an alarm when any stranger approaches the vicinity. On some large farms and estates they establish wild colonies in the woods and forests where they elude natural predators with the usual success until such time as their numbers interfere with local game and are reduced by shooting and night netting. At this level of regeneration, economics scarcely enter the scheme, any more than for similar groups of foraging chickens and ducks. A few settings of eggs are found and incubated under a broody hen or bantam or the guinea is allowed to brood them for herself. The keets are reared in any convenient enclosure and fed on spare grains and refuse. Finally they are sold locally at a few months old to provide some 'pin' money. In these circumstances and in such small proportions few difficulties arise. However, as with all other poultry, multiply the number of stock by a factor of 10 or greater and the happy arrangement becomes unworkable without a proper management system.

Figure 4 – 4 Guinea Fowl will roost on sheds or in trees and provide an excellent alarm system **(Courtesy: Dengold Guineafowl Ltd and Photo: Scotpix)**

EXTENSIVE REARING

Whether maintained on farm or on small holding, birds and animals require sustained dedication and an interest in increasing ones knowledge and practical understanding of them. They will then become a flourishing and self supporting colony contributing to their owners economy and providing a source of enjoyment.

The common guinea fowl will thrive under most conditions suitable for chickens. They are however more excitable and prone to fly when disturbed. This is unimportant on a large farm but creates a problem for the small holder with only a few acres. As with game birds they are likely to fly right off the property and while they would normally return at feeding time, heavy losses are likely to be suffered from human and non human predators. If on the other hand one wing is clipped and pinioned, the birds will be unable to escape into the trees when attacked. This brings us to the necessity for secure enclosures. Even large pens need to be moved or rested every year and the birds allowed access to fresh ground. This also fertilises the land and diminishes pests and risk of disease.

The small holder who may have only one acre of ground available for poultry might fence and sub divide it into four main sections with a row of small pens at one end. Alternatively, the units could be smaller and the birds rotated four times a year around the field with movable fences and sheds. In the first scheme, two of the large sections would always be in use while the other two were resting; the smaller pens would be rotated in the same way. This allows differing age groups to be reared separately, as well as separating breeding groups and providing isolation areas. The entrance gate to each section should be wide enough to admit a tractor if the pens are very large or a wheel barrow if small. The external and main dividing fences can be of 5 cm mesh and 2 meters high with posts about 3 meters apart. If foxes are prevalent in the neighbourhood 13 gauge wire is preferable to normal chicken wire which they can bite through. At the top there should be a floppy anti–fox fringe of outward facing 0.3 m strip netting supported by wire running parallel to the ground. It is wise to strengthen the base of the fence with some material like 0.75 m corrugated sheeting which also provides screening cover. It is worth while making some of the smaller rearing pens completely vermin proof if keets are going to be reared outdoors with foster mothers. These would require 10 mm mesh wire top and bottom as well as sides, similar to that for the aviary pens.

Guineas prefer open fronted shelters to roost under but they can be trained when young to enter and roost inside existing hen houses. Shelters should be constructed with their backs to the prevailing bad weather and deep enough to afford protection against driving rain and snow. High roofs and perches will assist when cleaning out the droppings. The size obviously depends on that of the enclosures but a 3 x 3 m shelter with 5 cm slat perches at 40 cm apart will accommodate 100 birds. Perches should not be more than one and a half metres high as if the birds are pinioned, a fall from a higher roost may cause damage, especially to laying hens. Generally, about 18 cm of roosting space per bird should be allocated. While they can withstand it, guineas dislike constant rain just as much as chickens and it has an obvious effect on their condition and egg production. In wet regions, good scratching sheds are important. A structure 7 x 8 m long and 1½ m high will be adequate for 100 birds. The sloping roof can be corrugated asbestos or plastic (they are upset by the sound of rain on tin), with a good overhang in front to keep the floor dry. Dry peat moss makes a fine scratching medium.

Figure 4 – 5 A Silkie makes an excellent Broody **(Courtesy: Mr T. Penny)**
Black and White Hens

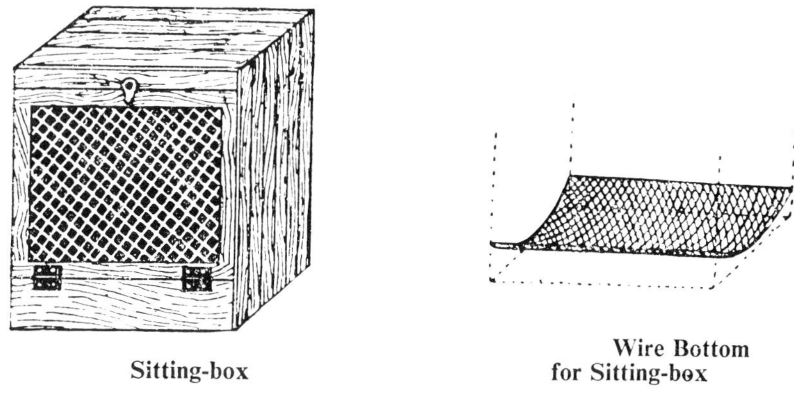

Figure 4 – 6 A Sitting Box

The areas which are being rested should be disinfected with a heavy dressing of lime and then reseeded. Mixtures attractive to guineas are cocksfoot, Italian rye grass, meadow fescue, Timothy, red and white clover and rape. Sheds must also be thoroughly cleaned and disinfected regularly. If a small section of ground has to be reused constantly or heavily stocked, it should be stripped to a depth of 15 to 20 cm (6 to 8 ins) and packed with hard core filling and topped off with cinders and sand. This will keep the birds dry and free of mud and once again, it is easy to disinfect.

This onset of laying is often preceded by a light moult. Large nesting boxes eg. a tea chest on it s side, should be located in secluded and sheltered positions and kept clean and dry with fresh straw or shavings. Guineas in outdoor pens tend to lay in the early and late morning. Eggs intended for hatching should be collected 3 to 5 times daily to ensure they are as clean and dry as possible. If numbers are allowed to build up in nests, the rate of laying is also likely to slow down. There is always a consumer demand for surplus eggs. Those intended for setting should be cared for as suggested in the section on incubation. The most usual method of brooding for pen and aviary keepers is by small incubator or foster mother. A successful hatch is more certain than when the guinea fowl is allowed to brood her own eggs. This would also interupt her egg production. Hens, bantams and hen turkeys are used as foster mothers. The latter are instinctively better at keeping the keets dry when they go wandering in wet weather, she also remains with them for a longer period than a hen. A severe wetting can result in a heavy keet mortality during the first 6 weeks, prior to adequate feathering.

It is increasingly difficult to obtain reliable broody hens from modern hybrid strains. The most satisfactory foster mothers in the authors experience, are crosses of Silkie bantam with Rhode Island Red or Light Sussex hens. These possess the excellent brooding and mothering qualities of the Silkie Bantam combined with larger size, which enables them to cover 15 to 18 guinea eggs in comfort. If one adopts this method of hatching it is best to follow a similar procedure to that used for pheasant eggs i.e. outdoor setting boxes and coops which can be moved to fresh ground every few days. A good foster mother can cope with a mixed group of eggs which vary in uniformity and freshness and which may continue hatching over 48 hours.

Satisfactory working breeds of bantam are the Silkie, the Cochin and the Orpington, any of these can cover about a dozen guinea eggs. Two or three years old are best if available. When a bird is broody, she will be found regularly sitting in a nesting box. When a hand is placed underneath her with fingers curled upwards, she should squeeze the fingers with her wings and ruffle her plumage. If still in doubt, try her on a few dummy eggs for a couple of days. The hen should be in first class condition, eyes clear and bright, breath clean and feathers shining, as four weeks incubation is a considerable strain. Ensure she is free of parasites by dusting her and the brooding box thoroughly. The brooding box should be a minimum of 40 cm^2 to give her room to turn around and the keets space to move when they hatch. The front should have bars or slots to allow the keets separate access to the coop which can be added when required, or built on as a complete unit. As with game birds, the setting of eggs should be put down on a thick fresh grass sod which fits snugly in the nesting box. If part of the earth is removed from the centre underneath, this creates a suitable depression or hollow in the grass surface of the sod and the eggs are less likely to roll around. If the depression is too deep or bowl like, the hen will have trouble turning the eggs in the centre. The sod should be moist but not soaking, as this helps retain the humidity under the foster parent. A little water should be added every few days as the sod dries out, by sprinkling it around the perimeter, especially during the fourth week. An old rural custom was to place a sheet of iron under the sod. This was thought to afford protection to the eggs during electrical storms which were believed to damage the developing embryos. A good foster mother will turn the eggs every few hours and reject those which are unsatisfactory, this can be checked by pencil marking the shells. She is usually the best judge of how long the eggs should be left, normally 10 to 15 minutes, depending on the exterior temperature. Some keepers allow them off only once daily, others twice but the timing should be regular. A high quality balanced feed should be waiting nearby, also water and grit. If the sun is shining she may enjoy a quick dust bath.

The correct amount of humidity at the chipping stage is most important. Control is more critical if using older type incubators. If the humidity is too low the shell membrane becomes dry, hard and tough. If it is too high the membrane will turn soft and rubbery and the keet will have difficulty in splitting it.

OPEN RANGE

On an open range farm where the flock is moved regularly, the concentration is often up to 700 birds per acre. This suits rough grassland and bracken or scrub belts which are relatively useless for other kinds of farming. Here the birds will rapidly strip the vegetation and foliage, as well as the grubs and insects appearing on the surface. As modern grassland tends to be herb deficient, scrub land and hedgerows provide a far more varied and nutritious diet which undoubtedly adds to the game flavoured meat of birds grown in such localities. Guineas on open range are normally supplied with feeding supplements on an ad lib basis. When the supply is restricted they tend to hang around the hoppers awaiting the feeding hour and lose valuable foraging time.

Various studies have shown that guineas are more susceptible to chemicals like dieldrin than chickens, when these were constituents of pesticides sprayed regularly on crops.

Open range keets are usually brooded under radiant heaters in houses with constant access to outdoor pens and are moved to open range at about 6 to 8 weeks old, depending on the weather. Because the keet feathers early, in warm dry climates they can be allowed into large outdoor coops as early as 15 days old. Absence of cold rain, wind and dampness is the decisive factor. It is best that they have open shelters under which to roost, or lock–up housing in fox country as the birds are normally pinioned. Under these conditions with a well balanced supplementary diet, the keets should attain from 2½ to 3½ lbs (approx 1.00 to 1.56 kg) live weight depending on the strain of bird, in 15 to 20 weeks. This compares with 11 to 13 weeks in confined pens with natural food supplements, and 8 to 10 weeks for broiler reared keets. The open range birds eat less supplied food stuff, estimates are around 50 kg daily per 1000 birds, of a balanced diet including vitamin and mineral concentrate which takes their foraging consumption into account. If birds in confined pens are supplied with natural organic foods, greens and herbs, the difference in flavour and texture of the meat should be negligible.

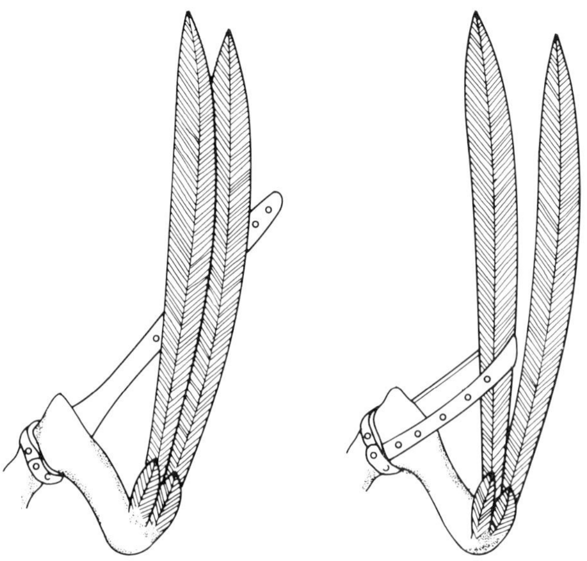

Figure 4 – 7 Brailing

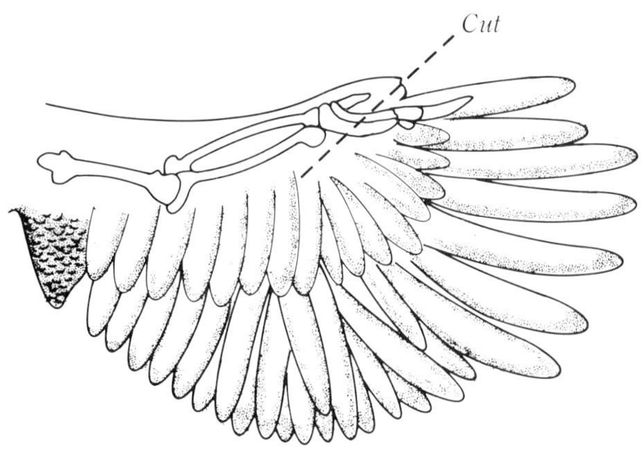

Figure 4 – 8 Pinioning

STRAW YARDS

Guinea fowl like other poultry can be kept in straw yards. This is generally a way of utilising pre–existing buildings and enclosures. The hard open ground is covered with straw which is renewed weekly or in wet weather two or three times per week. If it becomes sodden, worms and fungal moulds will quickly develop. Good management and skilful use of this arrangement is essential. The floor in the covered area should be slatted to keep the birds dry in poor weather and good air circulation is needed to avoid humid conditions but draughts must be eliminated. The food supply should include fresh greens and herbs as for birds in confined pens.

PREVENTION OF FLYING

To prevent the birds flying out of open systems one wing must be immobilised. The first method is to clip back the primary wing feathers to half their length. This needs to be checked and redone every 4 to 6 weeks after the birds are weaned, as the feathers grow again quite quickly. Ensure only the juvenile flights outside the most recent blood quills are clipped on the 6 to 7 week old keet.

A more radical and permanent method is pinioning. This should be performed during the first few days of the keet's life, or by 1 week at the very latest. The tip of one wing is cut through with a sharp knife or an electric cauteriser, (see fig 4.8) as close to the 'thumb' as possible. This inhibits the flight feathers from growing at the source.

A third method is called brailing and is used for ornamental or exhibition birds, where to cut or pinion the wing would impair the appearance. Leather or plastic brails must be of the right size and pliability. They can be purchased for about £8·00 to £10·00 per hundred. The two short arms of the brail are secured around the bird's humerus bone or 'forearm' with a split paper fastener, the long end is then passed underneath the wing and between the first and second or second and third flight feathers, finally it is bent back bringing the wing downwards (see fig 4.7) and connected to the paper fastener.

The brailed wing must be allowed a little movement and the brails should be changed from one wing to the other every 3 months. For short periods, taping is a useful alternative to brailing. Two equal lengths of approx 5 mm of tape are knotted together at one third their dual length. The long end of the double tape is then used to secure the flight feathers in the same manner as with the brail.

IDENTIFICATION

Marking breeding birds is done by leg ringing or wing tagging. While rings are more easily noticed a comfortable fit must be ensured and checked for size every few weeks as the legs grow, otherwise unpleasant injuries will be caused. A large sized adjustible game or pigeon type banded ring is preferable to the standard spiral chicken ring. The wing tags are fixed by special pliers to the leading edge of the wing usually between 5 and 8 weeks old. They must not be pushed too tight as space is required for growth.

SEXING

Efficient management is the 'sine qua non', regardless of the system operated. Properly set out records and strict routine provide the only solid platform for success in aviary, farm or intensive commercial unit. A regular daily inspection will reveal birds which are seedy or ill, those which are sparkling with health and vitality and those which are merely 'hangers on'. The undesirables must be isolated and treated or culled on a daily basis. A bird in full lay should have a large soft abdomen and a reasonable gap between the pelvic bones on either side of the vent. If she is not laying the abdomen will be leathery and smaller, the vent will be dry and puckered, with the pelvic bones closer together and nearer the sternum.

The breeding birds are best separated into small pens at a ratio of one cock to five or six hens. Too many cocks are likely to result in improper fertilisation as well as causing unnecessary aggression. This should be accomplished four to six weeks before laying might be expected to begin. The reproductive cycle is triggered by the lengthening daylight as well as by temperature (which should be around 20°C) and proper nourishment. There is a natural gap of about six weeks between the lighting stimulus, natural or artificial, and the commencment of laying. This is also important when it comes to sexing.

Keets can be purchased from some hatcheries already sexed and it is customary for males to have the wing pinioned on one particular side and the female on the other for identification purposes. There are generally some errors which usually turn out to be extra males. Normally however keets are purchased as plain day olds and if they are of good modern strain they can be sexed at eleven to twelve weeks by inspecting the genitalia. The development of these is tied to an adequate lighting stimulus which in the case of keets raised outdoors must be a minimum of twelve hours of daylight. Thus, if they were hatched at the beginning of June or July, they could be sexed at the end of August or September. If hatched even one month later, because of the shorter and decreasing length of daylight their reproductive system would not have received a sufficient development stimulus to enable sexual discrimination to be made unless they were kept indoors and subjected to artificial lighting like those under intensive systems. A final sexing can be made on seven or eight month old birds the following spring just prior to breeding, to eliminate possible errors, as some males in particular, at three months, are less clearly defined.

With the bird laid on its back across one's knee, hold its legs up with one hand and with the other separate the tail feathers to disclose the cloaca. Squeeze lightly with thumb and index finger on either side to expose the genitalia. In the male the cloacal orifice is slightly raised, it is circular and surrounded with a firm muscular ring. Under pressure the genital appendage should stand out with the cloaca remaining more or less circular, the appendage resembles a small bulbous tongue. In the female the cloaca is flatter, sometimes slightly concave and less easy to grasp. When pressed the orifice is less muscular and yields flexibly to the touch, appearing as an elongated slit. When the female is approaching lay at six or seven months, the separation of her pelvic bones will allow the width of from 1 to 3 fingers to be placed between them. If just before the point of lay this separation is greater than two and a half fingers wide, the bird can be marked as a potentially good layer who will probably be worth retaining for at least a second year.

Under natural conditions, a hen may lay well over five years, but the cock's semen production usually starts to decline after the third year.

CATCHING CRUSH:

A well designed catching crush or coop is an important item of equipment for any guinea grower. The individual birds should be inspected regularly and frequent handling helps to inhibit their nervous propensities. they must be caught with a minimum of fuss and without damage to plumage or body bruising.

These are usually constructed in the form of a narrow coop with a funnel shaped open end. They may hold up to six or ten birds in a single row. There should be a guillotine type division gate positioned along the length in order to isolate one or two birds at a time and a gate at the top to enable the grower to lift them out easily. The catching crush can be used at a ground level bird exit from a building or interior section or in the open pen in such a position that the birds can be easily steered into it.

KEETS FOR MARKET

For those who want to rear keets for sale to poulterers and restaurants or for their own use, the easiest and in western Europe the most commonly adopted method is to purchase day old keets from a reputable hatchery.

These are started under radiant heaters or in brooders (see Chapter 5) for the first 5 to 6 weeks and then grown on litter indoors, broiler style to approx 10 weeks, or outdoors in pens from 6 to 12 or 14 weeks. At this stage they should be ready for marketing at 0·9 kg to 1·25 kg live weight. During the winter months pen reared keets will also need indoor shelter to maintain rapid growth, but the market price is correspondingly high in compensation. After the brooder period, only one building or enclosure is needed and this can be cleaned and rested when the birds have gone. Such a policy eliminates most of the problems connected with keeping adult stock on a permanent basis. It also greatly reduces the risk of disease or parasitic infection. As each batch is a separate operation and can be repeated when desired, it suits many people who may be preoccupied with other things during parts of the year.

CAPONISING

Caponising male keets is practiced in a few broiler guinea production units and growers with outdoor pens who operate with sex linked keets.

The popular method is not to castrate the bird but to implant a tiny pellet under the loose skin of the neck about 6 weeks before slaughter. The pellets contain one of the female oestrogen hormones in synthetic form. Diethylstilboestrol, Thiouracil or Hexoestrol are amongst the compounds used. The aim is to stimulate the production of fatty tissue and thereby improve the texture of the meat, there is generally some gain in live weight and increase in blood plasma content. The effects are not always as uniform with guinea fowl as with chickens. The duration of hormonal activity may vary with the compound and in the author's opinion, there is uncertainty about the amounts of hormone remaining in the carcass after slaughter and as to whether the consumer might be affected by these, no matter how small the amount. They are of course officially declared as safe, providing the manufacturer's instructions are complied with.

HYGIENE

A planned cleaning and disinfecting programme should be established as automatic routine. This applies to all buildings, fittings and equipment as well as outdoor runs, pens, yards etc. Once the necessary daily and monthly frequencies have been decided, the work should be started at fixed hours on each occasion. Some micro organisms can renew residence within hours of the previous lot being liquidated. Certain viruses and bacteria have such survival ability that they are never totally wiped out, but at least their numbers can be kept to a minimum tolerance. Many of these tiny creatures are resistant to flame or steam cleaning alone and detergents are necessary to help remove dirt efficiently. There are hundreds of disinfectants on the market, many claiming an all purpose use. If so, they must hit pests, bacteria, viruses and fungal moulds. If in doubt about this consult your vet or chemist. Some of the phenol based compounds are made up for 'safe' use alongside livestock — these are non toxic and non irritant. Other more powerful, wide spectrum compounds are relatively stable and ideal for washing down surfaces, mats and dips. Some iodine combinations are most effective with viruses. all these can be used in conjunction with formaldehyde which as mentioned elsewhere, makes an excellent fumigant and spray. Anti–parasitic compounds like fenchchloros or malathion in dusting powder or aerosol form are useful for puffing or spraying into crevices to eliminate lice, mites etc. Small pieces of equipment and utensils should be disinfected after use or at least daily. Larger fittings which can be removed from a building should be taken out and powersprayed or soaked in detergent and germicide. In litter houses, after the removal of all litter, the floors and lower walls should be scrubbed, soaked with one of the strong disinfectants and allowed to dry out naturally. The areas around and between buildings should be sprayed and the approaches provided with vehicle and foot dips or mats. Sterile apparel should be worn by both staff and visitors entering hatcheries, interiors of aviaries and breeding houses.

INTENSIVE REARING

Where poultry are kept in dense concentration, problems arising from stress, infections etc., are multiplied. Successful management therefore demands a higher degree of scientific expertise and skill. The argument in favour of intensive systems for guinea fowl is as for turkeys, that only by employing these methods will sufficient quantities of birds be produced economically, to satisfy existing demands and to make them available to a wider popular market.

Only the specialised strains of guinea fowl which have been developed for the purpose will succeed and thrive under intensive controls, so the grower must ensure his stock comes from a known hatchery involved in broiler production. The aim is to produce keets which will be ready for standard market demand with a live weight of 2¼ to 3 lbs, (1 to 1·5 kg) or an oven ready carcass of 1¾ to 2½ lbs (750 gm to 1·25 kg), at 8 to 12 weeks old, with an average food conversion ratio of 3.00 : 1.

Environmental conditions can be similar to those for chickens. In large scale operations, age groups are always standardised so that an 'all in' and 'all out' system is obtained.

Figure 4 – 9 Modern Housing with Ventilation cowls (from **Pictorial Poultry Keeping, J Batty**)

Figure 4 – 10 Intensive (note brick walls) Housing with Food Hopper (**Courtesy: Harlow Bros Ltd. Photo: Smith Studios Ltd**)

Figure 4 – 11 Battery cages used for Poultry which may house Guinea Fowl **(Courtesy: Platchett)**

Figure 4 – 12 Guinea Fowl chicks

Whereas broiler chickens are stocked in single units of 10,000 to 50,000, broiler keets do better in small units or sub–divisions of a larger building containing 700 to 1,000, from 4 weeks old. Above this age they are considerably more nervous and sudden noises like car horns, supersonic bangs or thunderstorms are liable to create panic, with subsequent danger of a 'smother', i.e. mass overcrowding into the corners which causes large percentages to be suffocated or trampled to death. For the same reasons, the sudden introduction of strangers or even strange or differently coloured clothing is likely to cause considerable disturbance.

The twin fundamentals of intensive rearing are nutrition and controlled environment. For the latter, purpose built housing is preferable but old buildings can be converted. Because of soaring fuel costs, the proper insulation of roof, wall and floor is now vital. It should be realised that recommended standards in many countries, expressed as U values for the total building or in K values for specific materials, are not much above minimum requirements. By increasing the standard values from 50 to 100%, the energy saving achieved will more than repay the capital outlay. When choosing the type of insulation, acoustic values should also be kept in mind. As with the former, it is the rating for the total structure which counts and if the building is not expertly assembled, high K and acoustic values will count for nothing. When there is correctly interlocked insulation, functional design and accurate control of ventilation and humidity, a fully stocked house should require little extra heating up to latitudes as far north as Stockholm. The same rules apply equally in hot climates, in order to minimise solar heat gain and save cooling costs. The structure should be windowless and all ventilators should be well baffled to eliminate natural light, acoustic and wind effects.

Highly reflective interior surfaces can reduce by more than 50% the amount of artificial light required. A sprayed polyurethane coating is one of the best ways to achieve this. It will also act as the interior vapour barrier while providing minimum anchorage for bacteria, being easy to keep clean. Pale reflective greens and blues are considered by some designers to produce a beneficial effect on laying fowl, even slow rhythm background music is being tested. Any stress factor lowers fertility in female and male.

The ventilation systems currently in favour are of the pressurised reverse flow type, where the air is drawn in by automatically controlled sets of high speed fans at ceiling level, through small inlets which reduce unfavourable wind effects. This air stream sets up secondary currents which ensure a constant and uniform distribution, regardless of whether deep litter or tiers of cages are being used. This conserves energy by retaining the coolest air under the ceiling surfaces. Whichever type of system is used, the air is usually extracted at the house ridges.

Design is all important and the system should be tailor made to the size, shape and contents of the building. The air flow for example, could be distorted or interrupted by the partitions which sub divide the guineas in a large building. There must be no draughts or dead spots and the rate of flow should be highly flexible. The fresh air needs of adult birds in summer would be almost 100 times as much as day old keets in winter. In case of faults, 'fail safe' arrangements must be inbuilt with temperature alarms. In the event of a mains failure an automatic standby generator is required, as deaths due to heat prostration would start within 20 minutes. Ventilation is interrelated with the temperature and humidity controls. Guinea fowl appear to thrive best at slightly higher temperature levels than chickens. In brooding houses, which are usually on floor systems, the day old keets are started at temperatures of 35°C (95°F) and gradually reduced to about 20 to 21°C (68 to 70°F) by 6 weeks old. Both radiant and space heating methods are in use. A relative humidity of 65 to 70% is optimum range, this is sometimes difficult to maintain in cold dry continental climates. At less humid levels, organic and inorganic particle concentrations rise and may required to be filtered out. A useful combination is an electrostatic dust filter and ioniser, connected to the ventilation system. The standard of feathering is adversely affected by low humidity levels and to surmount this problem a moisture spray which does not atomise too finely, can be fitted in the circulation system. Ammonia levels should be kept well below 20 ppm since anything over 10 ppm produces an unpleasant smell. The guinea fowls susceptibility to respiratory infections is increased when their breathing tracts become irritated.

Excellent data, tables and charts on all the above ratios are available and no one should venture into this field without working in, or acutely observing several commercial operations. They should study the copious literature on the subject and have discussions with all the experts available before embarking on their own project.

In a brooder house, the keets are started in a circular screened area, which is gradually widened when they are under radiant heating. Alternatively they are kept in chicken brooders for the first four weeks. In these they will need fine sheeting over the standard mesh grids to protect their feet, which are more tender than those of chickens and easily damaged. Being smaller, 120 keets will fit into a 100 chick brooder. On the floor litter system the keets should not have so much space, that they can stray far from the feeders and fresh water containers, hence the circular screening. The approximate space allocation for each keet is, 0.065 sq.m or 100 sq.ins for up to 10 weeks. For a semi intensive system 0.093 sq.m is adequate for anything up to 16 weeks (see also Chapter 5).

The response threshold between light and darkness for guinea fowl or standard poultry, is 0.04 ft candles or 0.4 lux. Day old keets are started at a high light intensity of 15 to 20 lux, to encourage feeding and drinking. This is reduced down to around 2 lux after 3 to 4 weeks, dimmer switches with fluorescent daylight tubes are useful, to avoid fast falls in contrast and also save electricity. For broiler guineas stronger light is unnecessary and may encourage pecking or even depress growth. High internal reflectivity may mean the difference between using 25 or 40 watt tubes with obvious savings in costs. Some producers maintain the lighting on a 24 hour basis over the entire fattening period, others allow 1 hour of darkness in each 24 hour cycle, to accustom the birds in case of power failure. (See Chapter 5 Lighting Programmes).

5

SELECTIVE BREEDING

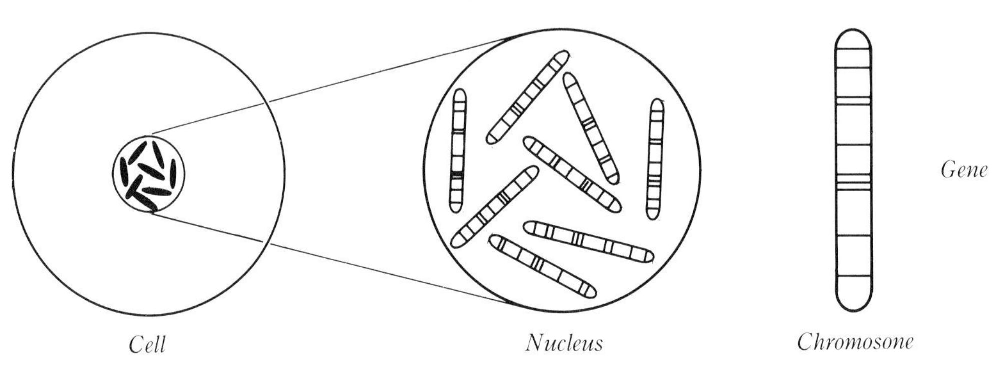

Figure 5 – 1 Location of Genes

CHAPTER 5
SELECTIVE BREEDING

ACQUIRING STOCK

The initial bird stock which the breeder will procure, is going to constitute the nucleus of his future flock. It is most important that these birds should be of the highest quality and obtained from as wide a range of sources as possible, in order to make available the maximum number of desirable genes. Circumstances of course vary enormously. The aviculturalist when starting with a new species, may consider himself fortunate to obtain a setting of fertile eggs from any source. Show and commercial breeders will have the opportunity to study each available strain and compile as much information as they can about their antecedents. Commercial strains from a hatchery should be bought on details of their flock records and current performance.

Considering that substantial expenditure will have been laid out, it is surprising how many people fail to make adequate travelling arrangements, so that the birds travel securely and arrive in good condition. Similar attention should be given to preparing their accommodation which should be scrupulously clean, disinfected and ready to receive them. Here the new stock should be isolated for a few weeks even when they have a clean certificate of health or were previously quarantined, in case of infections picked up in transit being transmitted to existing stock.

When breeding to establish new strain leaders who are intended to influence the flock for many generations, it is worth remembering that a fowl in unforced conditions reaches its maturation peak at about 18 months. The following season is the optimum laying period from which to anticipate the finest specimen keets. This applies equally to aviary, show pen or production unit.

FUNCTION OF CHROMOSOMES AND GENES

An understanding of the principles of genetics and a knowledge of the mode of inheritance of specific defects as well as qualities, can help us to avoid particular errors when a mating is projected. It will not necessarily produce all the qualities for which we are aiming.

In the cell nucleus are thread like structures called chromosomes, they occur in pairs with differing numbers for different classes of bird — guineas are thought to have 39 pairs. There are two types, the autosomes or body chromosomes are normally constant in number and as cells divide, each new cell carries the same number. The sex chromosomes are contained, together with half the autosomes, in the reproduction cells, e.g. a spermatozoon or an ovum, which are both known as gametes. When these fuse together, as at fertilisation, the resultant complete cell is known as a zygot. There are two sex chromosomes in each male zygot, but only one sex chromosome in the female; in place of the second is what is called a Y chromosome (see fig. 5.1). In fowls the female cell decides the sex of the offspring. Each chromosome contains many genes and it is these which control the development of the hundreds of characteristics appearing in the bird. The full development of any characteristic in a bird is also affected to some degree by the bird's environment, which is another reason why no two birds are ever exactly alike although they may be similar. For example, suppose the gene combination in a particular bird's chromosomes which control its weight, would allow the bird to grow up to 2 kilos in weight, by acting through enzymes which stimulate growth to continue until the full weight is reached. These may be deflected from enabling that bird to reach its potential because of poor management or deficient feeding. The bird may then only attain 1·5 kg.

Forms of genes are said to be dominant or recessive to each other in their effect on a characteristic, so if we know that for example yellow is dominant to green, it is easy to work out the result of a cross for a single factor inheritance (see fig. 5.2). The pairs of genes which an organism possesses are called its genotype, the physical expression (visible effect) of the genes in the bird is called the phenotype. If the bird has one dominant and one recessive gene form (Aa) for a certain character, it is heterozygous for that character. If it has two dominant (AA) or two recessive (aa) gene forms, it is homozygous for that character i.e. it will breed pure. These alternative forms of gene are called alleles. A test, or recessive back cross will reveal whether an individual is homozygous or heterozygous for a particular character, when it is crossed with another which is known to be homozygous recessive. The recessive allele can only appear in the phenotype of the first generation progeny if it was present in both parents, so if any of the progeny are homozygous recessives then the parent being tested was heterozygous.

There are many complications which can upset particular breeding programmes, especially those of the show breeder who is usually operating with small numbers. Sometimes a dominant allele will not exercise its full effect on all the birds which carry it and it appears only partly or not at all in the phenotype, this is described as incomplete penetrance. A similar situation in reverse may happen with homozygous recessive alleles but these and other exceptions do not invalidate the general theory. The dominant allele may not fully mask the recessive one or the two may be in certain conditions, of similar strength. The monohybrid or dihybrid ratios do not always work when dealing with small numbers. The general theory is based on the result of thousands of crosses. Mendel's 3:1 ratio is actually a mean of 2.84:1 to 3.15:1. Some of his individual results ranged from 1:1 to 32:1.

Another factor which often upsets dominant/recessive relationships is that although genes at a precise locus on a chromosome bear a particular character, their action may be modified by genes at other loci of the chromosome, creating an epistatic effect.

Chromosomes are also subject to other aberrations. With some genes which affect colour, it is easy to detect the heterozygous state in the phenotype; in the Blue Andalusian fowl the alleles are simple (AA) black, (aa) white, (Aa) blue. Sex linkage occurs because there are genes on the sex or X chromosome, not connected with sex, for which there are no corresponding alleles on the smaller Y chromsome. If one of these gene forms is recessive on an X chromosome in the male, it will be masked by a dominant form on the other X chromosome. In the female there would be no corresponding dominant gene, so the carrier would appear as homozygous. As previously mentioned, in the ornamental buff Dundotte guinea strain, for 95% of cases, all the keets bearing dark stripes on their heads were found by their breeder to be female and those with light stripes were males. Commercial sex linked guinea strains have also been developed in France. These are valued by growers, as sexual dimorphism is not apparent under 10 to 12 weeks but is inverted above this age. At three months the male is usually heavier than the female but subsequently the female will increase in weight and pass out the male which is lighter when adult.

Hybrids are the result of cross mating between parents who differ genetically but whose desirable characteristics may complement each other, with the premise that favourable alleles are likely to be dominant. The crosses may be between unrelated strains, varieties or in some cases even species.

As an out cross breeding will tend to increase heterozygosity, this method frequently increases the average merit of the individual. There is usually an increase in size and viability which may even exceed the performance of the better parent. This is known as hybrid vigour or heterosis and is frequently most apparent when the genetic difference is widest. It may also be non existant between similar but unrelated strains. In ornamental breeds the result is sometimes spectacular in terms of changes in colour or conformation. Commercially, it is undertaken in the hope of eliminating or raising the standard of some character in a few individual birds, which can then be selectively crossed back into a breeding flock. The new hybrid will normally first be tested out by breeding it with sample birds from the flock in order to determine the effects.

In general, outcrossing is also likely to import other adverse alleles which may lower the general standard of a flock for a considerable period. In a variable strain, there may well be a higher first year mortality because of the hereditary constitution. A proper diet can improve the condition. The F2 generation is often genetically stronger. Hybrids also

Blue Andalusian Fowl
(see text for colour breeding)

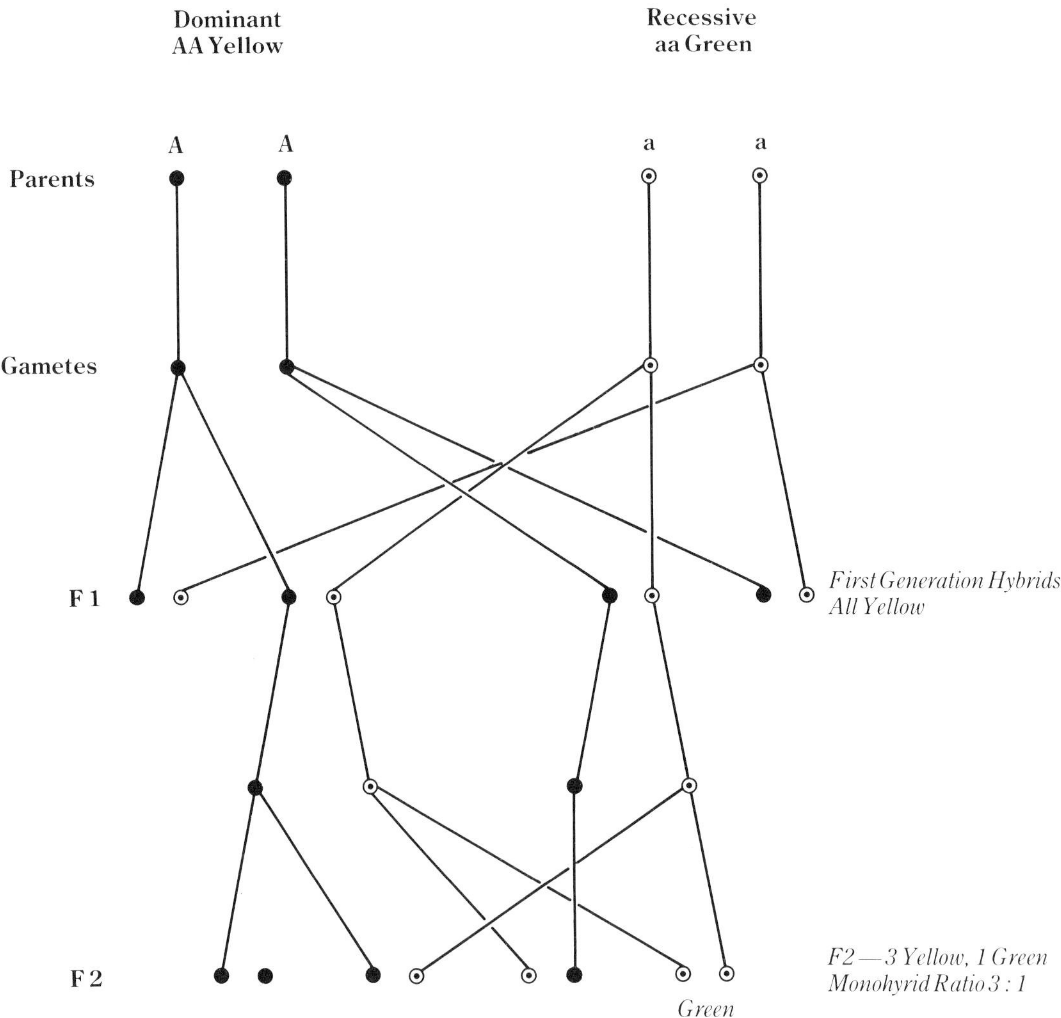

3 possible Genotypes; AA, Aa, aa
2 possible Phenotypes; Green, Yellow
1 Homozygous Green AA, 2 Heterozygous Green Aa, 1 Homozygous Yellow aa

Figure 5 – 2 Basic Genetics

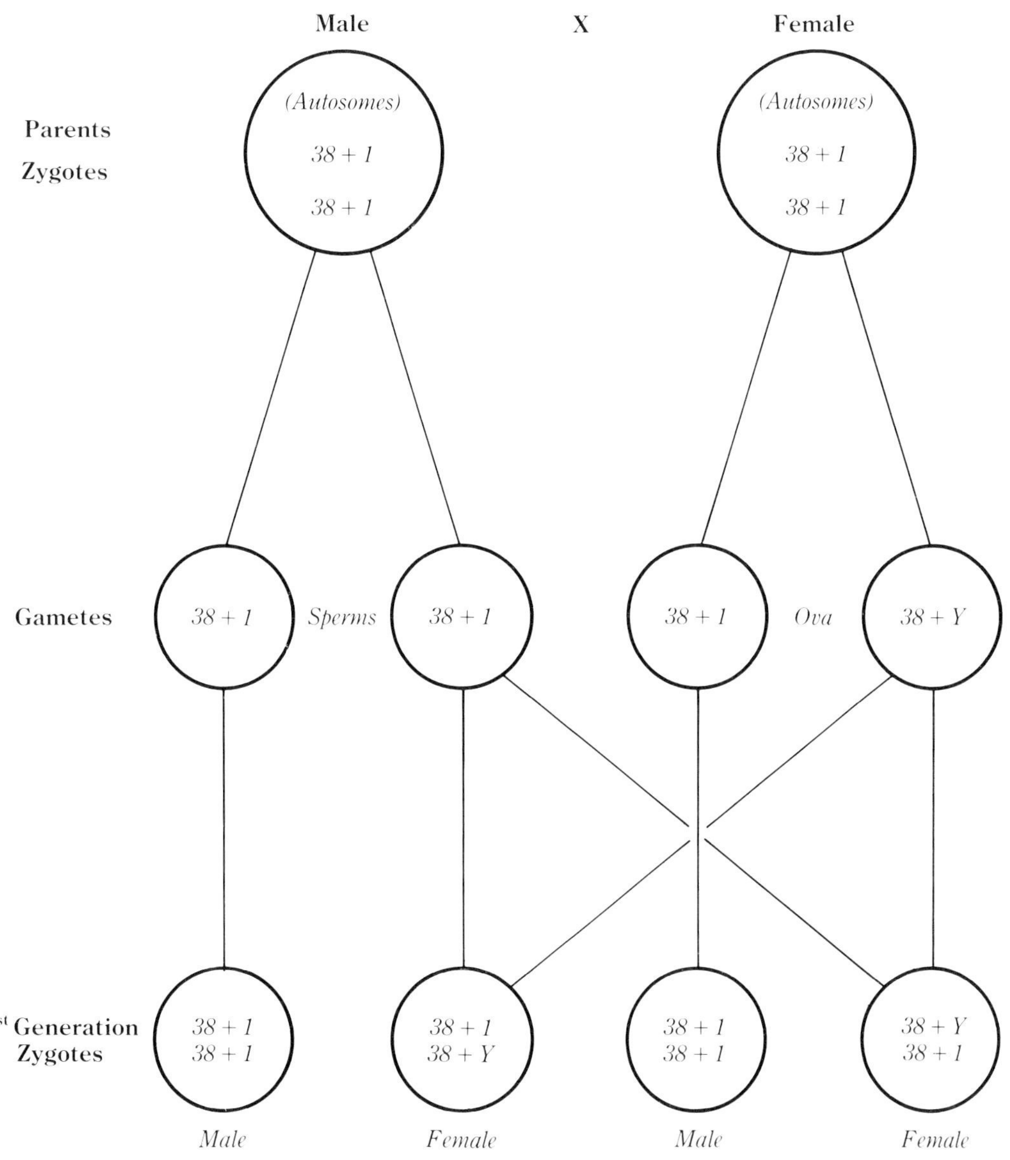

Figure 5 – 3 Reproductive Cells

tend to hatch less easily from large eggs. Commercially there are several recognised systems, a favourite being variations of reciprocal recurrent selection. By this method, two and sometimes three or four flock strains are established; size and ratios vary. A minimum size would be 250 hens and 50 cocks. Two thousand keets would then be bred and reared up to 10 weeks old and from these, 500 hens with 100 cocks would be selected, a further selection of 250 hens and 50 cocks is again made at 20 to 25 weeks. The flocks are closed to other stock and selected male progeny is tested against the opposite flock of hens on individual performance. Every cross mating in both directions is recorded and ranked and the next season the most proven sires are mated to the proven hens in order to reproduce them as pure bred. The cycle can then be repeated. Selections are made on the records of families rather than individuals, also on the physical handling qualities during rearing and at point of lay. Any individual which shows loss of vigour or is physically incapable of making suitable breeding material must be eliminated.

Unlike breeding for colour, where gene combinations are often fairly small, all the desirable commercial traits are affected by multiple gene combinations. Additionally, the two sets of characteristics are mutually antagonistic i.e. the larger and better fleshed strains have greater difficulty in reproduction and a fertility factor often has to be introduced. As table production is the primary concern with guinea fowl 12 to 20 characteristics are involved. Good breast width and body weight at 8 weeks, limb size, succulent flesh, rapid maturation, low mortality or sturdiness, ratio of meat to bone, feed efficiency, handling qualities and good semen production are frequently known as the 'male line'. The 'female line' includes, fertility, maturation, fecundity, intensity of egg production, high persistency during first laying year, egg size, hatchability also viability or livablility in terms of disease resistance, immunity and feed efficiency. Handling quality is particularly important in breeding guineas by artificial insemination because of their inherent nervous disposition.

A large hatchery may keep five or six strains with 5,000 to 8,000 cocks per pure strain. Progeny tests are made on eight hatches per strain per year. Keets marketed will often be the result of a triple cross, where the female is already the result of one cross and the male is of a pure strain. If these keets, as sold for fattening, were to be bred together by a hopeful grower, the progeny would almost certainly be inferior to the parents. Certain guinea strains have now evolved in some French hatcheries which seem to possess a degree of genetic resistance to infectious enteritis and these are being concentrated upon in the absence of any virus having yet been isolated and vaccine developed.

Within a subspecies, members interbreed with each other and the total of their genes constitutes a gene pool, interbreeding with other subspecies is known as gene flow. This is well exemplified amongst many of the *Numida* subspecies which exhibit strong similarities in the border regions adjacent to the next subspecies. There is some evidence of genetic change or drift between the three or four main groups. Apart from natural selection and geographical isolation, the third factor, variation, is derived from mutation and recombination i.e. after crossing over at meiosis. Considering the size of the area involved on the African continent, the large number of genes in each cell and the endless possible combinations of dominant and recessive alleles, it is interesting that the difference is not greater.

Interbreeding between species which is not usual, has been shown to be occasionally possible. Professor Ghigi found in experiments between species of wild jungle fowl that although the female hybrids were sterile, this did not preclude gene flow between the species. The cocks when fed a suitable diet proved fertile and produced unusual phenotypes when crossed back again. Cross matings between families have also been made. Guineas have been crossed with pheasants *(Phasianus colchicus),* chickens, peafowl and a Beltsville hen turkey (AW Schorger 1966). The resultant 'churkeys' and 'guinhens' etc. were all sterile in both male and female line. Similarly the hybrid mule is invariably sterile with an uneven chromosome count of 63, against that of the horse which has 64 and the donkey's 62.

No consideration is given here to recent experimentation or results achieved with implants, gene recoding by blocking undesirable alleles, inhibiting RNA transcription, somaticell hybridisation etc. Some of these techniques when established may well short circuit the theory and method of selective breeding as currently practiced, but adaptation to viable usage still lies years ahead.

MANAGEMENT OF BREEDING STOCK:

Intensive management of breeding stock in large numbers is at present really feasible only in cage systems because of the necessity to maintain a calm atmosphere and accustom the birds to regular human proximity and manipulation. Strictly hygienic conditions are equally imperative for successful fertilisation. Housing should be as described in Chapter 4; i.e., properly designed in order to provide full environmental control of the microclimate. It cannot be emphasised sufficiently that dedication, knowledge, skill and responsibility must be of the highest standard not only to provide a basis for successful breeding but to avoid causing stress or cruelty to the birds. All electronic or mechanical systems must be fail safe. Atmospheric control, food and watering mechanisms, even droppings collection belts require in–built alternative breakdown arrangements. Equipment faults and failure account for 80 to 90% of all problems. Cages may be of the stacked, stepstair or flatdeck varieties but they should be ergonomically arranged to allow easy access to the birds. The flatdeck system is probably the most satisfactory to maintenance and is becoming more popular.

The keets intended for replacement breeding are floor reared, in a similarly controlled microclimate. Several lighting programmes are in current use. Some commence with extended light during the keet's first 24 to 48 hours of an 18 to 23 hour period to ensure they are feeding and drinking properly, this is followed by a series of rapid steps down to 8 hours by 2 weeks old and then gradually increased to 17 hours by 12 to 13 weeks. Reducing again to 8 hours at an intensity of 1 to 5 lux over the next 15 weeks. From point of lay onwards at about 28 weeks the light is again increased by half an hour per week up to 16 to 18 hours; sometimes 2 hours are kept in hand for a boost towards the end of the laying season. Densities are 50 per m^2 for first three days, 25 per m^2 after one week and from two weeks onwards 12 per m^2. For older birds allowances for hens are 8 per m^2 to 28 weeks at low light level, cocks 6 per m^2 to 28 weeks at higher light levels. The initial brooding temperature of 35° to 36°C (95°F) is gradually reduced over the following three weeks to 28° to 29°C (84°F) with fresh air volume and humidity in phase. After 6 weeks they can be held at 20° to 21°C (68° to 70°F).

Another programme discriminates between males and females. The females are normally prepared in artificial lighting increased or decreased by half hour graduations:

0 – 4 weeks	20 hours
5 – 10 weeks	16 hours
11 – 15 weeks	12 hours
16 – 24 weeks	7 to 8 hours

From 24 to 28 weeks they are graduated back to 14 hours. At 28 weeks they are placed in cages with the light held at 16 hours or 14 and slowly increased to 16 over the laying period.

During the first 3 months, the males if unsexed are raised with the females in artificial light. After being sexed they are removed to normal daylight type conditions. If they have been kept on an 8 hour lighting schedule during the growth cycle; they are given photostimulation from about 21 weeks old. This is two to three weeks earlier than the female and should ensure synchronization of the peaks of sperm and laying production. Sperm production commences 8 to 10 weeks after photostimulation has begun and should attain its peak 3 weeks later. They are sometimes placed in the cages two weeks before the hen for habituation to handling and milking. This enables poor donors to be weeded out and ensures the selected cocks are ready when the hens arrive.

The selection of quality males can be decided earlier than with many other species of fowl (see de Reviers 1982). If during one to five weeks after the first ejaculation the quantity of semen and the motility of the spermatozoa yield high results, this situation will be maintained throughout the breeding period.

Tests on the ambient temperature, whether 12°C, 21°C, or 23°C, in which the males are reared showed it to have little effect upon testicular growth.

Some programmes eliminate the initial high intensity long light pattern during the first week. The object of these patterns is to encourage growth and to ensure that maturation is at peak development by 28 weeks, whatever the season. An excessively precocious development and therefore low body weight, must be guarded against, as this will create a depressed rate of laying and small eggs. Late maturity will give a depressed rate of laying and large eggs. The optimum chronological age for maturity should be established previously, by assuming a statistical average for the particular strain of bird. Because guinea fowl can be so disasterously upset by noise during dark periods, some producers leave 'dim' lights in operation at these times. The importance of light intensity is sometimes insufficently understood. For laying birds, the highest intensity should be 10 to 15 lux, uniformly distributed at all levels. This may be diminished to a 'dim' contrast of approximately 1 or 2 lux. The latter level is adequate to give a photoperiodic response which triggers the timing of the ovulation cycle. In younger birds where daylight stimulates maturation and development of the reproductive organs, a contrast to 'dim' may result in cessation of eating or cannibalism, but only 'darkness' i.e. below the 0.4 lux level will trigger the photoperiodic response and remove the daylight stimulus. For this purpose a level of 0.2 lux, which is about cinema intensity, is recommended. These levels should be checked with an accurate light meter.

There is still no hard evidence that red lights inhibit aggressive pecking and they consume 2 or 3 times as much power as a white tungsten bulb to produce a similar intensity. Daylight fluorescent tubes are now available with dimmer controls and consume 4 times less power than tungsten bulbs. These are better than tungsten because they give more light in the blue green spectrum. A pink tube could be substituted if desired, with the appropriate savings.

ARTIFICIAL INSEMINATION

Cocks and hens which have been chosen for breeding should be humanised as much as possible by walking amongst them and handling them regularly. if possible they should be caged well before breeding commences and conditioned to the insemination team by daily handling and stroking. The ratio of males to females reared from day old should allow for up to 50% rejection of unsuitable cocks.

Both sexes should be allotted reasonable space in the cages, a high concentration of birds per cage increases stress. Normal poultry cages require closer mesh floors in order to protect the feet of guinea fowl. Cocks and hens are usually accommodated in the same building so that insemination of the females can be completed in the minimum time and to assist in keeping accurate records. Depending on the strain the hens commence laying at about 28 to 31 weeks and some extra days should be allowed before using the eggs for incubation. The cocks should start producing high quality semen in desired quantities between 6 and 8 months again depending on the strain, the individual and good management. the quantity of semen yielded by the guinea cock varies from 0.05 ml to 0.15 ml. This is a considerably lower volume than most other fowl, e.g. turkey stags average 0.15 to 1.25 ml. and roosters 0.2 ml. to 0.35 ml. The concentration of spermatozoa in millions per mic-microlitre or billions per millilitre is 6.0 to 9.0 for guinea fowl, 5.0 for chickens and 9.0 for turkeys. The quality of guinea semen is normally good. The high density appearance should be pearly white, a low density is greyish and watery, a distinctly yellow colour should be rejected. Males can be milked 3 times per week on alternate days and a routine once established, should not be altered; the quantities collected however may vary. If the bird becomes accustomed to only one handler, the introduction of a different team member is likely to result in lower yield. Any form of stress may-not only inhibit the volume of semen but also reduce the sperm count. Several weeks training is necessary before a rapid response can be elicited.

When milking, one person who should be seated, holds the bird breast downwards across their knees with the cloaca raised on one side, they massage the back towards the base of the tail with one hand and with the other massage the abdomen around the cloaca. Another person gently squeezes the copulatory appendage between thumb and forefinger and aspirates the semen as it appears at the tip, into the collection tube. The erectile organ is longer than that of the rooster and consists of elongated bulbous folds with a central groove. After the bird is conditioned, one person can make the collection with the aid of a small bench, leg clamps and air or suction gun in about 10 seconds.

The hen also needs preliminary conditioning. She may be held in a similar way to the male but pressure on the abdomen must be very gentle. She quickly learns to respond and the slight pressure causes the cloaca to evert and expose the opening of the oviduct. The cannula is inserted to a depth of 25 to 30 mm and pressure is relaxed on the abdomen, this allows the oviduct to resume its normal position. The semen is then injected by using a plunger or blowing tube. If the hen is squawking there will be a corresponding pumping action in the vaginal passage and the cannula should be given a gentle half turn and carefully removed to ensure that the semen is placed deeply enough to enter the primary stor-

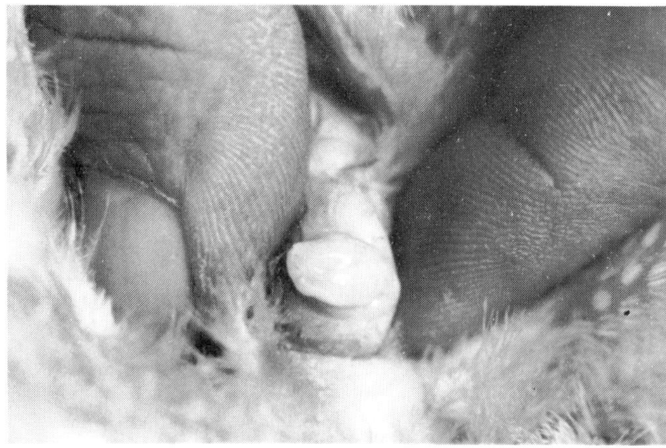

Stage A
Erection of Compulatory
Appendage after massage

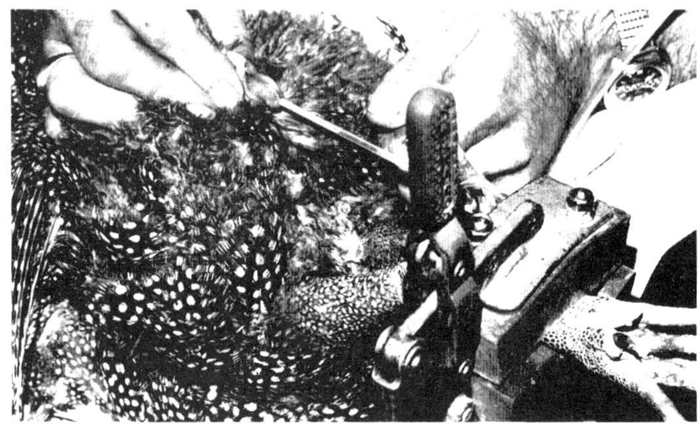

Stage B
Semen being aspirated into
collecting tube

Stage C
Semen flowing from male —
(food quality essential)

Figure 5 – 4 Artificial Insemination — collection of semen from Guinea Fowl

age glands at the utero vaginal junction. With practice the female can be injected without removal from her cage. The insemination process should take place after the majority of the day's eggs in the unit have been laid. The presence of a hard shelled egg in the lower oviduct is indicated when the distal part appears widened when it is everted, rather than tube like. This would probably cause mis–insemination and result in a series of infertile eggs.

The optimum time for insemination in the guinea hen is every sixth day. The recommended minimum injection of pure semen is 0.03 to 0.05 ml. and this must be given within a maximum of 20 minutes following ejaculation. To avoid risk of infection, many breeders use plastic cannulae on the end of a syringe and these are discarded after each insertion. In theory, 2 or 3 females could be inseminated from 1 male who produced 0.1 ml of good quality semen. A diluent is available called "Dilavia", which can be added at 1 : 1 and the solution adminstrated in 0.05 ml doses, this must also take place within the viable 20 minute holding period. The number of hens inseminated would thereby be raised to 4 or 6 per session or 10 to 15 per week for each male. Conditions in the breeding house vary considerably from those in a laboratory, a team with perhaps several thousand birds to cover, are limited by their capabilities and the type of equipment in use. The utilisation of fewer males or greater speed are less important factors if a high level of fertilisation is not achieved.

In order to ensure the latter, some breeders simply inseminate 1 female with the total ejaculation from 1 male. This can be done at high speed with a small team of three people, it also reduces the likelihood of recording errors, as to which crosses are being made.

Other breeders operate on a principle of pooled semen, which allows the most vigorous spermatozoa from a group of males to fertilise the ova and they use the diluent in whatever amounts they judge will achieve the highest level of fertility for their particular method.

Temperatures during the operation should not be below 5°C (approx 40°F) or over 20°C (approx 68°F). Before commencing the procedure, all equipment should be rinsed 6 or 7 times to ensure that no detergent has been left on it.

Breeders who are interested in non commercial traits and are working with only small numbers of fowl, can more easily emulate laboratory conditions, when fertilising a group of females from a male with valuable characteristics but low semen yield.

The design of equipment in use, collectors, containers, cannulae, suction devices, multiple shot syringes and diluents, varies from year to year and regular information on this subject should be obtained from the agricultural poultry advisory service in respective countries. Although the process of insemination is not complicated, intending practitioners would be well advised to avail of some practical training with an experienced breeder or poultry research establishment. Investigation into storage of frozen guinea fowl semen is being pursued, as it is with that of turkeys. Both have so far been found more difficult to preserve without degeneration than chicken semen. The maximum period over which a male can be expected to produce reasonable amounts of quality semen is about 8 months, with good management. Volumes may well diminish somewhat earlier. Egg production at the end of the season tends to be similarly affected. Both sexes may be stimulated to some degree by an extra daily boost in light duration of 1 to 2 hours, i.e. 16 to 18 and additional food supplements. Natural fertility which is known to reach its peak nearer the commencement of the laying season can also be improved towards the end by corrective diet. In commercial production, only birds of exceptional quality or special charac-

Figure 5 – 5 Eggs being candled in trays **(Courtesy: Ark Foods Ltd)**

Figure 5 – 6 Guinea Fowl eggs in incubation **(Courtesy: Ark Foods Ltd)**

teristics are retained for a second season's breeding. If cessation or postponement of laying to later in the season is desired, an early moult can be induced by breaking the lighting patterns e.g. 24 hours full light and by reducing the protein value and regularity of the diet for a few days.

After five or six months of lay, if the returns are falling, the birds are often rested for three months, usually in the cages. It is not advisable to put the hens outside into open air unless the second period of lay is planned for that environment.

INCUBATION

Apart from the ease with which eggs can be identified, another of the advantages of breeding cages is that eggs intended for hatching are not soiled. Nevertheless they should be disinfected as a preventative measure within hours of collection. Once infections like salmonellosis or aspergillus fumigatus enter the hatchery, they are very difficult to eliminate. Eggs may be irradiated with ultra violet rays for 4 to 6 mins., fumigated with formaldehyde gas in sealed cabinets, or dipped in various clean solutions like sodium hypochlorite for 15 minutes at 80 to 90°F (27° to 32°C) and allowed to drain and dry for 1 to 2 hours before storing. Never wipe eggs with a damp cloth as this will force harmful bacteria in through the shell pores.

If dirt is adhering to the shell, remove while dipping it in warm solution. The gas may be made by heating paraformaldehyde crystals or by mixing 40% formalin with potassium permanganate at 3 : 2. Pour the formalin on to the potassium permanganate crystals, **NEVER** the other way round, to avoid an explosive reaction. **ALWAYS** wear a mask over eyes and nose when handling these substances. Amounts of 120 gm formalin plus 75 gm potassium permanganate are sufficient for 100 cubic feet, 30 minutes is the minimum fumigation time. It is also advisable to spray the hatchery air space, (but **NOT** the set eggs or the chicks), daily with a 1 : 1 formalin and water solution. All cracked or irregular eggs should be removed. Handling should be as gentle as possible because this affects the hatchability more than gastrulation, i.e. adequate development prior to laying.

Eggs which have travelled should be 'rested' for several hours before setting. The correct storage temperature is 13° to 16°C (55° to 61°F), with relative humidity at 70% to 80% and proper ventilation. It is important the temperature does not fall below 10°C (50°F), as this is harmful, or rise above 20°C (68°F) as this might initiate embryonic development. They should be stored with large ends uppermost and turned daily to prevent interior adhesion to the shells. The settings should be of uniform size, as larger eggs will take 6 to 12 hours longer to hatch. Incubator settings should be made twice a week if possible. Experiments have shown that there is a decrease in hatchability of about 19% in eggs which are 14 days old.

Incubators are usually of two types. The still air variety are designed for from 20 to 500 eggs although in some machines larger quantities are feasible, whereas the larger ones tend to be forced–draught type. They should all be test run for several days before setting is commenced. If the eggs are marked with the strain and parents coding, this will also show whether they are being properly turned. The larger incubators have two processes, in the first the eggs remain for 24/25 days. Usually they are automatically turned through an angle of 35 to 45 degrees every hour, in the semi upright setting position with broad end up. Temperature is 37.8°C (100°F) R.H. 50%. Escaping gases except carbon dioxide, should be kept below 0.4% and the oxygen supply should be at least 18%. For the final 3 days, the eggs are moved to the hatching section, here the relative humidity should be higher at 70 to 75% and turning is not necessary. The actual hatching may occur between 26 and 27 days depending on the strain of bird, age of egg, size of egg etc. In the smaller still air incubators, the eggs are often set on their sides in trays. These have to be hand turned over 180 degrees at least every 6 hours, in alternate directions each time for the first 10 days. This is the most critical period, thereafter they can be turned 3 times a day up to the 24th day. If the humidity control is not automatic it should be carefully checked when turning eggs and adjusted if necessary. For the last three days, the atmosphere around the eggs should be kept moist. If the relative humidity is too low it will prevent some of the keets from breaking out of the shell and cause delay to others; too high relative humidity may cause premature hatching and less sturdy keets. Ideally, the hatching temperature at the centre of the egg should be 37.7°C and on the outside shell 39.3°C (99.8°F and 102.7°F), depending on the model being used, but the temperature if taken underneath the eggs will read about 36°C (97°F). Some incubators run a little too hot for guinea fowl and indeed for chickens, if in doubt test the shell temperature both above and below. This is important as a difference of more than 0.2°C (1°F) degree may result in poor quality chicks and a number of 'dead in shell'.

Egg inspection by 'candling', is more difficult with guinea fowl eggs due to the much thicker shell and a more powerful ray of light is needed. An ultra violet inspection lamp is used. Even then all the details visible through the shell of a hen egg will not be apparent. It can be done before setting the eggs, to check for hair cracks. An inspection at the 8th day stage should reveal the embryo in a fertile egg as a dark mobile blob. The infertile ones will show clear like newly laid eggs and should be removed. A third inspection at 24 days should show a substantial enlargement of the embryo, a dark red ring or a lack of increase in the size of the blob will probably indicate embryonic demise. Normal eggs should begin to pip or chip between the 23rd and 25th day with full hatch 24 to 30 hours later. The newly hatched keets contain sufficient nourishment to remain alive up to a maximum of 70 hours, but they should be introduced to food within 40 hours. Late hatched keets and those which have difficulty breaking out of the shell should be noted or marked. Avoid confusing the coding information written on the egg shell, by temporarily isolating the chipping eggs, and/or trays, with high cardboard rings. Placing a dab of coloured dye on the down of the keet's back is a helpful method of identification prior to permanent leg or wing banding.

Sometimes the hatching trays are too slippery for the soft toes of the baby keets and a layer of fine sacking or corrugated paper is used to provide a better grip. Some late hatching keets which need assistance to escape from the shell can still be quite healthy and viable but usually need a little extra care during the first few days.

Russian experiments carried out on cooling the incubator, involved lowering the temperature by 5°C for half an hour twice each day. They reported a 2% to 5% improvement in hatching out. The reasoning is that these variations occur in the natural state when the bird leaves the nest.

The highest incubation losses have been caused by the fact that 2% to 10% of battery eggs have had an excessive porosity, this can be seen by a higher than normal loss in weight during incubation; average losses are 4% to 5% at eight days and 13% at twenty four days. A high percentage of 'clears' and dead embryos results from the use of these eggs.

Many problems may contribute to a less than successful hatch. Too many infertiles at the start could be due to eggs being stored too long or roughly handled, infertility in the parents because of age i.e. males were too old, misinsemination or lack of sufficient nutrients during and towards the end of the laying season. The latter may be one of the reasons for 'dead in shell' between 10 and 24 days.

A secondary nutrient deficiency may be due to a parasitic infection of the breeding stock. This is known as 'mushy chick disease', yolk sac infection or omphalitis. It causes the greatest mortality 24 to 72 hours after hatching. Examination will show a wet navel, unpleasant smell and swollen abdomen. The yolk sac has not been absorbed and is filled with a dirty yellow or brown fluid.

Increasing the brooder warmth and medicating the drinking water with antibiotics and vitamins may curtail the spread of the infection which is usually due to Escherichia coli. It may be caused in numerous ways, often through low resistance in the stock or poor hygiene in the hatchery. Laboratory tests should be made to establish the exact type of bacteria and veterinary advice obtained as to appropriate treatment.

Intensive brooding is usually on a floor system. Where overhead heaters are employed for large numbers of day olds, the highest mortality is frequently a result of dehydration and starvation. This is due to the keets in the centre being unable to reach the drinkers and food trays frequently enough. These should be carefully positioned and the keets reactions closely observed. A general heating system throughout the room relieves this problem and that of too high a contrast between pockets of cold and hot air.

Figure 5 – 7 A small Still-Air Incubator with Viewer **(Courtesy: Reliable Thermostat Co)**

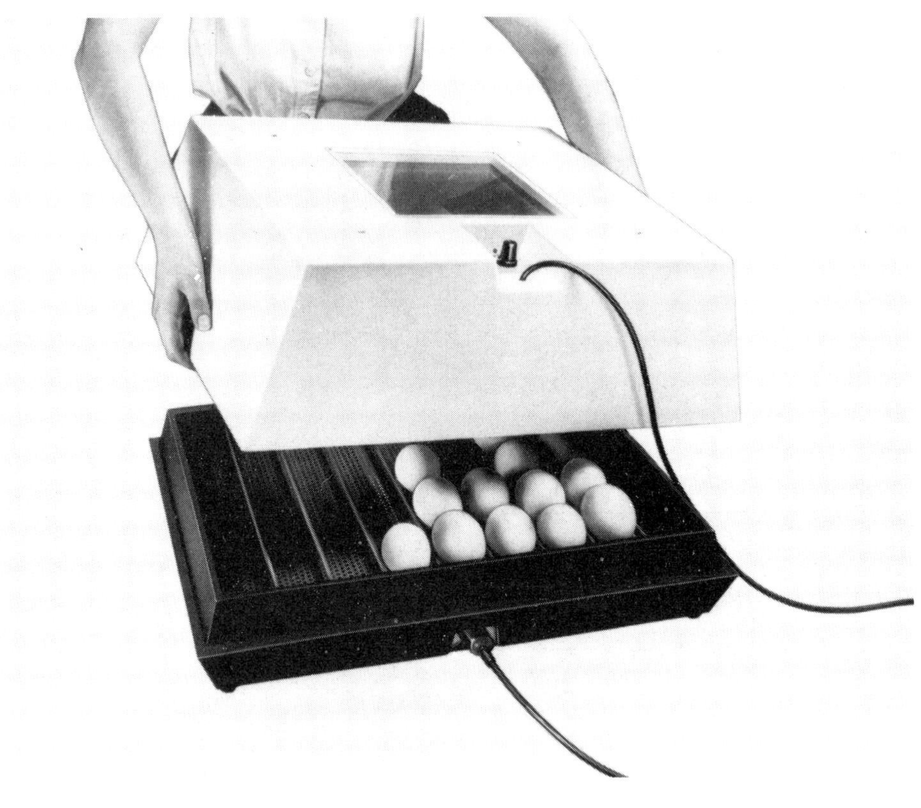

Figure 5 – 8 An Incubator with Electronic Temperature Control **(Courtesy: Brinsea)**

6

NUTRITION

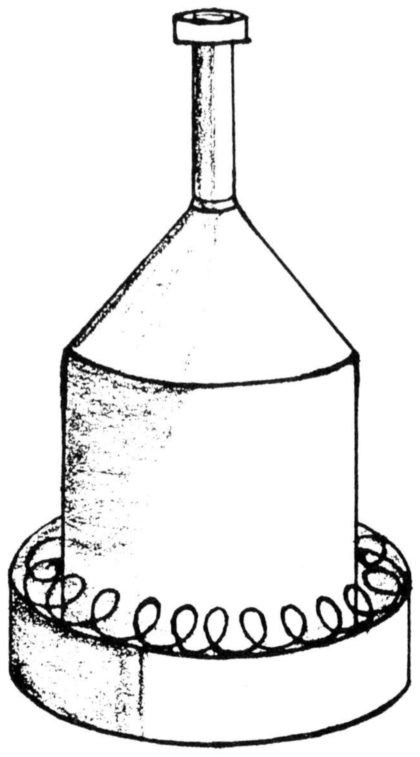

A metal or plastic coil placed inside rim of drinker prevents young birds getting wet or even drowning

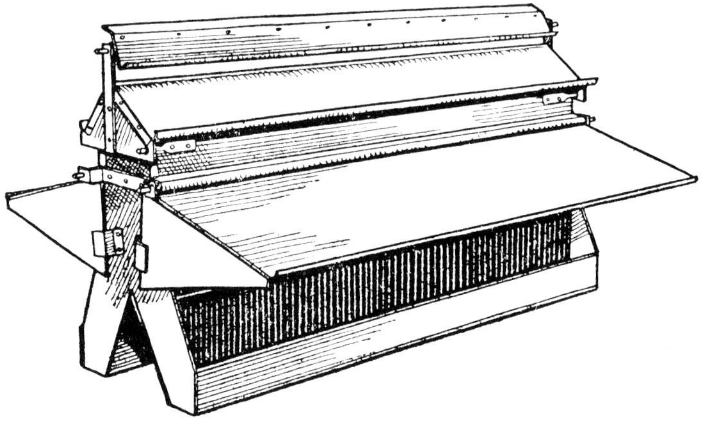

Figure 6 – 1 Basic Food and Water Equipment
Top: Water Fountains
Bottom: Food Hopper for Outside Use

CHAPTER 6

NUTRITION

The nutrients which constitute any balanced diet include water, carbohydrates, fats and oils, crude fibre, proteins, minerals and vitamins. Probably more experimentation has been devoted to, and experience gained from, the composition of poultry foods and birds' reactions to them than the feeding of any other animal.

Much more still remains to be unravelled in the biochemistry of nutrition. There is also a temptation for some nutrition experts and growers to try out new chemical discoveries, after the regulation tests have been run, on fowls, because of their relatively fast growth and breeding rates and the lure of improved commercial returns. All these discoveries get lumped into the category of additives which now comprises a rather alarming miscellany.

WATER

The primary essential for all poultry is permanent and easy access to fresh clean water. This applies particularly to guinea fowl because of their high protein intake. Approximately 60% of the birds body is composed of water. It is the main constituent of the blood and internal secretions. It assists nutrient absorbtion, lubricates tissues and joints, helps regulate body temperature and removes toxic products from the kidneys. The amount consumed depends upon the state of the constituents and the amounts of food eaten, as well as the prevailing temperature and humidity. An average daily consumption for keets in the first week is around 2 cl. At 4 weeks consumption is likely to be from 6 to 9 cl; at 12 weeks, 18 cl and from 20 weeks onwards 22 to 30 cl. Baby keets should have a minimum of 2 cm drinking space per bird; failure to drink sufficient water from the beginning is reflected in poor health and retarded growth. As water in many parts of the world has become more acidic due to the sulphur dioxide and nitrous oxides precipitated by acid rain showers, the pH of drinking water should be checked regularly and when much below 7.20 a balance can be restored, if the water is either treated or filtered with soda ash or hydrated lime. If well or spring water is used a chemical and bacteriological analysis should be made annually. Nitrate level should be below 10 p.p.m. Highly chlorinated water should be avoided or treated.

ENERGY

Food values in a diet are calculated by the nutritionist in terms of energy. The metabolizable energy (ME) of a food is what remains in the bird after voiding the faeces, urates and waste gases. The energy content is expressed as a unit of energy measurement per unit weight of food. One calorie (1 cal) is the amount of heat required to raise the temperature of one gram/1cc of water through 1 degree at 15°C. Since in mixing poultry food, one operates in kilograms, the scale is raised by 100 or 1000, i.e. kilo = k cal/kg or mega = m cal/kg. The ME of wheat is 2.91 m cal/kg; 2910 k cal/kg or even 12.18 M.J/kg. It has recently been agreed to use the Joule measurement in European publications as the rate of heat production should also be expressed. Not all food is digested or converted at once. The Joule is the output in 1 second of an energy flow of 1 watt. A practical conversion is 1 k cal = 4.18 k J. A further discrimination is made between net energy and productive energy. Net energy represents the amount remaining to the bird after subtracting the heat increment used up in the course of the normal metabolic processes. The energy still left is divided between that used for actual body maintenance, breathing, internal and external functions. The remainder is that which can be directed towards the specific productive purposes required, i.e. growth, egg or semen production, body weight and meat gain. Obviously, to be able to quantify production or net energy, many circumstantial factors need to be taken into account as very few individual systems have the same standards or conditions.

Energy intake should be related to energy requirement by each producer. In a tropical country, the increased climatic temperature will cause a bird to consume a smaller daily amount of food, but if the energy constituent of its ration is computed from a table of averages in energy requirement for a particular strain of breeding guinea fowl, the calorie density unless increased, may be correspondingly short of its energy requirement for that country. Further, even the balance of constituent proteins, minerals and vitamins will need revision.

If one is working from tables prepared for chickens or turkeys, remember that the guinea fowl consumes fractionally less than the light strains of chicken. The smaller the daily intake of food, the higher the amino acid content needs to be.

CARBOHYDRATES

From the carbohydrates which, as their name implies, are compounds of carbon, hydrogen and oxygen, fowls mainly use the starches and sugars which they can absorb quickly. Most of the polysaccharides pass on out of their system. Fats and oils are similar compounds but more than twice as concentrated. Small amounts are necessary to utilise the fat soluble vitamins but high levels of rancid fats will act adversely on the vitamins and their value may be dissipated. Vegetable oils are rich in linoleic acid which is especially important in a low fat diet. In cold climates, it is useful to have oil rich foods in the mixtures, as the triglyceride molecules of some of the fatty acids are utilised directly to construct fatty tissue, with a large saving in energy compared to that required to break up starches for the same purpose. The crude fibre constituent provides negligible energy and should be low in a finishing diet but it can be from 2½% to 7½% (max. 15%) for growing birds and for laying birds 15% to 25%. This allows the digestive juices to function well by keeping the food in an open state. Although the intestinal enzymes of a bird are unable to deal with the polysaccharide chains, a partial decomposition by interaction with bacterial or fungal flora may occur in the caecal tubes, as with non ruminants like the rabbit. Some of these chains contain substances like pectin and hemicellulose. These absorb large amounts of water and the bulking action affects the consistency of the faecal matter and promotes muscle tone by encouraging peristalsis. They also remove chemicals and minerals contained in the water which are surplus to metabolic needs. The fibrous content in the intestine of a young keet is about 10 to 12% and about 15 to 25% in a grown bird.

PROTEINS

As the basic components of cellular protoplasm, proteins are the feather and body building nutrients, they include many hormones and all the known enzymes. They are not stored by the body, the excess intake is either filtered off and converted by the liver for energy purposes or excreted. They are therefore most important during the primary 8 to 10 weeks of growth and during breeding and moulting periods. The constituents utilised for these purposes include over twenty molecular combinations known as amino acids. The majority are termed non–essential which means that they do not have to be incorporated in the diet as they can be synthesised from other nitrogenous compounds or from the essential ones by the birds internal mechanisms. Average percentages of the amino acids contained in feeding materials are listed in most feeding charts but it should be noted that individual samples of a given food may vary a good deal in content. Any particular consignment of feeding material intended for home mixing, of which the quality is in doubt, can be microbiologically assayed in a couple of days. The ten essential amino acids are: Arginine, Histidine, Isoleucine, Leucine, Lycine, Methionine, Phenylalanine, Threonine, Tryptophan and Valine. Glycine and Proline may be inadequately synthesised during periods of fast growth and should therefore be supplied in addition at these times.

MINERAL IONS

The mineral content of a diet is described as ash because it is the non combustible portion. It represents about 40% bone and a tiny percentage of flesh content. The importance of some of the major mineral ions is vital and well known, but that of some of the minor inorganic elements, which appear in minute amounts in the body, is still under investigation. Five are calculated in the diet on a percentage basis and the first three are often described as bulk minerals. With calcium, 99% goes into the bone cells, as does 80% of phosphorus. They are also inter related in the context of blood plasma and other body fluids, as well as in egg production. Calcium is stored in the bone marrow cavities during the fortnight prior to egg laying, in sufficient quantity to provide the first 6 shells and the female continues to secrete it from her skeleton for shell formation, as well as using it from the diet. Daily skeletal replenishment is therefore necessary and calcium is required at 3% of the diet throughout the breeding season, usually in the form of limestone flour.

Additional supplements are often necessary for prolific layers, in the form of oyster shell or limestone grit supplied ad lib, also in hot climates as carbonated drinking water, if the skeletal stocks become depleted. In very hot weather fowl keep cool by panting, this reduces the level of carbon dioxide in the blood and initiates chemical reactions which give the blood proteins a negative charge. Positive calcium atoms link to the proteins thus reducing the amount of available calcium to the metabolism. A supply of carbonated drinking water reverses the situation by replenishing the lost carbon dioxide.

Calcium and phosphorus should be supplied at a ratio of 2 : 1 or 2 : 1.5, for the growing keet or a dietary minimum of 1 to 2% calcium and 0.5 to 1% phosphorus. Adequate absorbtion of both these elements is closely linked with sufficient supplies of vitamin D and manganese. A deficiency of any one of the group results in improper bone formation. Inorganic phosphorus as a phosphate is more readily useable by the body. It is needed for the activation of sugar before it is broken down in cell respiration. Phosphorus is obtainable from fish or bone meal and dicalcium phosphate.

Salt is the third bulk mineral, its daily inclusion rate should be 0.25 to 0.4%. Sodium and chlorine are necessary in blood formation, protein digestion and growth. Sodium ions perform vital functions in the maintenance of correct pH balance in the blood, as electrolytes, and in conjunction with potassium and chlorine ions, in the transmission of nerve impulses. Animal proteins are rich in salt but vegetable proteins contain little. Guineas are more vulerable than chickens to salt poisoning and it should be remembered that if the drinking water is saline a similar amount in solution is more accentuated in its effect than in solids.

Kelp, alfalfa and soya bean meal are rich sources of potassium and it is usually unnecessary to add it or manganese as separate supplements in a broad spectrum diet as long as they are taken into account, like the other essential trace elements. Manganese, of which the daily requirement is only 30 to 60 parts per million, is available in many substances like wheat or lime. It is an essential link in the calcium metabolism and is used in bone and shell formation. A deficiency is quickly noted in embryo malformation or the chondrodystrophy syndrome, and also by a marked drop in hatchability. If the keet's diet is deficient, a perosis condition will develop between 2 and 10 weeks, where the achilles tendon detaches from its groove behind the hock joint. When both legs are affected, the keet will be seen walking on its hocks. This condition may also result from a lack of choline and vitamins of the B group. The deficiency can be caused by giving a high level of calcium without a compensating rise in the manganese level.

A lack of iodine will cause lethargic behaviour. It is vital to the proper functioning of the thyroid gland and assists in developing energy and stamina, and it relieves excess tension. It is obtainable from fish or seaweed meal. Zinc contributes to good hatchability, bone and feather growth. Iron and copper are needed for haemoglobin formation. Also important are, cobalt as part of vitamin E, fluorine, silicon and sulphur. Other trace elements listed below, have been identified in the avian body but their use is only partially understood; chromium, vanadium, molybdenum, aluminium, arsenic, bromine, boron, lead, cadmium, nickel, strontium, rubidium and titanium.

VITAMINS

These are equally necessary in a balanced supply to keets and breeding birds, especially when kept indoors. Vitamin A (retinol, derived from the pigment carotene as a pro vitamin), plays an important part in growth and disease resistance. It may be destroyed within a few weeks under poor storage conditions or contact with rancid fats. It is supplied in fresh greens, maize meal, fish liver oils or as dry stabilised supplement. A deficiency in young keets will lead to high mortality; in adults, the salivary and tear glands will dehydrate and the nictitating membrane may become keratinized.

Vitamin D (calciferol) is rarely synthesised in sufficient quantity from sunlight in northern latitudes. It may be obtained from fish liver oils or dry, along with vitamin A, in the form of cholecalciferol or D3, which is more potent for birds. A deficiency causes rickets in keets and in adults can inhibit laying.

Vitamin E (tocopherol) is important for hatchability, especially between 24 and 28 days, also general health. A deficiency produces crazy chick disease. It is easily destroyed in mixed food rations. It can be supplied in wheat or maize germ oil and fresh green food or as a dry preparation.

Vitamin C (ascorbic acid) is normally synthesised by the bird within its own body. Sources are fresh greens.

Vitamin K (quinones group); the main functions are in promoting blood coagulation. K1 is available in lucerne meal and fresh greens. K2 is produced by bacterial flora in animals. Two synthetics, K3 and K5 have been manufactured. Fowl are unable to produce sufficient quantities, as do most other animals, by intestinal microbial synthesis. In fresh food, it can be destroyed by a few hours exposure to sunlight, or by an alkali. The administration of drugs like sulphaquinoxaline create a much increased requirement and this can be supplied as K5 and menadione sodium bisulphite.

Vitamin B, complex; all the B vitamins promote optimum growth. Certain deficiencies are associated with particular members. In B2, riboflavin, a deficiency results in perosis, dermatitis, poor feather development and impaired hatchability. B1 thiamin or aneurine is required for the metabolism of carbohydrates; B1 and B2 are found in rice and wheat husks, unextracted live yeasts and fresh greens. Higher amounts of B2 are required in rations, 2 to 3 mg/kg. It is also found in dried grass, dried milk products, dried yeast, dried liver meal and condensed fish solubles.

Pantothenic acid, niacin or nicotinic acid, folacin or folic acid; deficiencies of these are associated with paralytic symptoms, weak growth, deformities, poor feathering and with folacin depigmentation of the plumage. All three are found in yeast and liver meal, fresh greens, milk products and fermentation residues. B6 (pyridoxine) regulates metabolism of proteins and amino acids; if synthetic amino acids like methionine are fed, B6 supplements are helpful. It is also associated with the adrenal functions and is therefore important as a stress easing factor for intensive rearing. Found in fresh greens, grains and dried yeast.

Choline, is mainly associated with perosis and must be given in sufficient quantity to allow the breeding female to transmit it, as the young keet cannot manufacture it for itself. Found in fish, liver and soya bean meal.

Biotin deficiency results in depressed growth, dry feathers, perosis and dermatitis. It may also be associated in a condition known as FLKS (fatty liver kidney syndrome); fairly common with broiler chickens but it has not so far appeared with guineas. It occurs where rations have been low in protein or have not included sunflower, soya bean or groundnut meal (soya bean seed is low and sunflower seed rich in methionine).

B.12 (cobalamin) is also carried over from breeder to keet. Growth rate and hatchability are severely reduced by a deficiency in the diet, it also affects haemoglobin formation. Found in high quality white fish meal, liver extracts, seaweed and possibly comfrey.

At least five other unidentified factors which improve growth and hatchability have not yet been isolated. One known as APF (animal protein factor) is a complex of B12 but two other components are known to be present in liver extract and seaweed. Substances which are biologically different but having similar chemical and physical properties to cobalamin have been converted by bacteria from cattle dung. It is also known that in deep litter systems of some months standing, controlled groups of poultry deprived of animal protein have achieved growth rates equal to those where it was included. A fish factor found in meal and solubles may be part of the APF complex. Another factor appears to be adequately supplied when fresh greens, grass or hay is included in the diet. The whey factor is obtained from the remaining whey, following the isolation of proteins, in yeast, liver and milk products. A further factor seems to exist in some protein fractions, which suggests a peptide–like structure.

ADDITIVES

These fall into two main groups; Group A is concerned with the control or preservation of food stuffs and prevention of diseases. Group B covers all those agents or compounds, generally given to broiler birds, to accelerate growth or increase weight and improve finish. The ingredients in this group fluctuate as new products are added and old ones withdrawn.

GROUP A Antioxidants are incorporated in feeding ingredients, either in the final mix, when they are usually stated on the label of the commercial sack, or in some of the premixes; in which case they are unlikely to be named. The object is to protect fats and oils which are themselves added to the ration to boost the energy content, either in order to supplement a cheap low energy food or to increase a higher energy one. Additional vitamins and minerals will therefore be required to balance the extra energy. The antioxidant delays the period, over which the fats will go rancid, up to twice as long. This in turn similarly delays the rancidity from destroying the potency of the fat soluble vitamins and xanthophylls. In the finishing diet of broilers prior to slaughter, antioxidants are sometimes incorporated along with extra vitamin E to improve the stability of the actual body fats. In 1954 the British ministry of food committee reported that no health hazards should arise if 0.2% of butylated hydroxy anisole (BHA) were added to edible fats and oils. The AO's in most common use are BHA, BHT and EQ (ethoxyquin), all of which appear under various brand names.

Pellet hardening agents are used to bind the pelleted food, thus keeping it free from dust and stopping it from crumbling and clogging up food hoppers. This causes wastage and may prevent the birds from ingesting sufficient quantities. A commonly used agent is sodium bentonite. Molasses is also an effective binder at about 2.5% of the mixture.

Propionic acid or its salts at 300 to 400 g. per tonne is sometimes added, to control mites, weevils and moulds in the meal and pellets during storage.

Commercial growers often add a triple prophylactic in the premix consisting of a coccidiostat (Robenidine at 25 ppm) anthelmintic (Emtryl at 50 ppm), antibiotic (Nystatin at 50 ppm).

Antibiotics for disease control are added at full therapeutic levels by the producer to treat infected birds. Small doses, which were intended to prevent early attacks and allow birds to develop immunity, were often added by the food manufacturer. This practice is being discontinued and is now banned in many countries.

GROUP B Antibiotics have also been used at low levels of up to 10 g. per tonne to promote increased growth in broilers. The fact that an active response is frequently obtained in less than optimum conditions may be because growth was not actually stimulated, but rather, allowed to proceed at a normal rate, due to severe reduction of bacterial flora in the lining of the intestinal walls. This would permit more nutrients to be absorbed and improve the appetite. They are also administered to laying birds, usually on floor systems, at 5 to 10 times higher levels to control stress which may be causing out of season moulting, pecking or cannibalism.

Tranquillizers are also used to relieve stress, reduce hyperactivity and to control reactions to noise and movement. It has been claimed that they thereby improve the birds appetite and digestion, leading to faster growth rates.

Synthetic oestrogens used in caponising have already been mentioned. Other synthetic hormones have been used to suppress broodiness or boost growth. As the effects last from 3 to 8 weeks, implantation in broilers is calculated so as to last the desired period before slaughter. Official regulations exist for most countries, as to when the use of particular hormones should be withdrawn before slaughter to ensure they have been fully metabolised. Experiments have shown that some hormonal residues remain in the carcass in any case, particularly in the legs, after slaughter. It is felt that possible side effects on consumers have been insufficiently monitored.

Where pigments are concerned; in some countries a preference is shown for deep coloured egg yolks or well pigmented, golden skinned carcasses. In such situations, additional pigmenting xanthophylls are sometimes added to the ration at 10 to 15 mg per kg. They are not needed for Guinea Fowl.

Numbers of organic arsenic compounds which were devised for the prevention of certain diseases are often included in rations to promote growth. The toxic levels may vary from 2 to 10 times the amount recommended. Their use has been officially restricted in some countries and a veterinarian should be consulted if their inclusion is contemplated.

This caution applies to all additives. A further point is that possible synergistic or antagonistic effects may result if these are used in conjunction with each other or with extra vitamins and minerals. Arsenical compounds include, nitarsone, carbarsone, roxarsone, sodium arsanilate, arsanilic acid. Yet another popular growth promoter is nitrovin, sold under various trade names. Most growth promoters claim to achieve an improvement of 3 to 7% either in weight gain or in saving by food reduction.

A few marketers, prior to slaughter, add to the drinking water a polyphosphate solution. This is alleged to tenderise the carcass meat. It certainly increases dead weight by 5% to 10%.

COMMERCIAL FOODSTUFFS AND FEEDING SYSTEMS

A majority of countries have legal requirements for poultry feeding stuffs, offered for sale. They must state minimum percentages of protein, oil and fibre. The presence of other materials which are considered deleterious in regularly revised government schedules, must also be indicated, as must the amounts and shelf life of vitamins A, D and E, the presence of antioxidants and colouring agents and the amount of copper if it exceeds 50 mg per kg.

All antibiotics, growth promoters and other medicines must carry suitably comprehensive instructions as to use, storage life and safety.

During the past ten years, French researchers in the INRA have established a number of specific nutritional levels both for fattening keets up to twelve weeks old and for breeding birds, (see bibliography and tables reproduced at the end of this section). As however, commercial feeding stuffs are as yet compounded especially for guinea fowl in very few countries, the producer is often obliged to select from broiler chicken, turkey or game rations and modify those which best suit his particular conditions. If compounded pellets are too large, guinea fowl will experience difficulty in swallowing them. Dry mash has been found to be as effective as pelleted foods in maintenance and fattening up to 8 weeks old provided undue wastage can be avoided. The starter rations should be in the form of chick crumbs or mash and is normally fed from 0 to 4 weeks, but pellets or granules of not larger than 2.5 mm may be given from 15 days old up to adult status.

It was previously thought that guinea fowl required a high protein and energy diet throughout their growing and breeding periods but it is now known that this is only the case for the starting period. During this phase the keet will respond with an immediate decrease in growth to a drop in the energy level and particularly to a lowering in available protein with the recommended amino acid balance. The limiting factors are the necessary amounts of the sulphur amino acids i.e. methionine plus cystine and of lysine. It is most important to incorporate the supplementary amounts of these as recommended in tables 1 to 7. Costs need not prove too high as the keets' appetite is relatively small in the starting period. On an intensive system and assuming a diet assayed at ME 3000 k cal/kg, after four weeks the live weight gain should be in the order of 330 g with a food consumption of 620 g.

Requirements of vitamins and minerals are about equal to that for the lighter breeds of chicken except perhaps in niacine and vitamin E as if these are low the keet shows a higher tendency to perosis or pseudoperosis.

In growing and finishing rations for fattening keets, 4 to 8 weeks and 8 to 12 weeks, experiments have shown that it is actually undesirable to incorporate similarly high levels of protein in the diet. Beyond 4 weeks the guinea self–regulates its energy intake to satisfy only its bodily needs, an excess of protein and calories if not voided will merely accrue in the form of lipids or fat deposits and may in the end lower the value of the finished bird on the consumer market. However, a protein deficiency leads to a noticeable drop in energy consumption, unlike the chicken it is the amount of protein consumed which determines the guinea's speed of growth after the first 4 weeks; so maintaining a correct proportion and amino acid balance, though at a lower level, continues to be of the utmost concern.

From 4 to 8 weeks the average live weight gain is approximately 560 g with food consumption rising to 1550/1600 g per keet. The final 8 to 12 week period shows, as might be imagined, the highest food consumption which is about 50% of the fattening cycle. The speed of growth tends to slow down after the keet attains a live weight of around 900 g.

The researchers have been careful to point out that the three recommended dietary formulations should be applied to keets not so much on the basis of chronological age as on the attainment of satisfactory growth and weight levels for each phase of the fattening period. Thus if for any reason a slackening of growth is observed, it would be advisable to prolong the starting or growing ration beyond the standard length of time or even increase the protein level until parity is restored. It should be noted again that these and all formulae are standardised for particular strains in a given environment and so are liable to require some modification when adapted by individual producers where conditions are different. Keets for example on extensive systems will have slightly larger appetites so the calculated ME and crude protein levels may be decreased by a similar degree.

Beyond the 12 week period, the female achieves a superior live weight gain of about 20%. This is mainly due to fat deposit and the development of the reproductive organs. To produce a relatively lean bird of larger size for some market requirements, it is preferable to rear the males separately to 14 to 16 weeks on a diet with energy levels of ME 2900/3000.

Feeding trials for potential breeding stock raised indoors have tended to show that quantitative rationing from 12 to 24 weeks at approximately 60 g of food per bird per day provides a better control on the rate of growth and can produce savings in the order of 2 kg of food per bird, partly by reduction in wastage. The rationing is gradually relaxed a few weeks before commencement of laying. It was noted that diets comprising slightly reduced amounts of protein achieved better results when supplemented with DL methionine. Compared to the chicken, the guinea fowl at all stages is more exacting in its sulphur amino acid requirements than in lysine. Levels of 14% to 17% protein with an energy constituent of 2850 to 2950 k cal per kg are indicated for breeding stock. Optimum results for laying and hatchability of eggs were obtained with the level of calcium carbonate (pulverised) at 4% of the ration and available phosphorus at 0.44% or total phosphorus at 0.68% (see table 66). This applied especially in the case of caged or litter reared birds, the specimens were healthier and their eggs showed better hatching rates.

Dry feeding methods for guinea fowl are usually on an ad lib. basis as they prefer to eat little and often. Whichever system is employed wastage or spoilage should be avoided. In principle all birds should have enough space to be able to feed at the same time. Young keets are tiny for the first week and should be fed on corrugated sheets of cardboard or similar type trays to get them well started. These are followed by chick feeding troughs which minimise spillage. There are many systems for older keets; troughs, small and bulk circular hoppers or tubular units suspended from rails on ceilings.

For birds in cages there are many types of automatic belt and chain feeders which also help to prevent boredom. Choices must be geared to design of housing, number of birds and whether food will consist of pellets or dry mash supplemented with grain. Outdoor dry feeding is best with weather and verminproof circular metal hoppers which come in many sizes, double sided troughs with weatherproof lids are also widely used. All hoppers should be screwed down so that only small amounts of mash or pellets can trickle over the bottom to a depth of 5 to 15 mm, otherwise considerable quantities will get pulled out and wasted. Wet mash is offered in open troughs or containers and anything remaining after one hour should be removed.

Water must be easily available at all ages. It should not be too cold for baby keets and ideally should be presented in containers in which the whole beak can be dipped but not the whole chick. The highest cause of mortality during the first 4 to 5 days is dehydration, particularly when under brooding lamps, as the keets simply cannot reach the drinkers often enough. They should not have to travel more than 30 cms at day old, as they need three times as much water as food. A clove of fresh garlic placed in each drinking trough is an excellent health measure. Nipple drinkers are now very popular for older birds in cages or on floor systems at about 1 nipple to 4 birds. There is some evidence to show that birds thrive better when they can physically dip and wash their beaks even though circular drinkers or troughs create extra cleaning labour.

Recommended spacings are:

Baby keets — 2 cms per bird at feeding trough and drinker.
Growers — 4/6 cm feeding space and 2 cms drinking space.
Adults — 10 cms feeding space and 3 cms drinking space.

Insoluble chick grit should be sprinkled on the floor with the food for the first fortnight and thereafter should be freely available in small grit hoppers or containers. The grit is usually granite, like the soluble calcium grit of limestone or oyster shell, it is available in several sizes. Grit should be changed according to age as too fine a stone for larger birds only irritates the intestine and may cause enteritis.

DIETS

Diet formulation is an exact science and poultry keepers intending to blend their own mixes should arm themselves with a book which contains detailed compositions of all the feeding materials which they plan to use. One such is, the *Poultry Nutrition Bulletin 174* from the British Ministry of Agriculture. The basic information needed is an analysis of each food ingredient and the maximum percentage inclusion level for each age group, combined with their nutrient, vitamin and trace element requirements. The critical equation for the intensive guinea fowl raiser is to compound economical rations, sufficiently high in energy and protein, for starter and broiler feeding. The high density ingredients are usually purchased commercially. The extensive raiser who will be growing his keets up to 12 or even 16 to 18 weeks has a greater flexibility to vary the preparation and range of foodstuffs. He must also control the food texture and quality, avoiding stale or rancid mixes but he has a wider choice in his nutritional specifications. Unwanted additives and vaccines, which are often included in the commercial mixes, can be avoided and if desired, only organic foodstuffs incorporated.

When cereal grains are being purchased for inclusion in a mix, one should make certain that they have not been dressed with insecticides or fungicides as these may contain mercury, lead, gammexane etc. When there is any doubt, the grain should be analysed as the temptation to mix excess sowing grain into clean grain for foodstuffs is understandable. Laying birds which were fed grains dressed with arasan have produced soft shelled or misshapen eggs. Mixing rations on the premises can be simplified by using home grown foodstuffs. No more than 4 to 5 ingredients need be selected from the following list, depending on which are locally appropriate to grow. Cereals can be combined with a purchased protein concentrate. Remember that all birds and animals respond to some change and variety in their diet.

The necessary equipment is a small grinding mill and mixer, combination units of differing sizes are now designed for large and small poultry farms and these can be set up so that the mixes pass into moveable hoppers or holding bins for the supply of automatic feeding systems.

Energy protein ratios should approximate to those indicated on the sample tables. Adequate levels can then be set for amino acids, vitamins and minerals. Cereals comprise 70 to 80% of the diet, they supply most of the energy and about 40% of the dietary proteins.

Most cereal grains can be fed whole or bruised to guinea fowl, or ground into finer particles and mixed with other ingredients. Mixes should always be fresh, especially in hot climates where they are likely to turn rancid and destroy the vitamin content. Guinea Fowl prefer coarsely ground particles and this keeps down the dust levels, for the same reason fine granular limestone is better than limestone flour.

If dry concentrates or amino acid supplements are being included, pre mixing on a small scale is normally adopted to gain a uniformly even distribution. Very small amounts are added to, say, half a kilo of meal and thoroughly mixed, increasing amounts of meal are then added and mixed each time until the desired ration is attained. Manganese salts should be premixed with sodium chloride, not with bone meal or limestone which will absorb the manganese and restrict it from the birds metabolism. If fats are added they should be melted, stabilised and mixed with a carrier such as vegetable protein supplement. A small amount of grains fed whole tends to increase intestinal acidity which in turn reduces the numbers of harmful bacteria in that region.

They can be fed separately from dry or wet mash and green stuffs. As cereals vary in content, two or three types are better, mixed together with fish or meat and bone meal, pulses etc. to create a balanced ration. A good cereal component combination might be maize grits with cut wheat or millet.

FOODSTUFFS

Maize *(Zea mays):* has the richest energy content, 65% available carbohydrate, ME 3160 k cal/kg. Where it can be grown or purchased cheaply it is usually the main cereal ingredient. It is low in vitamins and minerals and has only 6% to 7% digestible protein. Subsequent to grinding, the oil content quickly becomes rancid. The meal when stored is also prone to fungal attack and may cause deformities in keets under a week old or a reduction in growth or egg quality. It must therefore only be used freshly ground in amounts of not less than 10% and not more than 70% of the total ration. White maize is recommended to avoid the yellow pigmenting of egg or carcass. By–products are maize germ meal which contains about 20% crude protein and can be included at 2½ to 10%, maize gluten meal has 40% crude protein and is a good source of methionine and pro-vit. A, Hominy grits contain the maize germ, bran and starchy portions whereas maize grits are simply small particles of the actual ground meal.

Wheat *(Triticum SP):* Is not far behind maize in ME with 2910 k cal/kg 8.8% digestible protein. If ground, the particles should be coarse because wheat has a high gluten content and if it is included in the ration at a high level when finely ground, can form a sticky paste which creates impaction troubles. The protein levels fluctuate depending on the strain and other factors and should be regularly checked. Rich in vitamins and some minerals, birds prefer wheat to most other cereals and it can constitute the basic grain in the ration at from 20 to 60%. The germ meal while expensive for a normal poultry ration is valuable for special birds, with 25% digestible protein and high levels of choline, alpha and beta tocopherols, riboflavin and manganese.

Barley *(Hordeum vulgare)* Has lower energy and protein levels than wheat and is not normally included above 50% of the ration. It is useful for fattening and the naked berry has an ME of about 3000 k cal/kg.

Oats *(Avena sativa):* Lower than barley in the ME scale at 2640 k cal/kg. They have quite a high fibre content and the inclusion rate is not over 20%. They are often given to young

breeding fowl to slow down maturation and postpone 'point of lay' to later in the season. When the husk is stripped, the food value is similar to maize, likewise, when the ear is bruised birds can pick out the berry content.
Triticale: A genetic combination of Rye and Durum wheat, it has a higher ME than maize with 3350 k cal/kg and 11.8% digestible protein. It can be fed at a similar rate to wheat and is patently well worth growing.
Millet: Has a similar composition to barley, the tiny grains are a useful size for mixed starter cereals.
Sorghums: Of various types; kaffir or guinea corn, milo, darso, feterita, etc. resemble wheat in food value. The white varieties are preferred as the brown coated varieties, unless decorticated, are high in tannin which may create harmful conditions with eggs and small keets.
Brown Rice: If available, is an excellent ingredient, ME 3600 k cal/kg low fat, 8.5% digestible protein, especially for aviary and exhibition birds.
'Roots' such as:
Manioc SP (cassava, tapioca): The rhizome has an ME of 3200 k cal/kg but no digestible protein. It can be fed to adult birds at 2 to 30% and keets at 2 to 5% of diet.
Carrot *(Daucus carrota):* Chopped raw, about 25 gm per keet daily, contains 3000 IU pro vitamin A. Calcium phosphorous balance is 1:1. The leaves are even more nourishing than the roots.
Mangolds *(Beta vulgaris)* **swedes** *(Brassica napus),* **turnips** *(Brassica rapa):*
These are not high in any nutrients but most useful when suspended in pens or litter as a pecking medium to relieve boredom.
Potatoes *Solanum tuberosum):* Are a useful fattening material when cooked in their skins and fed in mixed wet mash at 5 to 15%. Potato meal is also high in available carbohydrates, ME 2900 k cal/kg.
Seeds: Seed meals for poultry are prepared after the oils have been extracted. These included the residues of Cotton seed, *(Gossypium* SPP), rape seed *(Brassica campestris* and *napus),* safflower seed *(Carthamus tinctorius),* sesame seed (Sesamum orientalis and radiatum), sunflower seed *(Helianthus annus),* linseed *(Linum usitatissimum),* they are usually deficient in at least one or two of the important amino acids. Rape, cotton and linseed meals contain toxic agents which must be destroyed by cooking. They are all included in food mixes at low volumes of 2 to 5% (not in starter rations). Quinoa seed — related to fat hen *(Chenopodium)* was grown by the Incas in the high Andes. It is gluten free and well balanced in amino acids. Varieties low in saponin are now being developed for poultry food; 12% to 14% protein.
Nuts: Decorticated nuts are also prepared as meal following extraction of the oil. Groundnut meal *(Arachis hypogea)* is used in amounts up to 20% as a protein source but care must be taken to ensure it is not invaded by *Aspergillus flavus.* Coconut *(Cocus nucifera)* as copra is used from 5 to 20% but is not highly nutritious. Horse chestnuts *(Aesculus hyppocastanum)* can be made into a palatable meal by crushing and steeping them in lime water for 8 hours to remove the bitter flavour, then lightly cooked for 30 minutes, they are rich in carbohydrates and useful for adding to a fattening ration. Palm kernels are one of the guinea fowl's favourite foods (see chapter 4). A meal is prepared from *(Elaeis guineenis)* and used at levels up to 20%. The South American seje palm *(Jessenia batava)* kernels have an amino acid content which is as high as meat and better than the soya bean.

Beech mast *(Fagus sylvatica)* and acorns *(Quercus robur)* are both nutritious and contain tonic properties. The acorns, which must be fully ripe, are crushed and dried to remove the bitter flavour. They can both be added at from 2 to 10%.

Pulses: Meals are made from the broad and haricot beans, also gram or chick peas, cow peas, peas and lentils, all of which contain about 25% protein but are low in methionine and are incorporated at 10 to 20% levels.

The soya bean *(Glysine max)* which must be cooked to destroy the toxic soyin protein and a trypsin inhibitor, is one of the best balanced vegetable protein sources and can be used at up to 40% of ration.

Animal proteins: Because of their superior amino acid balance to the vegetable protein and the fact that they usually contain some essential vitamins and minerals, it is normal practice to include a small amount in most rations.

Fish meal is the most important because it has all the essential amino acids and is particularly rich in methionine and lysine as well as choline, calcium, phosphorus, riboflavin and B12. It has an average of 60% protein and an ME of 2800 k cal/kg but varies a good deal in quality. White fish meal is considered the best quality. Krill, herring etc. are also most useful. They are prepared by cooking, drying and mincing. An adequate rate of inclusion is 2 to 5% with 10% as maximum.

Meat or meat and bone meal is also a rich source of protein but not so well balanced in amino acids. It should contain a minimum of 50% crude protein and is fed at rates from 2 to 10%.

Milk: Skimmed, sour, or dried, is a valuable and easily digested protein and B complex source, especially for young keets.

Poultry By–Products: Processed from offal, feathers etc., the meal can be as high as 70% in crude protein, but is deficient in some of the main amino acids. These meals are sometimes avoided in case they might be carriers of pathogenic organisms.

Greens: Grass meals and lucerne or alfalfa *(Medicago sativa)* contain 12 to 20% crude protein, carotene, riboflavin, vitamin K and xanthophylls. Good quality dried grass if cut when young should have a similar content. It is usually a mixture of grasses, clovers, sainfoin *(Onobrychis sativa),* lucerne and young corn shoots. The inclusion rate is 2% to 10%. Fresh greens, normally in the form of kale, cabbage and lucerne can be fed separately as a year round supply.

Algae: One of the varieties which is increasingly grown in bulk is spirulina. This is produced in open sunlit ponds but requires warm temperatures over 35°C for heavy cropping. It is a most useful feeding material, well balanced in amino acids with a crude protein content of 65 to 70% and is rich in pro vitamin A, B12 and nucleic acid.

Fungal Proteins or 'Yeasts': These are variously described as micro organisms (NIC), single cell proteins (SCP) or 'bacterial and yeast SCP'. They are also grown commercially in large quantities. Organisms may be algal, fungal, or bacterial and the culture media range through potatoes, wood pulp, methane, wheys, farm and urban wastes, petroleum products and molasses. The protein content may be up to 80%. Unlike algae, fungal proteins can be grown independently of light and temperature. It has been calculated that if 3% of the total oil production were to be employed in this way, the available protein output in the world could be doubled. It is presently added to diets at rates of up to 10%. Wet brewers yeast ferments are also good sources of protein and B complex and are added fresh to wet mashes at the same rates.

FEEDING TABLES

The following tables, numbers 57 – 67 are extracted from and reprinted by permission of, *'L'Alimentation des Animaux Monogastriques: porc, lapin, volailles'*, I.N.R.A. Editeur C.N.R.A. Versailles — 1984.

Requirements have been determined with primary foodstuffs whose composition corresponded to that set out in the tables produced in France (A.E.C., Protector, I.N.R.A). The security margins adopted in the formulation of these tables do not take into account the nutritional variations which sometimes occur in different consignments of feeding materials produced or compiled in other countries. These should be determined by analysis before compiling the rations.

PRESENTATION AND ENERGY LEVEL OF FEEDING MATERIAL FOR FATTENING KEETS

An alteration in the energy level of the diet produces little change in the keets growth rate. Above an ME level of 2900 k cal/kg an increase of 100 k cal/kg only results in a live weight gain of 1% at 12 weeks and of 1.1% at 13 weeks and the weight increase merely corresponds to extra fat deposits. To produce large lean birds at 13 to 14 weeks, the males should be retained and provided with a relatively low energy level diet of ME 2700 – 2900 k cal/kg. As high energy diets are expensive, a slight improvement in the conversion ratio will fail to compensate for the additional outlay.

PROTEINS AND AMINO ACIDS

The requirements in protein, lysine and sulphur amino acids indicated in table 59 apply to live weight gain realised during each period. They are given as an absolute value; the total requirements for one period of growth.

The values given for protein requirements may appear low. They presuppose that the supplement of synthetic lysine can be applied and are only effective within that context.

The amounts recommended for starting, growing and finishing rations, tables 60 — 62, take these requirements into account and generally produce the performances indicated in table 57. They can at any time be raised if, at an equivalent energy level, a significantly lower food consumption is envis aged because of a higher ambient temperature, e.g. consumption index below 3.05 for ME 3000 k cal/kg at 0 – 12 weeks or below 2.85 for 3200 k cal/kg. If through accident or illness the growth rate is retarded, then the earlier diet should be prolonged until the required weights have been regained.

It will be noted that the relationship between the sulphur amino acids (methionine & cystine) and lycine should be higher for guinea fowl than for chickens.

MINERALS AND VITAMINS

For guinea fowl floor raised on litter the requirements for minerals are similar to those for chickens. The standard recommendations for amounts of phosphorus, calcium, sodium and chloride are given in tables 60 — 62.

The additional supplements of trace minerals indicated in table 63 allow a margin of error to take account of variations in the composition of feeding materials. This table also contains recommended additions of vitamins. The higher levels of vitamin E and/or niacin in the starter ration are intended to prevent the occurrence of perosis type conditions.

Table 57

AMOUNTS OF WEIGHT INCREASE, FOOD CONSUMPTION AND CONVERSATION RATES DURING THE KEETS GROWTH.

Period	Weight gain (g)	Food consumption (g) (x)	Conversion index (x)
0–4 weeks	380	670	1,76
5–8 weeks	590	1690	2,86
9–11 weeks	400	1735	4,34
12 weeks	110	630	5,73
13 weeks	100	635	6,35
0–11 weeks	1370	4095	2,99
0–12 weeks	1480	4725	3,19
0–13 weeks	1580	5360	3,39

x. Ration assayed at M.E. 3000 k.cal / kg.
Ambient temperature 20°C.

g. grammes

WEEKLY CONSUMPTION OF WATER AND FOOD (Table 58) IN GROWING KEETS.

Week	Food (x)	Water
1	55	75
2	130	180
3	210	290
4	275	380
5	340	460
6	395	530
7	460	620
8	495	670
9	540	730
10	585	780
11	610	810
12	630	835
13	635	845
14	640	850

x M.E. 3000 k.cal / kg.
ambient temperature 20°C.

REQUIREMENTS IN PROTEINS AND AMINO ACIDS FOR (Table 59) GROWING KEETS (in grammes / period / bird).

Period	Proteins	Lysine	* Sulphur Amino Acids
0–4 weeks	165	9,0	6,4
5–8 weeks	295	14,8	13,7
9–14 weeks	225	11,3	10,9
12 weeks	70	3,0	3,0
13 weeks	70	3,0	3,0
0–11 weeks	685	35,1	31
0–12 weeks	755	38,1	34
0–13 weeks	825	41,1	37

* Methionine + Cystine

Table 60

RECOMMENDED AMOUNTS IN PROTEINS, AMINO ACIDS AND MINERALS FOR KEETS; STARTER RATIONS (0 — 4 weeks) (in percentages).

M.E. k.cal / kg.	2 900	3 000	3 100	3 200
CRUDE PROTEIN	23,2	24,0	24,8	25,5
Lysine	1,26	1,30	1,34	1,38
Methionine	0,52	0,53	0,54	0,55
Methionine + Cystine	0,92	0,95	0,98	1,00
Tryptophan	0,23	0,24	0,24	0,25
Threonine	0,82	0,85	0,88	0,90
MINERALS				
Calcium	1,00	1,03	1,06	1,10
Total Phosphorus	0,64	0,65	0,66	0,67
Available Phosphorus	0,39	0,40	0,41	0,42
Sodium	0,16	0,16	0,17	0,17
Chloride	0,14	0,14	0,15	0,15

Table 61

RECOMMENDED AMOUNTS IN PROTEINS, AMINO ACIDS AND MINERALS FOR KEETS.
Growing ration (5 — 8 weeks)
(in percentages).

M.E. k.cal / kg.	2 800	2 900	3 000	3 100
CRUDE PROTEIN	17,3	17,9	18,5	19,1
Lysine	0,89	0,92	0,95	0,98
Methionine	0,38	0,39	0,40	0,42
Methionine + Cystine	0,78	0,80	0,83	0,86
Tryptophan	0,20	0,21	0,22	0,23
Threonine	0,68	0,70	0,72	0,74
Glycine + Serine	1,52	1,57	1,63	1,68
Leucine	1,56	1,62	1,67	1,72
Isoleucine	0,78	0,81	0,84	0,87
Valine	0,86	0,89	0,92	0,95
Histidine	0,43	0,45	0,46	0,48
Arginine	1,11	1,15	1,19	1,23
Phenylalanine + Tyrosine	1,51	1,56	1,62	1,67
MINERALS				
Calcium	0,87	0,90	0,93	0,96
Total Phosphorus	0,59	0,60	0,61	0,62
Available Phosphorus	0,34	0,35	0,36	0,37
Sodium	0,16	0,16	0,17	0,17
Chloride	0,14	0,14	0,15	0,15

Table 62

RECOMMENDED AMOUNTS IN PROTEINS, AMINO ACIDS AND MINERALS FOR KEETS.
Growing ration (9 — 12 weeks)
(in percentages).

M.E. k.cal / kg.	2 800	2 900	3 000	3 100
CRUDE PROTEIN	12,8	13,3	13,7	14,1
Lysine	0,60	0,62	0,64	0,66
Methionine	0,30	0,31	0,32	0,33
Methionine + Cystine	0,60	0,62	0,64	0,66
Tryptophan	0,11	0,12	0,12	0,13
Threonine	0,48	0,50	0,51	0,53
Glycine + Serine	1,13	1,17	1,21	1,25
Leucine	1,38	1,43	1,48	1,53
Isoleucine	0,55	0,57	0,59	0,61
Valine	0,64	0,67	0,69	0,72
Histidine	0,33	0,34	0,35	0,36
Arginine	0,74	0,77	0,79	0,82
Phenylalanine + Tyrosine	1,19	1,23	1,27	1,31
MINERALS				
Calcium	0,77	0,80	0,83	0,86
Total Phosphorus	0,56	0,57	0,58	0,59
Available Phosphorus	0,31	0,32	0,33	0,34
Sodium	0,16	0,16	0,17	0,17
Chloride	0,14	0,14	0,15	0,15

Table 63

RECOMMENDED ADDITIONAL SUPPLEMENTS OF TRACE MINERALS AND VITAMINS FOR FATTENING KEETS.

		Starting Ration	Growing and Finishing Ration
TRACE MINERALS (p.p.m.)			
Iron		25	15
Copper		3	2
Zinc		40	25
Manganese		70	50
Cobalt		0,15	–
Selenium		0,15	–
Iodine		1	1
VITAMINS			
Vitamin A	IU/kg)	12 000	10 000
Vitamin D_3	IU/kg)	2 000	1 000
Vitamin E	(ppm)	25	12
Vitamin K_3	(ppm)	3	2
Riboflavin	(ppm)	5	5
Pantothenic Acid	(ppm)	8	8
Niacin	(ppm)	30	15
Pyridoxine	(ppm)	1	–
Biotin	(ppm)	0,2	–
Folic Acid	(ppm)	0,2	–
Vitamin B_{12}	(ppm)	0,01	0,01
Choline	(ppm)	500	250

FUTURE BREEDING GUINEA FOWL

As the female guinea fowl above the age of 10 weeks tends to develop adipose deposits, she should be rationed during the holding / on growing period. This practice leads to no deleterious effects over the breeding period and indeed reduces mortality at the commencement of laying. Rationing slightly retards the development of sexual maturity but this can easily be compensated for in the lighting programme. The principles which govern the rationing of the poulet can be adapted for the guinea fowl. In practice, growth can be moderated during the first 10 to 12 weeks by lowering the protein content of the diet. The figures for these amounts are shown in table 64. Byond the 10 — 12 week stage, quantitive restriction is more economical. The daily quantities of food allowed per bird are based on the figures set out in table 65.

BREEDING GUINEA FOWL

The best laying performances are obtained when the ration contains an energy value equal to or above M.E. 2800 k.cal / kg. The female's daily requirements during the most productive months are given in table 66. When these requirements are associated with normal raising conditions and environment, the amounts recommended in table 67 should assure maximal productivity and hatchability of eggs.

Table 64
RECOMMENDED AMOUNTS IN PROTEINS, AMINO ACIDS AND MINERALS FOR FUTURE BREEDING GUINEA FOWL (in percentages).

M.E. k.cal / kg.	Starting ration 0-4 weeks 2 900	Growing ration 5-12 weeks 2 800	Holding ration 13-22 weeks 2 800
CRUDE PROTEIN	20,0	14,0	12,0
Lysine	1,20	0,55	0,48
Methionine	0,40	0,28	0,22
Methionine + Cystine	0,85	0,60	0,50
Tryptophan	0,25	0,14	0,12
MINERALS			
Calcium	0,85	0,80	0,50
Total Phosphorus	0,65	0,60	0,50
Available Phosphorus	0,40	0,35	0,25
Sodium	0,17	0,17	0,17
Chloride	0,15	0,15	0,15

Table 65

RATIONING SCHEDULE FOR FUTURE BREEDING GUINEA FOWL *

AGE (weeks)	TYPE OF RATION	RATION g/day/bird	CUMULATIVE TOTAL CONSUMPTION g.
0 – 4	Starter	ad-libitum	500
5 – 12	Grower	ad-libitum	3 000
13 – 15	Holding	55	4 155
16 – 17	–	63	5 040
18 – 22	–	72	7 560
23	–	80	8 120
24 to point of lay		85	
From 25% of full lay		ad-libitum xx	

* Ration assayed at M.E. 2800 k.cal / kg.
Mean ambient temperature 18°C.

xx It may be beneficial to maintain light rationing during the laying period.

g. = grammes

Table 66

DAILY REQUIREMENTS FOR BREEDING GUINEA FOWL
(in grammes)

M.E. K.cal / kg.	310 Kcal (variable according to temp.)
CRUDE PROTEIN	13,0
Lysine	0,58
Methionine	0,30
Methionine + Cystine	0,53
Tryptophan	0,14
Threonine	0,41
Glycine + Serine	1,20
Leucine	0,75
Isoleucine	0,62
Valine	0,51
Histidine	0,17
Arginine	0,54
Phenylalanine + Tyrosine	0,97
MINERALS	
Calcium	3,8
Total Phosphorus	0,68
Available Phosphorus	0,44
Sodium	0,14
Chloride	0,13
Linoleic Acid	0,80

Table 67

RECOMMENDED AMOUNTS OF CRUDE PROTEIN, AMINO ACIDS AND MINERALS FOR BREEDING GUINEA FOWL (in percentages)

M.E. K.cal / kg.	2 800	2 900	3 000
CRUDE PROTEIN	13,5	14,0	14,5
Lysine	0,77	0,80	0,83
Methionine	0,30	0,31	0,32
Methionine + Cystine	0,54	0,56	0,57
Tryptophan	0,14	0,15	0,15
Threonine	0,36	0,37	0,38
MINERALS			
Calcium	3,70	3,85	4,00
Total Phosphorus	0,67	0,68	0,70
Available Phosphorus	0,42	0,44	0,45
Sodium	0,140	0,145	0,150
Chloride	0,130	0,135	0,140
ANTICIPATED DAILY CONSUMPTION (in grammes) at 20°C.			
From 30 to 50 weeks	105	102	100
From 51 to 70 weeks	100	97	95

* All other constituents including trace minerals and vitamins are recommended at the same levels as for breeding turkeys.

TABLE A

SAMPLE HOME RATION FOR FATTENING KEETS (in percentages)

In compiling home based rations it may be desired to use lower concentrations of maize as in the alternative mixes suggested below. It is often easier to use a commercial feeding material for the starter diet to ensure an adequate protein concentration, i.e. approximately 24% crude protein.

	4—8 weeks	**9—12/14 weeks**
Crude Protein (approx.)	18	14
Maize	40	60
Wheat	15	15
Barley / Oats	10	–
Bran	5	5
Meat meal	5	4
Soyabean meal	17	6
Lucerne meal	5	5
Maize Gluten	–	2
Vitamin + Mineral Supplement	3	3

TABLE B

An example of a maize based ration formulated on standard recommendations. Amounts in percentages.

Ration	Starting	Growing	Finishing
Maize	58	72	75
Soya Bean Meal (48% protein)	32	18	7
Maize gluten meal	–	–	4
Fishmeal (68% protein)	2	–	–
Meatmeal (50% protein)	2	5	4.3
Lucerne meal	–	–	4
Rapeseed meal	–	3	4
Tallow	2.1	–	–
Calcium carbonate	0.9	1	0.7
Salt	0.4	0.4	0.4
Trace mineral premix *	0.1	0.1	0.1
Vitamin premix **	0.5	0.5	0.5
- containing DL methionine	(0.150)	0.140	0.020

* **Trace mineral premix, (see preceding tables)**

** **Vitamin premix — amounts recommended in Table 63 plus the indicated quantity of DL-methionine.**

Antioxidant, coccidiostat, anthelmintics etc., may be included in premixes.

TABLE C

EXAMPLE OF A BALANCED DIET FOR BREEDING GUINEAS PRIOR TO 1983

Composition in percentages

Analysis	Starter 0-4 weeks	Grower 4-12 weeks	Holding/ on–grower 12-24 weeks	Breeding
ME K cal / kg	3100	3050	3100	2850
Crude Protein	22.5	16.5	13.2	19.5
Methionine	0.5	0.36	0.25	0.34
Lysine	1.3	0.80	0.51	1.07
Calcium	0.85	0.98	0.30	3.75
Available phosphorus	0.40	0.47	0.26	0.42
Maize	40	60	62	33.8
Wheat	20	20	25	20.0
Soyabean Meal	30	13	–	28.0
Meat meal 48% protein	–	4.5	2	–
Fish meal 50% protein	3	–	–	2
Rapeseed meal	–	–	10	–
Tallow	4	–	–	4.8
Calcium carbonate (pulv.)	1	1	–	9
Dicalcium phosphate	1	0.5	–	1.5
Salt	0.3	0.3	0.5	0.3
Trace minerals premix	0.1	0.1	–	0.1
Vitamin premix	0.5	0.5	0.5	0.5
DL methionine	0.1	0.08	–	0.03

TABLE D

NORMS OF GUINEA FOWL BREEDER RATIONS IN COMMON USE

	Starter	Grower	Breeder	
			phase I	phase 2
	0-28 days	29 days-28 weeks	29-40 weeks	41 weeks-Culling
Metabolizable energy (Kcal/kg)	3000/3100	2650/2700	2750	2750
Crude protein (%)	23/24	15/16	17/17,5	16,5
Methionine (%)	0.48	0.30	0.40	0.36
Methionine + cystine (%)	0.90	0.60	0.75	0.68
Lysine (%)	1.20	0.70	0.90	0.85
Calcium (%)	1.10	1.10	3.20	3.20
Total phosphorus (%)	0.80	0.70	0.85	0.80
Available phosphorus (%)	0.55	0.50	0.60	0.55
Cellulose (%)	3.50	6.50	4.00	4.50
Input for 100 kg of food				
a) Vitamins				
A (I.U.)	1 500 000	1 200 000	1 500 000	
D 3 (I.U.)	300 000	240 000	300 000	
E mg	2 500	2 400	3 000	
K mg	500	500	500	
B 1 mg	150	150	200	
B 2 mg	1 200	1 000	2 000	
B 6 mg	500	300	400	
B 12 mg	1.25	1	1.5	
Nicotinic acid (mg)	6 000	4 000	5 000	
Pantothenic acid (mg)	2 000	1 600	2 000	
Choline (mg)	60 000	50 000	60 000	
Folic acid (mg)	150	150	200	
Biotin (mg)	15	15	20	
b) Trace elements (added)				
Zinc (mg)	8 000	6 400	8 000	
Manganese (mg)	10 000	8 000	10 000	
Iron (mg)	4 000	3 200	4 000	
Copper (mg)	1 250	1 000	1 200	
Cobalt (mg)	25	25	25	
Iodine (mg)	200	200	200	
Selenium (mg)	15	12	15	
c) Supplementation				
Anticoccidial (amprol +) (mg)	13 200			
Antioxydant (BHT) (mg)	12 500			

ORGANIC AND NATURAL FEEDING STUFFS

Organically grown foods have long been considered a fashionable luxury and particularly so for animals. Their production has been discounted by the majority of farmers because of the ensuing drop in crop yield which they could ill afford to suffer, geared as they are to expensive machinery and equipment. This was necessary to plant and harvest the huge fields of the industrial era. Now that the denuded land in many developed countries is yielding less each year, regardless of the amounts of inorganic fertiliser spread over it, many young agriculturalists are considering the possibility of experimental organic systems. The fact that these are more labour intensive may not pose a future problem when so many hands are being freed from the industrial society. There are already quite a number of organic farms, ranging from 40 to 4,000 acres, around the world. The ratio is higher amongst horticulturalists and small holders.

Warnings about polluted and adulterated foodstuffs from conservationist organisations like the International Union for the Conservation of Nature and Natural Resources and Friends of the Earth are beginning to impinge on public and political consciousness. People have been too preoccupied by social pressures and concerns of world conflict to realise that the potential result of the ecological damage already perpetrated amounts to a destructive threat as deadly to our planet as nuclear fallout. The pleasure of eating organically grown meat and vegetables is diminished by a consideration of the extent to which even they are likely to have been polluted already. Close to urban areas plants have suffered cellular distortion and birds and animals respiratory damage from atmospheric sulphur dioxide and heavy metals. Even when hundreds of miles away, oxidants converted into sulphuric and nitric acids are precipitated over us in rain as acid as vinegar. This accelerates the mobilisation of toxins in the soil and the disastrous results can be seen in the lakes and forests of Northern Europe and North America. Nitrate levels in drinking water and plants are up to three times the official "safe" 10 parts per million standard in many areas.

Escaped PCB's (polychlorinated biphenyls) have contaminated everything connected with rivers, lakes and seas from the Arctic to the Antarctic. A massive scientific campaign supported by the world's major governments, would require decades to reverse the tide of destruction, but it will still be unable to restore species now daily being rendered extinct.

COMPOST AND HUMUS

Composting is a scientific method in which we co–operate with the organic elements in our biosphere to produce a semidigested brown powdery substance which when raked into the soil at a depth of 3 to 6 cm is ingested by worms and earth bacteria to create humus. Any degradable material is heaped and compacted in flat level 15 cm layers on a well ventilated base, like a grid of sticks. Each layer is interspersed with an activator to initiate fermentation, this is usually poultry, farmyard, fish, blood or seaweed manure; as all these provide a balanced spectrum of nutrients.

Fermentation can also be initiated by sprinkling ammonium sulphate or a similar activator between the layers of waste. Decay is accelerated by the thermal process as the frenetic activity of the bacterial yeasts cause the pile to heat up to 50° or 60°C and slowly cool again. All diseases, pests, seeds, etc., are destroyed by the high temperatures. The cooling down period allows the reintroduction of a series of organisms ranging through aerobic bacteria, actinomycetes, fungal spores and hyphae, paramecium, tiny nematodes, fly larvae, manure worms and insects; all contributing to the complete compost breakdown. As the process takes about six months, a basic minimum of three piles are needed, one filling, one cooking and one ready for using. Piles should contain materials which will degrade at similar rates, i.e., soft material in one pile and the tougher cellulose like roots, cabbage stalks and hardwood cuttings in another. Dry materials must be moistened. Poultry manure is particularly suitable as a compost activator as it is dryer and richer than farmyard manure, guinea fowl droppings have a lower moisture content than those of chickens.

Percentages	Nitrogen	Phosphate	Potash
Poultry manure	2.75	3.00	1.50
Farmyard manure	0.5—0.75	0.30	0.50

The material from strawyards or open litter runs makes excellent compost, each fowl being responsible for up to 50 kg per annum, or 75 kg of actual droppings. Fresh harvested straw can now be sprayed with a recently developed cocktail containing a symbiotic group of cellulotytic fungi and bacteria. These rapidly break up the cellulose and hemicellulose forms encasing the 75% carbohydrate content and convert the straw to nitrogenous fertilizing material. It is either lightly ploughed into the soil before convertion starts or added to the compost.

By using this method of soil enrichment the only digging or ploughing required is to remove deep rooted perennial weeds. Only the top 5 cm to 8 cm of soil needs to be friable. Several years are required to build up a sufficient amount of humus in the land to get an organic system working to full capacity. The humus is a dark jelly like organic colloid with biological, chemical and physical properties. In a satisfactory medium the number and variety of micro–organisms is multiplied many times and it is the results of their work around the roots which creates biologically healthy and nutritious plants. Humus improves heavy or light earths, opening up the former and coagulating the latter. While it assists water retention, the earth does not become waterlogged; it provides protection for plant roots against heat, cold and drought and prevents the plant nutrients from being leached away; e.g. the vitamin B content of a plant is dependant on the amount in the soil as the growing medium. Organically farmed land in China which has been intensively cultivated for millenia remains fertile today.

Fast maturing, composting crops are specially grown on organic farms and gardens. These can be disc harrowed or lightly rotovated into the topsoil after 4 to 6 weeks growth, or cut and added to compost heaps while still lush. The most popular plants are, rape, lupin, buckwheat, tares, clovers, ryegrass and lucerne; black and white mustards are also useful as a disinfectant crop on land which has carried poultry with infected droppings. Russian comfrey *(Symphytum peregrinum)*, like seaweed, is an outstanding compost plant, rich in vitamins A, B & C with a 15% ash content. Twelve mature plants will produce about 2 cwts of organic material per season or 50 tons per acre, cutting four times per year. In Kenya, up to 100 tons per acre with twelve cuts, have been recorded. These plants thrive for as long as twenty years; clover sown between the rows provides additional nitrogen and keeps down grass. Lucerne which also has deep tap roots, when established, will thrive for 5 or 6 years and afford several cuts each season. Cereal growing is usually left to the farmer but it is not difficult for the smallholder to sow out a few patches. The grains can be broadcast by hand and harrowed into the soil. When harvesting, threshing is unnecessary for fowls in extensive runs. The heads can be cut from the top of the straw, stored and distributed separately on the scratching ground. Seed heads like those of sunflowers cannot be stored in this manner, but may be spread face down on wire racks, over paper, to catch the seeds. A green compost crop can also be undersown into cereals at 3 kg per acre, about a fortnight before harvest in harsh climates. This should be done just before or between rain showers. The young plants are sufficiently strong by harvest time to withstand the abuse. Carrots thrive in organic soil, particularly when following brassicas as a previous crop. Onions, garlic or sage planted between the rows have had great success at keeping the carrot fly at bay.

The most useful brassicas for guinea fowl are the savoys which will crop all the year round, and canson kale which is inexpensive, fairly frost hardy and pest resistant. It has a leaf like the marrow stem kale. Sage, thyme and hyssop will collectively help to repel cabbage root fly and the cabbage white butterfly. The legumes, as nitrogen fixators, should be alternated annually with other crops. Peas and lentils are fed directly but beans should be soaked and minced. Summer savoury, grown with beans, deters the black fly.

Derris dust, quasia, powdered tobacco leaves and pyrethrum are examples of safe natural insecticides. Eggs of some beneficial insects, wasps, beetles, flies, etc., which live on specific pests can now be purchased. There is even one slug, pestacella, which preys on other slugs. Compost itself inhibits many pests and diseases. The Mexican variety of marigold *(Tagetes minuta)*, when grown as a border will keep back couch grass, ground elder and even convolvulus. Varieties of fungi are also being developed to control pests and other harmful fungi. Some microfungi can trap and kill eel worms.

NATURAL FOODS

There are hundreds of wild plants which make useful additional foods and tonics for poultry, many have been mentioned in the preceding chapters. Two plant families are of paramount importance for general health and prevention of diseases in keets and adults alike. A little chopped garlic (one clove to 6 keets or 3 adults) or onion and rue added to the daily ration will provide a strong protection against the guinea fowl's main afflictions; worms, respiratory complaints and coccidiosis. The allium family have been successfully used against these and similar problems for thousands of years.

We understand that investigators in the USA have isolated a substance in garlic named crotonaldehyde, which was found to be highly effective against diseases of the respiratory system and intestines and which acts as a vermifuge and febrifuge. Russian chemists have also claimed another substance, allicin, which seems able to assist the white corpuscles in destroying foreign bacteria without harming fungi and bacteria native to the system, as do antibiotics. They also claim that garlic and onion emit an electrical field which appears to stimulate cellular activity, this is described as mitogenic radiation. Allyl disulphate which is a component of the volatile oils of garlic is quite a powerful germicide.

The second group comprise the seaweeds, or common marine algae which can be freely collected around the coasts. When washed and dried these can be fed at from 1% — 5% of the ration. The best known are: red dulce *(Rhodymenia palmata)*, chopped raw or boiled, the Pacific varieties *Porphyra tenera* and *P. yezoenis* have been cultured in Japan since 1700. Other varieties are purple laver *(Porphyra umbilicalis)*, boiled; green laver, sea lettuce, sea beet *(Ulva lactuca)* raw or boiled; brown rib weed, bladder locks, henware, winged kelp *(Alaria esculenta)* raw or boiled; brown tangle, sugar kelp, oar-weed, kombu *(Laminaria saccharina)* raw or cooked. The latter has been consumed by humans and animals in China since 3000 BC — when dried, a useful natural sugar (mannitol) forms on the fronds. Green wakame *(Undaria pinnatifida)* which may be fed fresh is useful and Ceylon moss *(gelidium)* and carrageen moss (Chondrus crispus), the latter used in Ireland for centuries, can be fed dried and powdered or as a solution in wet mash. Dulce as a typical edible seaweed contains 25% protein, 45% mostly digestible carbohydrates, 4% fats and 26% ash — mainly calcium and potassium with smaller amounts of iodine, sodium, magnesium, iron, sulphur, phosphorus, carotene, vitamins B1, B12 and E. As a tonic food, any of the group will promote digestion and general health, increase egg output and accelerate fattening. Seaweed meal is produced from the giant kelp *(Macrocystis pyrifera)*, recommended feeding level is 2%.

Another tonic factor which has not been identified but is associated with raw apple and apple cider vinegar is thought to be connected with acidic action in the protein metabolism. Tests on guinea fowl, turkeys and chickens where apple cider vinegar was added daily to the drinking water at 1 teaspoon per 8 keets, showed accelerated feathering and growth compared to that of the control group. There was also a significant reduction in the number of egg shells with high porosity amongst a test group of caged layers. On 'finished' birds, the meat was asserted to be leaner and more tender when cooked. The bone marrow was also said to show an increased redness. The author has found that when offered a quarter of a large cooking apple daily per bird, guinea fowl will desert even live insects and fresh greens to avoid missing their share. Reject quality cooking or crab apples (class 3) can be acquired for the removal cost.

As well as the greens already mentioned, nettles *(Urtica dioica)* are an excellent food, dried, fresh cut and wilted or blanched, for breeding fowl or fattening keets. Other greens which are appreciated and make nutritious conditioners are:–

Dandelion *(Taraxacum officinale)*, leaves, flowers and roots;
Land cress *(Barbarea verna)*
Water cress *(Nasturtium officinale)*
Spurry *(Spergula arvensis)*
Cleavers / goosegrass *(Galium aparine)*
Chickweed *(Stellaria media)*
Couchgrass and seeds *(Agropyron repens)*
Fathen / White Goosefoot *(Chenopodium Album)*
Fennel *(Foeniculum vulgare)*
Wormwood *Artemisia absinthium)*
Vetches *(Papilionaceae)*

Red Clover *(Trifolium pratense)*
Fenugreek *(Foenum graecum)*
Thistleheads and seeds *(Carduus species)*
Dill *(Anethum graveolens)*
Wild fruits include hips, *(Rosa arvensis(*, haws *(Crataegus monogyna)*, blackberry *(Rubus fructicosus)*, bilberry and cranberry families *(Vaccinium myrtillius, Vitis idaea* and *Oxycoccus palustris)*.

Other tonic substances are:–

Liquorice — powdered root of *(Glycyrrhiza glabra)*,
Dried edible fungi
Iceland moss *(Cetraria icelandica)*

Delicate or special baby keets can be given finely chopped; hard boiled eggs or (egg custard) with onion, cress, brown rice or millet, dill, garlic, rue, sunflower seeds, raisins and a pinch of powdered seaweed, moistened with skimmed milk. After 10 days any of the above together with other chopped greens and cereals as mentioned, added to approximately 15 to 25 gms of quality fish meal per head instead of the eggs and milk.

Figure 6 – 2 Automatic Feeding **(Courtesy: PAL, SA Products)**

Figure 6 – 3 Aviary-type of Accommodation giving fresh air (Note the feed hoppers)

Brooding House (25 sq.m) at each corner. Keets released 3–4 weeks with free access to "open" run (Photo: J.C. Cauchard)

7

DISEASES, PARASITES, PESTS AND PREDATORS

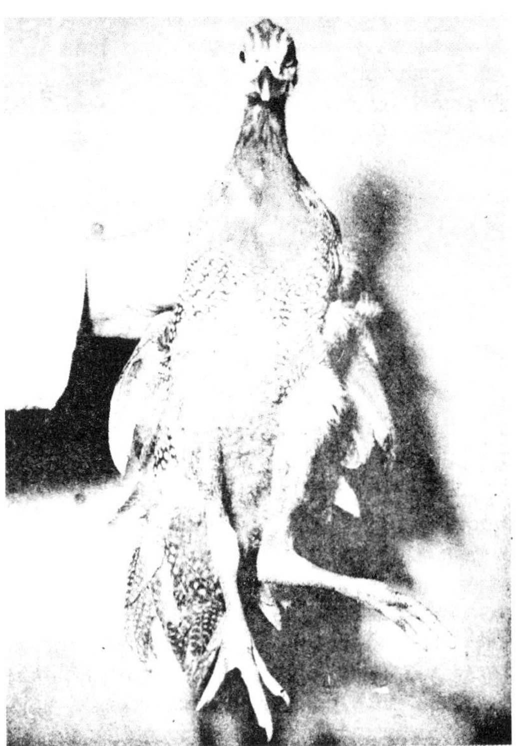

Figure 7 – 1 Top: Hėalthy 6 week old keet
bottom: Keet with vitamin deficiency showing Perosis in left hock

CHAPTER 7

DISEASES, PARASITES, PESTS AND PREDATORS

As previously stated the common guinea fowl are amongst the hardiest of the domestic birds. The family in general are vulnerable to respiratory infections and parasitic infestation. Provided adequate precautions against disease and parasites have been taken and a daily vigilance is enforced, severe problems should be avoided. However, for effective control in flock or aviary it is important to have some knowledge of the major diseases and afflictions, how they may be imported into the flock and the conditions and methods of their survival. As drugs are constantly changing, always consult with your veterinary surgeon or local department of agriculture before applying any of the treatments requiring vaccines and antibiotics in particular.

LIST OF DISEASES AND AILMENTS

There follows a list of diseases, ailments and possible treatment.

AVIAN ENCEPHALOMYELITIS (EPIDEMIC TREMOR):

Rare in guinea fowl, it is caused by a virus which may be egg borne or enter by the lungs or alimentary canal. The developing chick may, within the first week after hatching, show difficulty in walking or fall on its side, paralysed. Trembling in head neck and body are common signs among the under 8 weeks old, these also end in paralysis. The survivors may suffer blindness. In laying adults, egg production will fall by 10% to 50%, often rising again after three weeks but not back to normal. The eggs will exhibit poor hatchability. Diagnosis should be confirmed by PM examination which if positive will show changes in the central nervous system. It is possible to inoculate future breeding stock between 10 and 16 weeks old with live vaccines administered orally by dropper or in the drinking water.

INFECTIOUS ENTERITIS:

Currently this is a most serious infection, which appears to be specific to guinea fowl. First reported in Italy in 1957, it was confirmed in France in 1970 and during the next few years it decimated entire flocks.

Its aetiology in unknown but the clinical signs and cyclical epidemic character are suggestive of a virus. No effective treatment has yet been evolved. It seems particularly virulent from November to April and follows two clinical patterns. After a 3 to 5 day incubation period trembling or shivering and loss of appetite will be noticed, this is followed by foul smelling diarrhoea and prostration. Its duration lasts about one week and results in 30% to 100% mortality. Survivors are considerably retarded in growth and very susceptible to secondary infections.

In France this acute form subsided after a couple of years and gave way to a less acute one which affects keets from one to four weeks old. The signs are similar but the mortality rate varies from 5% to 50%. The acute form reappeared again during the winter of 1977 / 78. In diagnosis, the lesions are elusive, the intestine becomes dilated and has a very liquid content. The less malignant form can be confused with salmonellosis. The ambient temperature should be raised, vitamins and antibiotics should be administered to lessen the risk of secondary infections amongst possible survivors.

AVIAN PASTEURELLOSIS (FOWL CHOLERA):

Caused by the bacterium Pasteurella Multicoida / Aviseptica. Infection is via respiratory and alimentary tracts. It may be spread by the excreta of diseased birds, rodents, wild birds or on vehicle wheels and equipment. Incubation period is 4 to 9 days. The clinical signs may be listlessness, laboured breathing, thirst, nasal discharge, yellow green diarrhoea, lameness and swollen joints or simply the discovery of dead birds. Mortality is usually very high. The food, water and ground will have become contaminated. Diagnosis to be confirmed by PM examination which will isolate the bacterium from liver and heart tissue. Treatment may be attempted by subcutaneous injection of streptomycin or terramycin. Preventative vaccines have been developed.

ASPERGILLOSIS (PULMONARY MYCOSIS) (MYCOTIC PNEUMONIA):

Caused by the fungus *Aspergillus fumigatus.* It is usually imported on mouldy litter or grain, or it may also develop in damp conditions fostered by wet litter or nesting material and on soiled or damp eggs and on dirt in ventilation or heating ducts. It lodges on the lungs and air sacs causing laboured breathing and gasping, listlessness and loss of appetite. It may be observed in affected eggs or embryos. Keets are attacked from a few days old onwards. Losses can be 10% to 50%. Nystatin has been found quite effective. In large flocks the affected keet must be eliminated, all litter destroyed and all areas disinfected. The remaining flock should be given fresh wholesome food (see also chapter 4, section on hygiene).

COCCIDIOSIS:

This may be caused by any of a number of species of the large group of microscopic protozoa named *coccidia.* Guinea fowl are usually affected by *Eimeria Numidae* or *Eimeria Grenieri* when young. This genus has a peculiar life cycle involving asexual and sexual phases and several generations, which invade and reinvade the intestinal walls. They develop from oocysts or eggs expelled in the faeces of infected birds and are picked up and ingested by the next bird, thus enabling them to continue their life cycle. The disease is therefore soilborne and common on open range where wild birds may deposit their droppings. The signs are quite varied. Birds usually stand around listlessly and appetite fails, infection in young keets will produce a high mortality. There may be light brown diarrhoea but without fresh blood in the droppings as in the case of chickens. As recognition of the external signs is not always easy at 3 to 5 weeks, (the most susceptible time), one bird should be sacrificed and the caeca examined.

If the normally fluid contents have thickened to a cheesy consistency and the walls of caeca are inflamed, a veterinary confirmation should be obtained at once. There is no cross immunity, so the particular strain of Eimeria should be established and a separate immunity built up for each strain. Immunity can also be lost in as little as 10 weeks. There are many coccidiostats on the market, both for prevention when administered in dilute form and in stronger doses for treatment. Some of these must not be used on broilers for a number of days before killing to avoid leaving residues in the carcass. It is common for manufacturers to include the low level dosages in poultry feed from chick crumb and mash onwards. A 16% solution of sulphadimidene is frequently employed. Whichever products are administered, the manufacturer's recommendations should be carried out with great care in regard to the amounts for differing age groups and frequency of dosage in food or water. As some coccidiostats, like sodium monensin, are highly toxic to guinea fowl in the prescriptive amounts designed for chickens, it is wise to obtain a clearance from your veterinary surgeon for any of them which you wish to use. Robenidine at 25 ppm is a popular choice, The oocysts in the droppings can be destroyed with ammonia or methyl bromide, however, strict attention to overall hygiene and disinfection of the land should be the first objective. This requires several years exposure to weather, after ploughing and stripping off the surface layer.

FOWL POX:

The virus is usually transmitted by carrier birds and biting insects. More common in warm climates, incubation may vary from 4 to 20 days. Birds of any age can be affected. Yellowish white scabs can be seen on non feathered parts of the body. The scabs are soft at first but become hard and dark and could be mistaken for warts. Sometimes the eye lids become inflamed. The bird will rapidly lose condition and appetite and exhibit signs of stress. Trichomonas will grow in the mouth and nasal cavities, appearing in the form of yellow cheesy patches and breathing difficulties will be observed. Diagnosis should be confirmed in the laboratory. Infected birds should be isolated, but response to treatment in variable. If infected membranes can be removed from the mouth or larynx this will assist breathing. The external scabs, not around the eyes, should be dressed daily with a strong solution of iodine or mercurochrome. The rest of the flock should be vaccinated by follicular or wing web method, most vaccines preserve immunity for only 6 months.

FOWL PEST (NEWCASTLE DISEASE) NOTIFIABLE TO AUTHORITIES

This is caused by a myxo virus which is excreted by infected birds and spread in dust particles. It affects mainly chickens and turkeys, also occuring with pheasant, partridge and many smaller birds. The common guinea fowl appears to have considerable immunity, even when run together with infected birds during a test in England it exhibited no signs; but it can be a carrier of the virus. Some cases have been reported from Italy where vaccination is strongly advised.

SALMONELLOSIS

There are over two hundred of this type of bacteria, two bacteria of the salmonella group are particularly harmful to guinea fowl. Many countries have compulsory notification as they are trying to eliminate this disease.

Paratyphoid: Caused by *Salmonella typhimurium.* Infected food containing animal proteins is a frequent source, they should always undergo a heat process. Birds will stand or huddle listlessly with ruffled feathers. Pale green stinking diarrhoea will be noticed and sometimes vomiting. Convulsions are fairly common and death will occur in two to five days. Individuals can be treated by injection with tetracycline or furazolidone may be added to the drinking water, at 16 gm per 5 litres.

Pullorum Disease (Bacillary white diarrhoea): *Salmonella pullorum:* Transmission may be by infected equipment or staff, or contained in the fertile egg from an infected parent. The chick is liable to spread the infection to most others in the vicinity. Death may be swift or survivors will huddle listlessly together and produce the standard symptom of white diarrhoea. A high proportion will die of acute septicaemia. The mortality in adults is not high but acute cases will show weakness and produce greenish brown diarrhoea, chronic cases may exhibit no obvious symptoms. Diagnosis can be established from blood samples. Treatment produces variable results; furazolidone and sulphonamides will reduce losses but not completely eradicate them. These drugs treat the disease but leave the birds as carriers. Future breeding must only be from flocks that have had a complete clearance result after blood testing.

MYCOPLASMIC AND COLIFORM INFECTIONS:

The free living micro organisms *Mycoplasma Gallisepticum. M. Synoviae* or *M. Melegrides* may by themselves or when associated with an infection from specimens of the Escherichia Coli group, flare up and create conditions affecting overall performance. *M. Gallisepticum* may appear in the form of coryza i.e. watering eyes and nostrils, cough and sinusitis. Other combinations may produce anaemia or lameness through abscesses in the bone cavities of the leg joints. Antibiotics will relieve the severity of these afflictions but it is necessary to eliminate carriers of these bacteria from the flock. Eggs for incubation may be dipped in a medicated solution at a lower temperature, to allow it to penetrate the shell. Strictly enforced hygiene should prevent future outbreaks. Breeders often advertise day old keets as *M.Galtisepticum* or *M.Melegrides* free.

CHRONIC RESPIRATORY DISEASE:

Infection with a pleuro–pneumonia–like organism (PPLO). This is prevalent amongst guinea fowl and game birds. They exhibit a swelling around the face and a nasal discharge together with lack of appetite and emaciation. Furazolidone and antibiotics will usually clear up the symptoms but the birds may still be carriers. This organism develops rapidly when birds are housed in poorly ventilated or draughty quarters. These conditions are responsible for many more fatalities than is generally realised.

INFECTIOUS LARYNGOTRACHEITIS (I.L.T.):

This viral disease in confined to certain parts of the world. Symptoms are, great respiratory distress with coughing and blood stained mucus deposits. Mortality results from clots of mucus blocking the trachea. There is no effective treatment but an intraocular vaccine exists.

INFECTIOUS BRONCHITIS:

A contagious virus with numerous strains. In keets, one can hear sneezing and snicking accompanied by head shaking. Some strains affect the kidneys instead of the respiratory tract. Deaths are generally caused by secondary infections. In the female keet development of the oviduct may be interrupted or the hatchability of eggs affected. Prevention is by a vaccine programme.

TUBERCULOSIS:

This mycobacterium generally attacks old birds. It is contagious and is spread by infected droppings. Birds exhibit lack of condition and weight loss, joints may swell and cause lameness and wart like growths appear around throat, eyes and top of head. Affected birds should be destroyed and the quarters sterilised. Reputable hatcheries supply a TT test guarantee.

CANDIDOSIS (Thrush):

This may appear in the keet from two weeks onwards. Conditions contributing to the incidence are; inadequate sanitary conditions, too high a flock density, litter damp or of inferior quality, very high humidity, the result of administering preventative oral antibiotics as the digestive flora of guinea fowl in particular is most easily upset. However, the fungus *Candida albicans* sometimes appears when none of these errors have been committed as the guinea fowl is susceptible to it. The keet may exhibit loss of appetite, listlessness and slow growth or appear more nervous, lose coordination, suffer spasmodic neck contractions. Mortality may be as high as 30%. Pale lesions with a grey white secretion and a thickening of the crop wall will be evident and the crop will become stiff and inflexible. The secretions when examined will contain the Candida yeasts and pseudo filaments. A preventative dose of Nystatin at 50 ppm in the food should be given where an outbreak is feared or at 100 ppm if it occurs. Parconazole, copper sulphate and potassium iodide are also employed.

DEFICIENCY DISEASES

ENCEPHALOMALACIA (CRAZY CHICK DISEASE):

Vitamin E deficiency creates a loss of muscular control due to brain damage. The baby keet becomes unable to walk or feed properly. Recommended amounts of vitamin E must be added to the diet of the laying fowl. Dosage can be administered orally or in the drinking water.

NUTRITIONAL PARALYSIS (CURLY TOE DISEASE):

Lack of vitamin B 2 (riboflavine). The toes curl under the feet causing the bird to sink unto its hocks. Symptoms appear from 3 to 5 weeks old, and growth will cease; followed by high mortality. Recommended quantities of dried yeast, synthetic riboflavin or dried skimmed milk should be fed promptly.

OSTEOMALACIA (RICKETS):

Vitamin D 3 deficiency causes a deformity of the leg and rib bones in keets; created by an imbalance of phosphorous and calcium. In old birds, the bones soften and are prone to fracture and weakness. Guinea fowl require a slightly larger quantity of D 3 in their ration than other poultry.

OTHER AILMENTS

SINUSITIS:

This may be due to a vitamin A deficiency or to a local irritation started by a particle of grain or grit. Symptoms are shaking of head or closing of eyes and frequently nasal discharge. Birds will not be as listless or shaken up as with an infection. Check for foreign body and administer vitamin A.

BUMBLEFOOT:

Infection with a *staphylococcus* bacterium subsequent to a wound or injury. Inflammation may extend up the shank and cause lameness. A swelling or abscess will be noticed, usually on the soft parts of the underfoot. This should be lanced and cleansed with antiseptic lotion. Apply antibiotic dressing and if necessary dose with antibiotic or sulphonamides.

FAVUS:

A fungus which attacks unfeathered parts of the body and cloaca appearing as greyish white areas and forming scabs. Paint the affected area with Castillani's paint and disinfect the quarters. All diseases and especially fungal ones attack birds with lower resistance. This is usually due to another debilitating condition or sometimes a result of antibiotic treatment which has destroyed the natural fungal and bacterial contents of the bird's system.

BOTULISM (LIMBER NECK):

Partial paralysis of the neck muscles. The neck may be stretched out backwards, twisted or hanging limp. This is caused by Clostridial bacteria which build up in unhygienic conditions. Victims should be culled. If persistent, veterinary advice should be sought. Pay particular attention to hygiene.

OSTITIS OF CRANIAL BONE; (BIG HEAD)

Normally only individual birds are affected but occasionally a number in a flock may be stricken. Subjects withdraw from the rest of the flock and stand with the head held very low often the beak or helmet is actually resting on the ground. The head will appear somewhat swollen and the eyes will be either semi or fully closed. During the early development, the birds will attempt to run away when approached, after a few days this is no longer possible and death ensues from malnutrition.

An oedematous infiltration occurs at the top of the cranium. The porous part of the bone seems to liquify and form a large artificial sinus in the occipital region. This affects the nerve centres responsible for maintaining equilibrium. It has not been determined whether the cause is a virus or mycoplasmic infection and no effective treatment has been developed.

CROP IMPACTION:

The crop becomes noticeably swollen and hard to the touch. The bird shows disinclination to eat and occasionally there is a staggering walk. This is usually caused by eating debris such as plastic, wire, twine, etc., or long fibrous grasses in young keets. Administer luke–warm water with two teaspoonfuls of vegetable oil and massage the crop while holding the head downwards. The alternative is to make an incision through the skin and crop wall and remove the obstruction. Wash out with mild antiseptic solution and sew up crop and outer skin. keep bird on small amounts of soft food for a few days or until wound has healed.

SOUR CROP:

Sour crop shows a similar distension but with liquid contents which can be removed by massaging with the birds head downwards until the liquid is expelled. Dose with a pinch of sodium bicarbonate in warm water.

FEATHER PICKING:

Feather picking may be caused by cramped quarters, excessive light, lack of protein and cellulose, boredom or stress, or agression between males. The circumstances should be investigated carefully as they may be rectified fairly easily without performing beak trimming; this inhibits proper feather preening. The victim and aggressor should be isolated. A useful antipeck mixture is 16 ozs vaseline mixed with 1 oz of powdered aloes rubbed on the affected areas.

VACCINATION

Before embarking on any course of vaccines one should obtain professional advice from a local veterinary surgeon or agricultural department. Many factors are not dealt with or fully covered by the manufacturer's recommendations. These might be, suitability for different ages and species of bird, changes in local conditions for different geographical areas or alterations in vaccine.

A vaccine is not like a drug or antibiotic. The solution contained in the dispensing phials may be infectious. Wash and disinfect hands before and after vaccinating and destroy any surplus vaccine by boiling or burning. Vaccine should be kept in a refrigerator at 4°C / 39°F; carefully check the container dates, suggested methods of induction and period of immunity. Make sure that all birds are healthy and use each phial immediately after opening.

If using the spray method for baby keets, wear an eye mask, ensure the building is clean and disinfected and use distilled water at approx 25°C. Do not allow the keets access to heaters or under brooders during or shortly after spraying. It is essential that the spray particles should be extremely fine so use a special veterinary sprayer.

INTEROCULAR METHOD:

Nasal or occular drops can be used on birds under 2 to 3 weeks old. Dissolve the doses of vaccine in saline solution and instil only one drop per bird in eye or nostril.

ADMINISTRATION IN DRINKING WATER:

Use non chlorinated tap water or distilled water free from rust. All containers should be free of disinfectant or detergent. Skimmed milk may be added to the water at 600 ml per 10 litres in order to prolong the life of the virus. Open the phials under the water to be offered, and mix throughly before offering it to the birds. it is a good idea to withhold water beforehand for two or three hours. Ensure sufficient drinking space for each bird and that all the water is consumed within two hours.

ENDOPARASITES

Worms form the largest group of internal parasites. There are no typical symptoms apart from an unhealthy and listless look. Careful management of range, pens, litter, housing and feeding should keep these troubles at bay. If a severe outbreak is suspected, only a clinical examination will reveal the type of parasite and one should bear in mind that successful treatment of the birds will still only eliminate most worms for a few weeks.

ROUNDWORMS—NEMATODA *(Ascaris galli):*

These may populate the small intestine at any age. White and up to 8 cm in length, they may sometimes be seen in the droppings. Wet litter will encourage them. Loss of weight and alternating constipation and diarrhoea are likely symptoms. Piperazine Citrate is an effective treatment. The birds may be dosed with capsules, or have it added to the drinking water at 8 gms per gallon, for three days.

PIN OR CAECAL WORMS — NEMATODA *(Heterakis gallinae)*

These are hairlike and up to approx 1 cm long. They cause little distress but may harbour other parasites like the protozoa which causes Blackhead. Anthelmintic treatment e.g. Phenothiazine for three successive days at the rate of 0.2 gm per bird.

THREAD OR HAIR WORMS — *(Capillaria contorta), (C. retusa)*

These can be a plague with keets of 7 to 8 weeks old and the parents can also be affected. With the keets, an infestation shows in a general lowering of appetite and shivering; the severely affected ones stand still, feathers spikey, in a ball shaped stance characteristic of a sick guinea fowl. This is followed by yellow liquid diarrhoea with a pungent odour, and severe thirst. They rapidly grow thin and death follows after several days.

In adults progress is slower, showing in a slackening rate of lay and diarrhoea, they get thinner and eventually die in a few weeks.

With birds raised outside, the worms usually appear in the oesophagus and crop, these are less common and less serious.

With intensively reared keets the worms appear in the small intestine, these are long and thin and deeply embedded in the mucus membrane. Both they and their lemon shaped eggs can only be seen under the microscope.

Treatment: administer Mebendazole for five days or from seven to ten days in severe cases, at 60 ppm in food.

GAPE WORMS — NEMATODA *(Syngamus trachea):*

These can be troublesome in range reared keets. About 2 cm long and coloured deep red, due to sucking blood; they bury themselves in the wall of the trachea and are difficult to eradicate. Laeramisole may be added to the drinking water or Thiabendazole to the rations. Fertility in the male birds will be greatly reduced for the duration of the latter treatment. Birds with these worms will not thrive well and will be noticed coughing and wheezing. Gape worms frequently appear in conjunction with skin parasites.

TAPE WORMS — CESTODA *(Davainea proglottina), (Raillientina), (Cesticulata)*

These may be up to 25 cm long, they are segmented and ribbon shaped. The tail sections separate when full of eggs and pass out in the droppings. The head section or scolex remains attached to the intestinal wall. An old treatment which is still effective is to dose once a day with half a teaspoonful of grated male fernroot mixed with a little castor oil in bran. The previous night, administer half an oz of Epsoms salts per ADULT bird. The modern anthelmintic is Cetarsol. The droppings should be carefully examined for the worm head which can be extremely small. If not found, consultation with your veterinary surgeon is advisable.

GIZZARD WORMS *(Acuaria hamulosa):*

These are reddish brown and 1 to 2 cms long. grasshoppers are thought to be the vectors. Symptoms are loss of weight and digestive difficulties. Carbon tetra chloride is a possible treatment but veterinary consultation is recommended.

PROTOZOA *(Trichomonas gallinae):*

These create an ulceration in the crop and top of the oesophagus, known as Trichomoniasis or Wet Canker. There is a loss of appetite and an unpleasant odour. As an outbreak can cause heavy losses amongst guinea fowl, laboratory tests should be made as soon as this condition is suspected. Treat with Emtryl or a 16% solution of Aminonitrothiazole at one dessertspoonful per two gallons for a fortnight.

ECTOPARASITES

External parasites enjoy a dark humid atmosphere and proliferate in old buildings where there are lots of ledges and niches harbouring dust and dirt. An annual cleaning and spraying of the entire interior with a carbolic product will protect against mites. A strong nicotine sulphate solution sprayed on roosts, perches, etc. and repeated a fortnight later, should clear out any lice.

FOWL TICK *Argas persicus:*

This is a carrier of the *Leptospiral* bacteria which cause Spirochaetosis. These ticks descend on the birds at night in order to suck blood and the larvae may remain on the birds for days. Malathion based preparations will destroy them on the birds and in the buildings.

Many more lethal varieties of tick exist in the Americas and Australia.

BUGS *Cimicidae:*

Bugs have broad flat bodies, are light to dark brown in colour and are 5 to 6 mm long. Their behaviour and effect are similar to that of ticks. As before Malathion, Pyrethium or Gamma isomer BHC preparations can be used as sprays or dusting powder.

LICE:

Lice are the most common parasites. They remain on the bird and do not suck blood but feed on feathers and skin, there are several varieties.

Head lice *(Lipeurus heterographus)* are light grey.
Body lice *(Menocanthus stramineus)* and
Shaft lice *(Monopon gallinae)* are both amber in colour.

When examining the bird look for greyish or light clusters on the skin or base of the feathers around the neck, vent and under the wings. Dust particularly with proprietory powders around these areas at several 10 day intervals as their eggs are not affected.

The Mallophaga or 'biting lice' have broader and larger heads than true lice and their colouring adapts to that of their host.

MITES:

Mites are difficult to see with the naked eye and the use of a magnifying glass is recommended for inspection. Their effects are more obvious, feathers may be plucked and broken by scratching and red patches and scales will appear on the skin, birds will be irritated and lose condition.

FEATHER AND QUILL MITES:

Megninia columbae, Syringophilus bipectinatus and *Dermoglyphus elongatus.* These can be found on feathers or at base of quills. The Northern Fowl Mite, *Liponyssus sylvarium* will gather around the vent area of the male and produce a scaly condition which discourages him from mating. For all of the above, a regular dusting with pyrethrum powder is recommended.

SCALY LEG MITE *(Cnemidocoptes mutans):*

This is considered to be species specific. It is widely prevalent among pheasants and guinea fowl, but should not be troublesome when conditions are sufficiently hygienic. It creates a white scab with a grey barklike crust on legs and claws by gnawing galleries in the skin, this has a honeycomb appearance and may create lameness, even making it difficult for the bird to perch. Treat by immersing the affected parts in an equal solution of lorexane and paraffin brushing it well in under the scales with a small brush (toothbrush) twice a week until the symptoms have disappeared. Very badly affected cases may require to be culled.

RED MITE *(Dermanyssus gallinae):*

Under 1 mm long and grey in colour, it emerges from crevices and descends on the birds at night, causing acute irritation and anaemia. It also acts as a vector for streptococcal infections. Infestation in a laying house may be recognised by reddish blue droppings on the eggs. The interiors of the houses and / or cages should be thoroughly cleaned, mites will congregate even under droppings adhering to the wire floors of cages. All areas should be sprayed or brushed with gamma benzene hexachloride weekly for several weeks and the birds dusted with pyrethrum powder.

RODENTS AND OTHER PREDATORS

Apart from causing structural damage by gnawing through walls, pipes and cables and acting as carriers of pests and diseases; rats and mice multiply very rapidly and will eat large quantities of food and even baby keets and eggs. An adult rat will eat 9 kg of food per annum and a mouse 2 to 3 kg. Young mice can enter a building through a quarter inch diameter (0.625 cm) hole; both mice and rats are capable of incredible ingenuity in scaling walls, roofs, wire fences, etc. No matter how well proofed buildings and runs are constructed one must be watchful in case they manage to sneak in and hide when gates or doors are open, with the idea of setting up house and multiplying. The brown rat will from the age of six months produce two to seven litters of between 5 and 20 offspring each year and the common mouse four or five litters of 5 to 10 babies.

The common spring trap is well known, but only suitable for the occasional individual rat. Various poisons are available, the most commonly used being the anti coagulant 'Warfarrin' based varieties. These are not suitable for poultry farm or aviary as most commercial foods contain vitamin K which is an antidote to the anti coagulant. Zinc phosphide or alphachloralose can be incorporated in a prepared bait as follows:

> **15 parts finely ground cereal grain, 2 parts whole grains, 1 part sugar, 2 parts vegetable oil; mix together well before adding 2 parts of the poison.**

Pre bait mixture, without the added poison, should be left for two or three successive nights in suitable small closed boxes with a hole cut in one side for a rat or mouse to enter. By including about 25% melted paraffin wax in the mixture and allowing it to set, the bait can then be cut in small blocks which will remain attractive to the rodents for some weeks. As sometimes the bait gets dragged out of the box and portions may lie around unnoticed until eaten by some other animal or bird, it is important to place the bait box inside another container with limited entry from the top, suitable only for rodents. It is also important to wear gloves during the entire operation as rodents are easily discouraged by human scent. Two useful commercial poisons are Difenacoum which is compounded at 0.005% by one manufacturer in blue pellets the same size and shape as growers pellets. The other is Liphadione which is usually added to whole wheat grains and remains attractive for long periods. An antidote to the former in case a dead rodent is eaten by a domestic animal is vitamin K 1 Phytomenadione BP administered intravenously 5 to 20 mg in aqueous suspension. The synthetic vitamin K 3 which is usually added to poultry foods, is not effective in this case.

A range of larger predators may annoy owners of open pens or free range systems. These include cats, feral mink, racoons, weasels, stoats, foxes and dogs. If the older birds have high roosts and keets are enclosed at night the fox is denied much opportunity. However, if losses are occurring, the simplest method of detecting the culprit is by setting traps. Special cage traps for cats are available from shops and game farms, these will take the animal alive and if it is found to be a wandering pet, can be returned to its owner with an appropriate account. The cage traps designed for rats and cats are also successful with mink when baited with fish or offal. Box traps are successful with weasels and stoats. The entrance hole is about 11 x 9 cm with the roof sloping up to 15 cm at the other end. The principle used is a see–saw pivoting on a metal spindle which locks in the closed position behind the animal, the advantage of the box trap is that it can be camouflaged in a tunnel through a hedge or ditch, or easily moved around and located in any likely spot e.g. a boundary furrow, a plank over a stream, alongside a wall or wherever small tracks are noticed.

When a guinea fowl is nesting on open range, she is at risk from all the terrestial predators mentioned. A fox may be suspected if the head is bitten cleanly off and left on the ground or if the bird has vanished completely and the eggs are cold in the nest. Other predators are more untidy. Unfortunately the only control for foxes is gun or wire snare. Unlike pheasant and partridge, nests on open range are not so vulnerable to attacks by crows and raptors as the guineas are more than a match for them. However, young keets fostered by bantams should be protected in covered pens if birds of prey are in evidence.

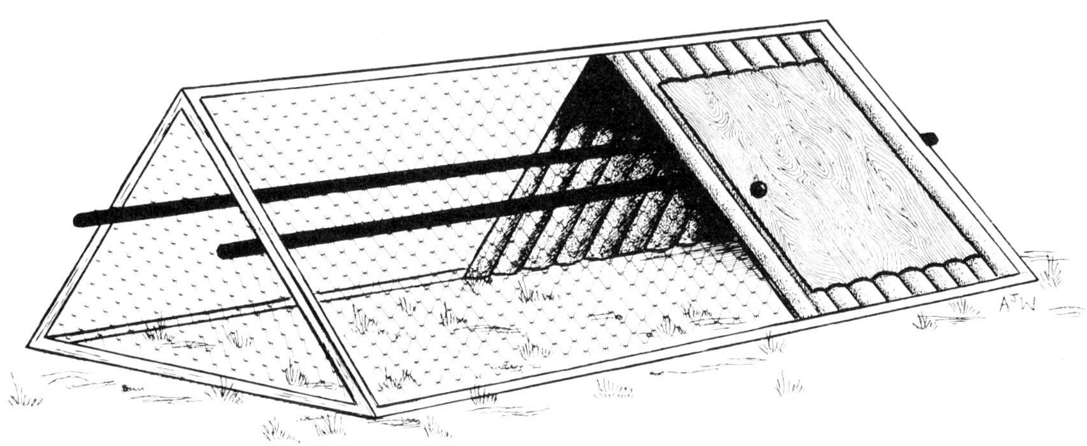

Figure 7 – 2 Fold unit which should have a wire base to keep out predators

Figure 8 – 1 An Example of Attractive Presentation **(Courtesy: Ark Foods Ltd)**

8

PREPARATION FOR MARKET AND TABLE

Figure 8 – 2 The branded product (alive)

Figure 8 – 3 Ready for Marketing **(Courtesy: Ark Foods Ltd)**

CHAPTER 8

PREPARATION FOR MARKET AND TABLE

FINISHING

A properly 'finished' keet should be well fleshed over all the bones with an even distribution of fat throughout the skin. The breast should be plump on both sides of the sternum, to the base of the keel. In a well developed modern strain, grown on to 1.25 kg or over, the leg and thigh should be sufficiently plump to provide a meal for one person. In a top quality bird, the skin on the breast and at the web of the wing should appear creamy, indicating adequate fat desposits.

The final feed should be a soft dry or wet mash, as grains can take quite a time to digest. The fowl should then be isolated in a quiet pen or building and food, but not clean fresh water, withheld for the last 15 to 24 hours. This should clear the crop and intestine, in order to avoid discolouration of the flesh in those areas. The birds must be handled with care and grasped only by the wings or legs, any bumping on the breast can result in extensive bruising.

CARCASS PREPARATION

KILLING

A method of killing employed by beginners is to stretch the fowl's neck tautly over a chopping block and sever the head by a clean sharp blow with an axe or hatchet. The more usual approach is to dislocate the spinal cord at the top of the neck. Place the first two fingers of one hand, or a V shaped piece of wood, firmly behind the head which should be angled back and facing outwards, stretch the neak as far as possible and then pulling sharply, give the head an upward twist. An easing of resistance will indicate the neck dislocation; this should leave a small cavity in the neck into which the severed arteries will start draining. Death will be instantaneous. A guinea fowl's neck is considerably more muscular than that of a chicken and a stronger pull is required. Sticking is a more professional method, here the jugular veins are severed with a sharp 10 cm knife, inserted through the beak aperture and piercing the veins at the junction of head and neck.

The blood is able to drain away quickly which gives the carcass increased keeping qualities. The back lobe of the brain is also pierced via the groove in the roof of the mouth, this loosens the feathers for dry plucking. If the last method is practised, the guinea fowl must first be stunned. This is required by the 1967 and 1978 Poultry Acts in Great Britain and similar acts in many other countries. If a lot of birds have to be dealt with, electronic stunners are available and there are specially designed instruments which kill the bird and cut the veins in one operation.

The carcass should be allowed to hang head downwards for a minute or two until the blood has completely drained or been funnelled off. If it is intended to 'hang' a bird or sell it as a feathered carcass, it is usual to remove part of the breast feathers to exhibit the quality of skin and flesh.

PLUCKING

Fullscale plucking should commence as soon as possible, because the feathers come away more easily while the body heat remains. Guinea fowl are frequently dry plucked as this gives the skin and carcass a more attractive appearance and the feathers would be ruined if they were removed by scalding or the hot wax processes. A regular sequence saves time when hand plucking. Some prefer to remove the breast feathers first for the reasons mentioned above. Others leave them to the last on the principle that the remaining blood and juices get more opportunity to drain away. To avoid tearing the skin, which spoils the appearance and impairs the keeping quality, hold it with one hand and with the other, pluck the feathers out in the same direction in which they lie. When the rough plucking is completed, the stubs and pin feathers are removed with the thumb and a blunt knife. The remaining hair like feathers can be eliminated by rapidly passing the carcass over a gas or spirit flame.

SHAPING

If time allows, the plucked fowl should be left for 24 hours before drawing and cutting. The carcass will stiffen as it cools, and it can be shaped by pushing the hocks back against the body and tying them with string, from the toes, along the thighs and across the back. Another length of string is passed around the front of the hocks, crossed behind them and tied to the 'parsons nose'. This forces the breast into a prominent position.

HANGING

The amount of time for which a feathered carcass should be hung depends upon the age of the bird, the humidity and temperature and in the final analysis just how 'high' the chef and the consumer like their meat to be. Preferences extend from three days to three weeks. There are a few who apply the test of whether the tail will fall away when lightly grasped. Ideally, the carcass should be left hanging in a current of cold dry air. If the fowl has been shot and food is found in the crop, it will also be in the intestine; unless it is 'roped' this will cause a greenish discolouration within twelve hours.

ROPING

A small cut can be made at the back of the neck, level with the top of the wings. Insert two fingers and carefully loosen and draw out the crop and its contents. A second small cut is made from the vent to the tail, again insert finger, loop the intestine around it and withdraw gently in order not to tear it. The fowl can then be hung in the game larder.

PRESERVING FEATHERS

A traditional way of preserving feathers is to let them soak in lime water for 3 to 4 days. Mix half a kilo of burnt lime in 5 litres of water, stir and remove the sediment. This should take out the grease and impurities; rinse the feathers well and dry in a very low heat. if it is planned to store them for long, add a little paradichlorbenzine as a moth deterrent.

DRAWING AND TRIMMING

Chop off the wings at the first joint; cut around the skin just below the hock joints, break the joints over the edge of a bench or table top, do not twist the joint as a straight sharp pull will remove the leg tendons more easily before cutting off the feet. Place the fowl breast down and make an incision along the back of the neck skin, cut off the neck at the junction of head and body leaving the long flap of neck skin to be pulled over and tucked underneath the locked wings. Loosen and take out the crop, trachea and oesophagus. Insert a finger into the cavity and loosen the lungs and organs around the top of the rib cage. Next make a deep cut between vent and tail, cut around vent and remove. loosen the intestine, inserting the fingers and thumb inside the body cavity, find the gizzard and pull out together with intestines and liver; if the lungs and heart have been properly loosened from the top end, these should also come away in one mass. Take great care not to break the green gall bladder attached to the liver as this would spoil the meat by imparting an unpleasant bitter flavour to it. Cut through the outer muscle of the gizzard and remove the grit and horny inside lining; wash throughly gizzard, liver, heart and neck. Wrap the giblets in a small polythene bag and replace inside the fowl, do not omit to wipe the interior of the carcass with a spotlessly clean cloth before replacing giblets in it.

TRUSSING

Thread a trussing needle with fine sterile string; fold the flap of neck skin over the opening, towards the back and secure it under the ends of the wings by folding them over the back. Pass the needle and string through the wing below the joint, under the back and through the other wing. Press the legs well forwards and down to raise up the breast then pass the needle through the thigh just behind the leg joint, through the fowl and the thigh on the other side and tie the two string ends at the side of the body. Re–thread and pass the needle through the back under the pelvic bones, bring the thread over the leg joint, through the breast skin below the end of the sternum then over the second leg joint and tie tightly down. Alternatively, a skewer may be passed through both thighs via the body cavity and the legs tied with string and secured to the parson's nose.

JOINTING OR SECTIONING

Standard size broiler keets are usually halved before or after cooking. They are split down the back bone with poultry shears or a heavy knife and cut through on each side of and close to the centre of the breast bone. Larger guinea fowl of 750 gms (dead weight) or more may be sectioned in four pieces. The legs and thighs are severed at the body joint, the wings are removed together with the adjacent breasts by dividing the rib cage at back and sternum.

BONING

This technique improves with practice, an expert will do the job in well under thirty minutes, allow up to one hour for your first attempt at it. Cut through the skin and meat along the backbone with a sharp narrow blade, work the flesh away from the rib cage on both sides down to the thigh joints. Sever the joints and scrape the meat from thigh and leg, pushing the bones inwards. The effect is like pulling an arm from a coat sleeve while the sleeve turns inside out. Repeat this process with the wing bones. Scrape away the remainder of the meat from the rib cage and then from the breast bone. Lift out the body skeleton. After stuffing, the skin is sewn together along the back and any tearing repaired.

GUINEA MEAT

One may consider the higher cost of guinea to chicken meat to be off–set to some degree by comparison studies made in France and Italy. Analysis of the male and female keet at 13 weeks old by Rouet shows that:

Content	Male	Female
Water	71.02%	69.4%
Protein material	20.8%	20.6%
Fats	3.18%	4.8%
Mineral material	5.0%	5.2%

A breakdown of the cooked carcass compared with a similar sized Cornish chicken in three different studies quoted by JC Cauchard in his excellent book *La Pintade* shows that:

Content	Guinea	Cornish chicken
Meat	77% — 79%	62% — 66%
Bones	15.7% — 16.8%	27% — 31%

According to Auxilia and Borde (see bibliography):

100 g guinea meat = approx 129 cal

100 g chicken meat = approx 100 cal

Guinea meat is shown to be almost 50% of live weight or 70% of the carcass prepared for cooking.

WEIGHTS AND AGES:

Many game restaurants offer small keets as a substitute for partridge or large quail; these are served whole at from 350 to 750 (live weight) or 250 to 500 gms when drawn and trussed. The standard range in demand by most restaurants is from 900 to 1250 g (live weight), or 750 to 900 g trussed and drawn. These can be split and served in halves like a large pheasant. To provide a substantial meal for four people, one requires a fowl of 1.5 kg (live weight) or 1.150 kg trussed and drawn. Adult hybrid strains whose breeding life is over may weigh from 1.75 kg to 2.25 kg after a few weeks conditioning; these will 'kill out' at from 1.17 kg to 1.50 kg approximately. After a little hanging, they make excellent boiling fowl.

A broiler fed hybrid keet of 8 to 11 weeks should have a flexible breast bone, soft feet and short sharp claws with little helmet or wattle development. Feral or wild birds taken on a shoot, require five to seven months to reach comparable weights of 900 g to 1.4 kg.

FREEZING

Quick freezing is one of the best ways of preserving freshly trussed fowl. The temperature is reduced so fast that the internal cells do not get the opportunity to rupture and the original quality is maintained. Place the trussed carcass in a heavy gauge freezer bag and mark with date, weight etc. The quick freezing temperature should be at least minus 25°C so it is preferable to have them frozen in a blast freezer and then transferred to a domestic deep freeze where the holding temperature is more likely to be minus 6°C. If the fowls have not been prestuffed they will store for at least one year. Thawing out times at room temperature, 18°C / 64.4°F. are 1 kg to 9 hours, 2 kg 11 hours. NEVER refreeze.

PRESERVING

The meat of older fowl is suitable for preserving in Kilner jars or similar containers. The carcass is jointed and sections packed carefully in well sterilised jars with a little salt. The tops and rings are loosely attached and the jars are steamed under 4½ kg pressure for 2 hours minimum, allow pressure to subside and tightly clamp the jar lids.

SMOKED GUINEA FOWL

Apart from the curing recipe and the smoking process, the texture of the meat in a particular batch of fowl, the external temperature and humidity all have a bearing on the final aroma and length of preservation. It is important to keep an accurate record of these factors, thus one can proceed by trial and error to a subjective criterion of excellence.

As soon as they are completely cold, the drawn carcasses should be immersed in the curing solution and weighted down. A standard mixture is 4 kg salt, 1.4 kg sugar, 95 gm saltpeter, and 30 lt. water. Proportions of salt and sugar may vary from 1 : 1 to 4 : 1, sometimes half a lt. of vinegar and or spices are added; occasionally beer is used instead of water, commercial smoked flavourings are also available. The interior of the rib cage should be opened up to achieve a uniform penetration. Some of the solution is often injected under pressure into the legs and wings to speed the process. The solution is boiled and then cooled and maintained at 15°C. If the carcasses have been pressure treated, three to five days immersion is sufficient, if they have not been under pressure, five to seven days immersion is needed. They are then drained, dried in stockinette and hung in a cold room for 24 hours. In the smoke room, a low temperature smoke of 40° to 50°C and near saturation humidity ensures less shrinkage. Apple or hickory provides the best scented sawdust or wood chips. If the fowls are hung by the wings, the entire surface skin should become a golden brown in 15 to 20 hours; the time allowed depends upon the degree of aroma preferred in the meat. A fresh, well cured and smoked carcass should keep for 3 to 4 weeks or can be frozen for at least one year. When cooking, the skin will tear easily, so the fowl should be slow roasted in roasting bags.

EGGS

Comparison studies of the guinea egg, made in France and Italy, record amongst other things that they will preserve for sixty days in a refrigerator without losing appreciable quality compared to ten days for the hen egg. A Russian study reports that guinea eggs can be kept at a cool temperature for up to one year without becoming dangerous to the consumer. A useful possibility for expeditions etc.

Guinea fowl eggs may be preserved and used in the same manner as those of other poultry. They may be submerged for up to 6 months in a sodium silicate and water 8 : 1 solution, or lime water 4 : 1 solution; they may also be coated with vegetable oil or warm butter and stored in sawdust. The yolks and whites can be stored frozen for approximately one year when they have been separated. The whites require no pre–freezing treatment, the yolks should be well stir mixed but not whipped and a half teaspoonful of salt or one tablespoon of syrup added per dozen eggs.

The preference shown by some people for the yolk rather than the white of an egg may be connected with the fact that the albumen contains a trypsin inhibitor which reduces the digestibility to about 85% when cooked. Some of the albumen is able to pass unchanged through the intestinal wall and may cause toxic symptoms in those who are allergy prone. The yolk on the other hand is so easily emulsified and digestible that it can be given to an 8 week old baby. Eggs have a useful content of potassium, iron, organic phosphorus and sulphur as methionine, the latter is the cause of the dark discolouration on the cut surface of a hard boiled egg when exposed to the air, as the sulphur reverts to its elemental state.

As well as being prepared in the normal varieties of ways, guinea fowl eggs are always in demand by chefs and gastronomes. Sixteen guinea egg whites are calculated equal to twelve hen whites. Connoisseurs consider them comparable with plover and quail eggs. Suggestions for serving. Oeufs en agar, hard boiled, halved and cold set in a jelly prepared from agar agar and clear chicken stock, suitably decorative vegetables are also set in the jelly. This can be served with fresh wakame, raw mushroom salad or any fresh salad of one's choice. Alternatively, either the yolks or the whole eggs may be whipped and prepared in the manner of a Zabaglione or a traditional English Sack Possit.

SUGGESTIONS FOR SERVING GUINEA FOWL

Recipes for guinea fowl may be found in cookery books the world over, each style of cuisine has its own delicious variations. Most of the arbitrary selection of dishes briefly enumerated below may be found in the bibliography or in national cookery books of the countries mentioned.

The popular method of cooking is to roast or grill as a game bird. They are best roasted in a moderate oven to avoid becoming too dry, as the meat is low in fats. The breast should be covered with strips of bacon and the limbs brushed with butter or oil. Small sized birds can be served on toast, slipped underneath when three quarters cooked, accompanied with watercress salad and game chips.

Stuffings for larger birds are legion; simple breadcrumbs and parsley seasoned with sage, thyme, salt and black pepper will reflect the guinea flavour. Additional blends can be achieved with spiced forcemeat, onion and apple, chestnuts, foie gras and truffles, mushroom, onion, garlic and liver etc.

A traditional Lombard recipe for the whole bird is **Faraona alla creta,** here the bird is coated and sealed in clay and roasted, to retain the aroma of herbs and spices. In many recipes the bird is sectioned into portions after a light cooking and braised or casseroled in a well seasoned stock prepared from the giblets with red or white wine or cider and supplemented with vegetables such as chicory, fennel, celery, mushroom and onion, or combinations like courgettes, tomatoes, onions and green peppers. Fruit accompaniments are equally popular; sweet and sour halved apples, black or green grapes, cherries, green figs, blueberries or loganberries. Sometimes after the preliminary light cooking the fowl is flamed with warm brandy to add a still richer savour.

There are many recipes incorporating breast of guinea fowl, a useful one for large limbs is, **Perlhühnerkeule;** the thigh and leg are deboned, fastened together, sauted in butter, then braised in a piquant fruit sauce. A different method of preparation is to section the raw carcass and marinate the portions overnight. One such marinade, composed of the juice and zest of limes with olive oil imparts a breath of the Caribbean, the bird is also served with lime butter. A subtle and more delicate variation of the Cantonese **Chiang–yu–chi,** for a guinea fowl, employs a marinade prepared from the following:

> 3 crushed garlic cloves, 1 teaspoonful of sliced root ginger, ½ teaspoonful of five spice, ½ teaspoonful of sesame oil and 225 cc soy sauce (non sweet variety); put all ingredients in a saucepan, bring to the boil, reduce heat and simmer gently for a few minutes, remove from heat and allow to cool. Next place bird in a close fitting dish and pour the marinade over the bird. Leave for approximately 4 hours, turning regularly to ensure that all parts are evenly saturated. Gently steam fowl over 750 cc of water until cooked (do not over–cook). Mix the remainder of the marinade with the resultant stock and reduce to the consistency of a light sauce. Place the fowl in a hot oven just long enough to crisp the skin. Serve in sectioned portions with a little of the sauce poured over the top.

Those who enjoy really spicy food may like the Punjabi **Tandoori chīn kī murgi:**

> The skinned fowl is first rubbed outside and inside with salt, lemon juice and garlic. After 20 minutes, a paste consisting of lemon juice, shallots, chillies, tumeric, cummin, fenugreek and mustard seeds is rubbed well into the carcass and left overnight. The fowl may be casseroled in a hot oven or spit roasted, but must not be allowed to become dry. Baste very frequently with a sauce of clarified butter, yoghurt, whipped cream, ground green ginger, paprika and lemon or lime juice.

A tasty stir fried meal is made with the meat of a steamed guinea fowl cut into bite sized pieces and stir fried with a finely sliced onion, two cupfuls of shredded white cabbage, finely sliced red capsicum, about 10 whole button mushrooms, 3 cloves finely chopped garlic, 50 gm chopped peanuts or almonds or 25 gm of each, add soy sauce (non sweet variety) and seasoning to taste. Stir fry all together in a lightly oiled wok for about 6 minutes, then add 1 cupful of fresh pineapple pieces or sliced fresh peaches, continue to stir fry for a further 4 minutes and serve immediately.

A large bird of 1.50 to 1.75 kg when deboned, stuffed and roasted can form the basis of a superb cold Galantine as the centre piece for a buffet.

One can prepare **Andouilettes de Pintade** by combining finely chopped cooked guinea meat and ham 2 : 1 or 3 : 1 according to taste. For six persons:

> **750 g of meat, 80 g butter, 4 or 5 finely chopped mushrooms, two chopped shallots or small onions. Lightly brown the shallots in a little of the butter, add about 75 cc of stock and bring to boil, then add the meat, mushrooms, one egg yolk, one teaspoonful of chopped parsley a few drops of lemon juice, nutmeg, salt and black pepper to taste. Stir until well mixed and hot, if necessary adding more stock to achieve a thick consistency. Turn into a dish to cool. Fill the mixture into natural cocktail sausage cases and seal. Fry the Andouilettes golden brown and brush with a meat glaze.**

The Greeks (and others) are extremely partial to guinea fowl soup, made as for Avgolemono but with small diced cubes of the meat added, after the eggs and lemon juice. A similar but more elaborate recipe known as Mattye was well known in the first century BC.

We could not end without mentioning **Guinea Fowl Pie,** or **Paté de Pintade.** These used to be popular dishes on the breakfast table.

> **Section and debone a large guinea fowl, fry the portions in butter until brown. Prepare a stuffing of spiced pork and veal or foie gras with chopped bacon and truffles, add a little stock and season to taste with herbs and spices. Line several small or one large pie dish with pastry and spread with the liver or spiced meat mixture, add the guinea fowl portions moistened with cognac, fruit or stem vegetables may be placed on top as required. Cover with the pastry crust and bake slowly for one to one and a half hours, glaze with egg yolk and decorate with land–or watercress and chervil.**

The guinea of two or three years old is of course tougher and should not be cooked in the same way as the keet. Its flavour is stronger, more appreciated by connoisseurs and ideal for casseroles, pâtés, soups and pies.

APPENDIXES

APPENDIX 1

COMPARISON RETAIL COSTS OF GUINEA MEAT AND EGGS: LONDON 1983

Feathered guinea fowl carcasses	£1:95 per lb
Oven ready guinea fowl	£1:20 per lb
Oven ready duck	£0:92 per lb
Barbary duck	£1:80 per lb
Oven ready turkey	£0:85 per lb
Oven ready chicken	£0:90 per lb

EGGS FOR CONSUMPTION:

Guinea fowl eggs	£0:12 each
Duck eggs	£0:18 each
Gull eggs	£0:36 each
Goose eggs	£0:55 each

APPENDIX 2

COSTS OF ORNAMENTAL STRAINS FOR BREEDING: USA 1983

Strain	Per Breeding Pair	Per 25 Keets	Per 15 Eggs
Pearl grey	\$25:00	\$40:00	\$11:95
White african	\$25:00	\$40:00	\$11:95
Lavender	\$35:00	\$40:00	\$12:95
Royal purple	\$35:00	\$40:00	\$12:95
Buff	\$50:00	\$50:00	
Coral blue	\$50:00	\$50:00	

Schubotzi's Plumed Guinea Fowl.
Now extremely rare.

Courtesy: Amsterdam Zoo

BIBLIOGRAPHY AND SUGGESTED READING LIST

Armstrong	*The Folklore of Birds*	(Collins)
Ayeni J S O	*The Biology and Utilisation of Helmeted Guinea Fowl* (Numida meleagris galeata), Ph D Thesis	University of Ibadan Nigeria, 1980
Bairacli Levi J	*Herbal Handbook for Farm and Stable*	(Faber), 1979
Balfour E B	*The living Soil and the Haughley Experiment*	(Faber), 1975
Banks S	*Complete Handbook of Poultry Keeping*	(Wardlock), 1979
Bannerman D A	*Birds of Tropical West Africa* Vols 1 & 8	1930 — 1951
	Birds of West and Equatorial Africa Vols 1 & 2	(Oliver & Boyd) 1953
Beeton E	*Mrs Beeton's Book of Household Management*	(Wardlock)
Boetticher H von	*'Die Perlhühner'*	(Neue Brehm Bucherei) Wittenberg, 1954
Boetticher H von	*'Fasanen Pfauen Perlhühner'* Bearbeitet von Dr H S Raethel	(Oertel & Sporer) Reutlingen, 1982
Bradley and Graham	*The Structure of the Fowl*	(Oliver and Boyd), 1960
Burton	*Human Nutrition*	(McGraw & Hill), 1976
Carrier R	*Great Dishes of the World, Cooking with Robert Carrier*	(Hamlyn)
Cauchard J C	*La Pintade*	(H Peladan) Uzes Gard, 1971
Cauchard J C	*Les Multiples facons d'accomoder la pintade*	
Chapin J P	*Birds of the Belgian Congo*	US, 1932
Cramp and Simmons	*Handbook of the Birds of Europe, Middle East and North Africa*	(Oxford University Press), 1982

Crawford D	*Kerkeosiris*	London
Crowe T M	*The Evolution and Ecology of the Guinea Fowl* (Galliformes Numidinae) Ph D Thesis	University of Capetown, 1978
David E	*A Book of Mediterranean Food*	(Penguin)
Erlich P & A	*Extinction*	(Random House)
Farner & King (eds)	*Avian Biology* Vol 1 – 6	(Academic Press), 1972—1982
Feltwell R & Fox S	*Practical Poultry Feeding*	(Faber), 1978
Florea	*A B C of Poultry Raising*	(Dover Pub Inc), 1975
Fracanzani C L	*La Faraona Domestica*	Edizioni Agricole, Bologna
Ghigi A	*Fagiani, Pernici e altri Galliformi – da caccia e da voliera*	Bologna, 1958
Ghigi A	Faraone et Tacchini	(Hoepli Edit) Milano, 1936
Ghigi A	*Monografia delle Galline di Faraone* (Numididae)	Piacenza 1927
Goodman & Schein	*Birds, Brain and Behaviour*	(Academic Press), 1974
Goodwin D	*Domestic Birds*	London
Graf	*Animal Life of Europe*	(Warne), 1968
Hache E	*Contribution a l'Etude de la Meleagriculture. L'oeuf de la Pintade.* Thesis Lyon No 30	University of Lyon 1966
Hannssen M	'E' for Additives	(Thorsons) 1984
Harting J E	*The Ornithology of Shakespeare*	London, 1864
Hodges R	*The Histology of the Fowl*	London, 1974

Howard & Moore	*A Complete Checklist of Birds of the World*	(Oxford University Press), 1980
Howe	*Poultry and Game*	London
Hyams E	*Animals in the Service of Man*	London, 1972
Jackson W	*New Roots for Agriculture*	(Friends of the Earth), 1981
Jarvis	*Folk Medicine*	(Allen), 1966
Karmali J	*Birds of Africa*	(Collins), 1980
Kordel	*Natural Folk Remedies*	(Allen), 1975
Long J L	*Introduced Birds of the World*	(David and Charles), 1981
Mackworth, Praed and Grant	*Birds of the Southern Third of Africa* *Birds of West Central and Western Africa* *Birds of East and Northeast Africa*	(Longmans Green), reissue 1970
Major A	*The Book of Seaweed*	(Gordon & Cremonesi), 1977
Mesnil R G	*Contribution a l'Etude de la Production Industrielle du Pintadeau,* Thesis Alfort 1970 No. 5	University of Alfort Paris (Foulon), 1970
Moreau R E	*The Bird Faunas of Africa and it's Islands*	(Academic Press)
Peters L J	*Checklist of Birds of the World*	Cambridge, Massachusets, USA
Portsmouth J	*Practical Poultry Keeping*	(Spur Publications), 1978
Reichenow A von	*Die Vögel Africas* Vol 3	Berlin, 1905
Richards A	*Chisungu*	London, 1956
Roberts A	*Birds of South Africa*	(Cape Times Ltd), 1957

Robinson	*Modern Poultry Husbandry*	(Crosby Lockwood), 1961
Rouet J C	*Contribution a l'Etude de la Pintadeau de Chair,* Thesis Alfort No. 56	University of Alfort 1967
Rutgers & Norris	*Encyclopaedia of Aviculture*	(Blandford), 1970
Sainsbury D	*Poultry Health and Management*	(Granada), 1981
Salzen and Parker	*Neural and Endocrine Aspects of Behaviour in Birds*	(Elsevier Scientific Pub Co), 1975
Savage	*The Cottagers Companion*	(Davies), 1975
Sclater W L	*Systema Avium Ethiopicarum*	London, 1930
Sclater and Stark	*Birds of South Africa* Vols 1—4	London, 1906
Shewell–Cooper W	*Compost Gardening*	(Sphere), 1977
Singh D	*Indian Cookery*	(Penguin)
Strickberger M W	*Genetics*	(MacMillan), 1964
Sykes F	*Humus and the Farmer*	(Faber), 1951
Sykes F	*Food Farming and the Future*	(Faber), 1946
Tremarne A J N	*Hausa Superstitions and Customs*	London, 1913
Weizmann	*Cessarka b. CCP* (Guinea Fowl in the USSR) *Biological Bases in Guinea Fowl Culture* Thesis: Novosibirsk, 1968	(Academy of Sciences of Siberian Region) 097, Zoologie 103
Wright L	*Wright's Book of Poultry* Revised	London, 1905
Thompson M A	*The Organic Poultryman*	(Thompson), Dorset, 1978
Toynbee J C M	*Animals in Roman Life & Art*	London, 1973
Webster Smith G	*The World in the Past*	(Warne)

White C M N	*Revised Checklist of African non Passerine Birds*	Lusaka, 1965
Williams J G	*Field Guide to Birds of East and Central Africa*	(Collins), 1978
Worthington J	*Natural Poultry Keeping*	London, 1960

EDITED WORKS AND COLLECTIONS

Catalogue of Birds in the British Museum Vol 12	1893
The International Zoological Yearbook	
Encyclopaedia Britannica	
Encyclopaedia Americana	
Encyclopaedia des Oiseaux	
Guinea Fowl, Van Hoesen Edited & Revised by L. Stromberg	(Stromberg Pub Co), Iowa, 1975
The Complete Book of Game Conservation Ed. C Coles	(Barrie & Jenkins), 1975
Man, Myth and Magic	(Purnell), 1970
The Living World of Animals	(Readers Digest), 1970
The Oxford Book of Food Plants	(O U P), 1981
The Oxford English Dictionary	
World of Wildlife	(Orbis), 1976
Larousse Encyclopaedia of Cookery	(Hamlyn)
ITAVI La pintade 1977	Paris
ITAVI L'elevage de la pintade dans le cadre d'une production fermière 1981	(Maison Rustique) Paris
Technique D'exploitation des Reproducteurs Galor	

Carnet de Bord de L'eleveur de pintades D'engraissement (Service Technique Galor) Amboise 1983

SPECIFIC ARTICLES

Bulletin British Ornithology cl vol 81 1961

B P Hall — "The Relationship of the Guinea Fowls Agelastes Meleagrides and Phasidus Niger"

Publ. Delle Stazaione Experimentale de Pollicoltura di Rovigo, II, 1 — 84, (1922)

A Ghigi — "Monografia delle Galline di Faraone"

Ibis 1944, C H B Grant and C W Machworth Praed
"*G.e. edouardi* and *G.e. verreauxi*"

Oiseau 1939, G M L Blancou "*N.m. blancoui*"

Ostrich 33, C J Skead 1962
"A Study of the crowned guinea fowl, Numida meleagris coronata"

Ornithologische Monatsberichte — No 2 1898 Oscar Neumann, "Die helmperlhühner"

Ornithologische Monatsberichte — No 8 1900 von Reichenow, "Neue Forschungen Deutsch–Ostafrika"

Ornithologische Monatsberichte — No 19 1911 K Kothe, "*Numida Frommi*"

La Revue de L'Elevage, 1966 M J Petitjean
"De Quelques applications pratique de l'insemination artificielle en aviculture. L'insemination de la Pintade"

L'Aviculteur — No 291 1973 "L'Insemination artificielle des Pintades"

Journal of Egyptian Archaeology — Vol 26 (1940) "Notes on the N H Bird", N M Davies

BULLETINS & JOURNALS

The Climatic Environment of Poultry Houses MAFF,
Charles & Spencer London HMSO No. 212

Understanding Hybridisation MAFF
London HMSO No 180 1959

Poultry Nutrition MAFF Bolton & Blair, London HMSO No 174 1973

Artificial Insemination in Poultry MAFF Lake Stewart, London HMSO No 213 1978

Incubation and Hatchery Practice MAFF Jones & Hodgetts, London HMSO No 148

Auxilia and Borda
'Composizione chimico–bromatologica della carne de faraone allevate in batteria e a terra su lettiera permante.'
Avicoltura No 3, 1966.

Auxilia, Masoero e Savio
'Studio sulle caratteristiche qualitative delle uova di gallina faraona'
Avicoltura No 10, 1967

Ayeni J S O
'Aspects of the biology of the helmeted guinea fowl *(Numida meleagris galeata)* in Nigeria
World Pheasant Assoc.
Journal V1 1980 — 81.

Blum, Guillaume and Leclercq
'Influence du tourteau de colza sur la croissance du Pintadeau — comparaison avec le poulet'.
Jour, de Recherches Avicole et Cunicoles Vol 1, 1973.

Blum J C and Leclercq B
Influence de l'age, du sexe et de l'alimentation sur la composition corporelle de pintadeau'
Congres mondial d'aviculture, Rio de Janeiro Vol 12, 1978.

Blum J C, Guillaume J and Leclercq B
'Etude preliminaire sur les besoins en vitamines du pintadeau'.
INRA, 1973

Blum J C and Leclercq B
'L'Alimentation des pintadeau'.
INRA

Blum J C and Leclercq B
'Besoins du pintadeau de chair en lysine et en acides aminés soufrés pendant les periodes de croissance et de finition'.
Ann Zootech 1976

Blum J C, Guillaume J and Leclercq B
'Studies of the energy and protein requirements of the growing guinea fowl'.
Brit Poultry Sci.
No 16 1975

Blum J C and Leclercq B
'Influence du niveau energetique et de la granulation de régime sur les performances de croissance et l'engraissement de pintadeau, comparasion avec le poulet.
Ann Zootech, 1979

Pliny the elder
Natural History No 10 and No 37

Bougon et Heuze
'Performances des poulets, pintadeaux et dindonneaux a differents âges'
INRA *Bulletin d'information*
VIII 45, 1968

Bougon et Heuze
'Influence de la supplementation alimentaire en divers pigments sur les performances et la coloration des pintadeaux'
INRA *Bull d'information de la station Exp. de Ploufragen*
1X, 1969

Buhtiiarova
'Kak my vyrascivaem cesarok'
Pticevodstvo, 1, 20, 1964

Cauchard J C and Stevens P
'La pintade en Italie'
Courrier Avicole
No 224, 1964

Colonna — Cesari M
'Les Principes de la selection généalogique des pintades'.
L'Aviculture, 1973

Crow T M
'Adaptive morphological variation in helmeted guinea fowl (Numida meleagris) and crested guinea fowl (Guttera pucherani).
Ibis No 3, 1979

Dias B
'Free range for the connoisseur'
Poultry World, Feb 1972

Farkas T
'Interesting facts about the crowned guinea fowl'
Fauna and Flora Eng. Ed.
16, 23 — 28, 1965

Fracanzani C L
'Elevage comparé de la pintade et du poulet'
Courrier Avicole XXV,
343, 1969

Ghigi A
'Ricerche sistematiche e sperimentali sulle Numididae'
Men R Ace *Scienze di Bologna,* 1911

Ghigi A
'Sulla eredita del colore nelle galline di faraone'
Nuovi Annali dell
'Agricoltura, IV, 1924

Ghigi A

'Note de nomenclature sur les pintades huppées'
Ann. Mus. Congo Fervuren IV, Zool. I., 1954

Ghigi A

'Les Pintades'
Zoo Societe Royal de Zoologie Anvers Science et Nature. Supplem. du No 59 1964

Gruaz R

'Experienze sulla perdita de peso delle uova durante L'incubazione'

Gruaz R

'Mezzi e metodi per sviluppare il consumo della faraona da carne'.
Il Giornale dei Pollicoltori XV1, 1965

Gruaz R

'Methodes pour promouvoir la consommation de la pintade de chair'
Il Giornale dei Pollicoltori, Jan 1965

Karapetian J K

'Influence of the modification of photoperioricity on the activation of the sexual function of guinea fowl'
No 3 Edit. An Arm CCP, 1961

Lamblard J M

'Developpement de l'Elevage des pintades en Afrique'
Roquemaure, Centre Etudes Meleagricules, 1972

Lamblard J M

'Incidence de comportement des pintades sur les rendements; methodes d'elevage appropriees'.
Rapport de BNA, 1965

Lamblard J M

'La Pintade dans le Gard'

Rev Elev 1970 (11)

Lamblard J M, Cauchard J.C. et Gruaz R.

'La Pintade, elevage Francais d'avenir pour L'Aviculture moyenne non integrée'.

XVII, *Journee d'etude avicole de BNA,* 1964

Laval A

'La Pintade — Aspects Zootechnique et Pathologiques'.

Le Point Veterinaire
Vol 8, 1979

Leclercq B

L'Alimentation des futurs Reproducteurs Pintades'.

INRA, 1982

Leclercq B and Sauveur B

'L'Alimentation des Reproducteurs Pintades en cour de ponte'

INRA, 1982

Leclercq B, Blum J C, Guillaume J and Stevens P

'Besoin en Protéines du Pintadeau en Croissance'.

INRA, 1974

Leclercq B and Blum J C

'Possibilities de reduction des apports proteiques chez le pintadeau de chair grace a la supplementation en lycine et en methionine'.

Ann. Zootech, 1977

Luhman M

'Untersuchungen über Gewichtszunahme und Futterverwertung wachsender Perlhühner'.

Arch. Geflugelk 34, 1970

Petitjean M J

'Essais d'Hybridation interspecifique coq X pintade et pintade male X poule'.

Revue de elevage,
1965, (5): 123

Reviers M

'Differents aspects de l'elevage des reproducteurs males (coqs, pintades) utilises en insemination artificielle'.
Extract from: *Fertilite et Insemination Artificielle en Aviculture*
INRA, 1982

Sauveur B

'Essai de determination de besoin en phosphore des pintades reproductrices'.
Ann. Zootech, 1979

Stevens M P

'Method de la selection de la pintade en France'.
circ. du SNAA
No's 1216 to 64

Szijj J

'The natural food of guinea fowl'.
Aquila Vol's 63 and 64, 1957

Tretj jakov

np pelstcer so
'Inkubacya' jaic cesarok
Inst. Pticev. 24, 33—39, 1954

Weiss I H and Basson N C J

'The oral toxicity of dieldrin to the crowned guinea fowl'.
South African Journal of Agricultural Science
No 10 : 697, 1967

'Le Pintadeau de Chair'
INRA, 3rd Ed., 1980

'Normes Conseillees pour les aliments composé destine aux pintades de chair'
Bureau de la nutrition animale et de l'elevage, Marseille, 1977

Salichon Y

'Dans son alimentation, la pintade a du caractère'.
Le Courrier Avicole
751, 1979

INDEX